WHEN LEMMINGS FLY

Helicopters in the Wilds of Alaska

By

Tom Smith

For Nancy & Normand Smith

ACKNOWLEDGMENTS

Van Santvoord and Craig Fielding for their thoughts and
endless support
Niki Kourofsky for her editing

Aerial Approach Inc.
PO Box 64
Keene Valley, NY 12943

TABLE OF CONTENTS

1. Cliff Dive

2. The North Slope

3. Whiteout

4. Devils Canyon

5. The Great Tanana River Raft Race

6. Good Friends and Ex-wives

7. Whitewater and Kathy

8. Dave Loses It

9. The Wolf and the Moose

10. The High One

11. The Other Side of the World

12. The Lifeless Heart of Winter

13. Kodiak

14. Death in the Family

15. End of an Era

CLIFF DIVE

Balanced on the edge of the 3,000-foot cliff, the helicopter rocked gently with the rotation of its main rotor blades. The cockpit and most of the passenger compartment stuck out over the sheer drop-off, giving us an excellent view of the rock face below. I glanced at the young woman beside me in the copilot seat.

"OK, Kat?" I asked over the intercom between our headsets.

She looked at me and smiled, her blue-green eyes warm in the soft rays of the evening sun, and gave me the thumbs up. I turned to Chris and Linda in the passenger compartment behind us.

Chris was checking her seatbelt, giving it one last tug. She looked up and said, "I don't know about this, Tom."

Linda, an Athabascan Indian and the only native Alaskan on the crew, didn't seem to be as concerned. She was gazing out her side window, placidly watching the evening sky turn crimson and gold far to the north. Then she turned, looked at me and smiled a very sweet smile.

"Hang on," I told them, and pushed the cyclic control stick forward. Linda squealed and Kathy grabbed the frame of her seat as the helicopter lurched and rotated nose first over the edge.

In a heartbeat we were in a vertical dive 10 feet away from the face of the cliff, staring at the apron of broken rock far below us at its base. It was as sensational as I thought it would be, but we were too close. Before long we were going to have to get out of the dive. To do that I'd have to bring the nose of the helicopter up, which, at our distance, would rotate the tail of the aircraft into solid rock.

Ever so slowly I eased back the cyclic control, tilting

the main rotor blades and bringing the nose up. Inch by inch we moved away from the rugged wall. That's when I noticed the low roar of the wind rushing past my open window vent. I glanced at the airspeed indicator to see if we were going as fast as the wind made it sound. The needle was just passing 40 miles an hour. But when I looked out the windshield at the ground coming up at us, we appeared to be going a lot faster. I checked the airspeed again. It was approaching 60. Then, as I watched, it jumped to 70.

My plan was to pull out of the dive around 90 mph, well below the helicopter's maximum speed of 150. However, things were happening so fast, I decided to get out of it right then, and eased the cyclic back some more. The aircraft responded with a tremble and the distance between the landing gear and the wall of rock grew to 30 or 40 feet. Plenty of room, I thought. A quick glance showed our airspeed was approaching 100 mph. "Shit," I said under my breath. I'd planned to be out of the dive by that speed.

No longer concerned about my tail hitting the cliff, I pulled the cyclic back further. The aircraft began to shake, but that didn't matter. I was more concerned we wouldn't get out of the dive before we reached VNE. At 150 mph we'd hit Velocity Never Exceed and the rotor system would go into a retreating blade stall, lose lift on the left side, and we'd crash. At the rate we were accelerating, that point was only a few seconds away.

I pulled back on the cyclic until the helicopter began to buffet and shudder violently. It felt like the damn thing was fighting me. Another glance at the airspeed indicator showed it climbing through 110 mph. I had to get out of the dive. I focused all my attention on the cyclic, pulling back on it until my muscles began to lock up in fear of ripping the aircraft apart. Then, reflexively, I pulled up on the collective with my other hand, putting lift in the main rotor blades. That made all the difference. The nose rose steadily and the shaking disappeared.

As we leveled out in normal flight, I paused. For the

time it took to let out a heartfelt sigh of relief, I looked out at what lay before me. The long winding river in the valley below, broad grassy slopes rising to the gray tops of rugged mountains set in a brilliant blue sky. It was the peak of summer, why we put up with Alaska's desolate winters. Few places are more alive.

Then I gave the instrument console in front of me a quick check. No master caution lights were on. Engine and transmission oil pressures and temperatures were in their normal operating range, as were the exhaust gas temperature, gas producer and torque, so I focused on the aircraft.

Helicopters have a lot of moving parts, and most of them create or transmit vibrations. Through the controls in my hands I could feel remnant forces of the main rotor system. The moving parts of the rotor system are connected to the controls by hydraulic servos, tubes and bell cranks that dampened the vibrations but didn't eliminate them. The pedals under my feet were more directly connected to the tail rotor and provided detailed information, and the frame of the seat I was buckled into transmitted vibrations from everywhere, including the engine that was turning at almost 50,000 revolutions per minute.

Vibrations are normal in helicopters, and in straight and level flight they are constant. That's what I was looking for, change in the vibrations I could feel, a sign that some part or system was not the same as it had been before I'd flown down the cliff. Most helicopters are tough, structurally sound, but when they come apart it happens fast.

Everything seemed normal so I relaxed and checked on my passengers. Kathy was uncharacteristically somber as she reached for a map that had ended up by her feet. Chris was slumped back in her seat, staring out the side window, and even Linda's dependable smile was missing. I rolled the helicopter into an easy turn to the right until we were on a heading that would get us back to our field camp on the other side of the Alaska Range. My helicopter and I were on a three-month contract with the U.S. Forest Service to fly these young women around Alaska, along with several other fledgling wildlife biologists, soil scientists and foresters who were conducting natural resource surveys.

"Goddamn," I muttered to myself, surprised how difficult it had been to pull out of the dive.

I'd put helicopters in steep dives before, not vertical, but close. They went down fast, but nothing like what we'd just experienced. And pulling out of dives had never been an issue. Must have something to do with flat pitch in that particular situation, I reasoned. Once I raised the collective and put lift in the blades, things returned to normal.

I shouldn't have done something like that without trying it by myself first, I thought. Then realized it hadn't been planned, or even something I'd considered before. We'd been flying along, dropped down for a minute to watch a golden eagle harass a tiny fox. Seconds later we were over the cliff and its perfect landing site, going slow enough to make a straight-in approach. Once we sitting on the edge, and I looked down and...

A promise that I would never point the nose of my helicopter at the ground again was forming in my mind when I heard Chris's voice in my headset. "You know, Tom," she said. "That was pretty cool."

"Is that the first time you've done that?" Kathy asked as she passed me the map she had in her hand.

"Well... yeah." I didn't know what to say. I thought they were upset. They should have been. I'd been showing off and could've killed them.

"First time! Really? You've never done that before?" Chris asked, surprise and pleasure in her voice. "I'm glad you didn't tell us."

"You mean a 'cliff dive'?" I asked, giving the maneuver a name. "I've never really done one exactly like that, but..."

I still was not sure how to handle the situation, so I leaned over and twisted the knobs on the VHF radio, figuring they'd stop asking questions if I was busy changing

4

frequencies. Critical time passed. I could feel the issue slipping behind us at 120 miles an hour. Then Linda keyed her mike.

"You're crazy, Tom," she laughed.

No one gave her an argument as we climbed steadily to clear the 6,000-foot pass between the Wood River and Yanert River valleys. We were well above tree line and went through the pass 20 feet above the ground. Now and then there would be a Dall sheep or a bear caught unaware because they didn't hear the helicopter coming from the other side of the mountain. We'd get a glimpse up close and, at a hundred miles an hour, be gone about the same time the animal realized we were there.

The only thing we saw in the pass was a marmot standing on a rock outcrop, but off to our left the Yanert Glacier appeared, winding its way to snowfields on the slopes of 12,000-foot Mount Deborah. We crossed that valley and climbed through another pass before we were out of the Alaska Range and on the wide plain that was the headwaters of the Susitna River.

I followed the river around the base of the Clearwater Mountains, first south then east, until I could see Alpine Creek and the stand of trees that was our field camp. At that point it was time to get ready to land. I checked the overhead switches and circuit breakers, pressing up on the forward fuel boost breaker to make sure it was all the way in. It had popped twice in the last week, meaning the circuit breaker was wearing out or the fuel pump was getting ready to fail. Most likely it was the breaker, because the fuel pressure gauge showed the pump was consistently developing the right amount of pressure. After a quick look at the flight and engine instruments in the console in front of me, I was down to the critical part of the landing, ascertaining the direction and speed of the wind.

Helicopters use 60–70 percent of available power in straight and level flight; however, landings and takeoffs when loaded with passengers and fuel often require 90–100 percent, particularly in the mountains. Landing directly into the wind gives the rotor system extra lift, and landing downwind can be disastrous.

5

The first thing you notice, if you are landing with the wind behind you, is the machine won't slow down when you bring the cyclic control back to level the rotor blades and come to a hover. Then the tail tries to come around and, if you don't do something, the helicopter falls out of the air because you've run out of power. Usually the aircraft rotates on the way down. It's the same thing if you take off downwind. The helicopter runs out of power.

During most of the trip back to camp the wind had been coming from the west. As we flew over a small pond I could see light ripples on the water and leaves dancing back and forth in a stand of aspens, but the wind was too light to tell if it was from the east or west. A moment later a duck climbed into the air from the far shore. He took off to the west, confirming the wind direction hadn't changed. Heavy birds like ducks and geese will always try to take off into the wind.

From a mile away I could see the bright red fuel truck parked off to one side of a knoll at the foot of the Clearwater Mountains, our landing spot. As we got closer Chris exclaimed, "Hey, look! We got a windsock."

She was right. Hanging limp from the top of a stick tied to the cab of the fuel truck was a red handkerchief. It was too heavy for the light wind that was blowing. "That Fred," I added. The makeshift wind indicator was undoubtedly the work of our camp boss and overzealous handyman.

Passing the fuel truck we were already down to 200 feet above the ground, so I rolled into a steep right turn to come around into the wind and land. The Bell Jet Ranger we were in, called "Alice" by everyone who flew her, was particularly smooth. The way she rolled in and out of turns personified what I felt about a partnership in the air. Alice responded to control movements as if they were her idea, without hesitation or waste of any kind, perfectly coordinated.

When we'd completed the 180-degree turn to the west, I leveled the rotor blades and headed for our landing spot, holding an altitude of 100 feet until we intercepted the approach angle I liked, around 30 degrees. Thirty is a little steep, but if my engine quit I stood a better chance of making my landing spot. Engines are most likely to quit under a load, like hovering, takeoff, and landing.

I lowered the collective control in my left hand, taking most of the lift out of the rotor blades to begin our approach to the ground. At the same time I brought the cyclic control in my right hand back about an inch or two, slowing us down, and pushed the right tail rotor pedal forward to compensate for the reduction in torque on the main rotor system. The constant whine of the turbine and the steady beat of the rotor blades lost some of their strength as we rode the approach angle to our landing spot on the top of the knoll below us.

At 50 feet I cross-checked the instruments again and brought the cyclic back even further to bleed off the last of our forward speed. Everything looked good in my final cockpit cross-check and the landing site was clear, so I continued my approach to the patch of smooth ground next to the fuel truck, came to a two-foot hover, set Alice gently on the ground, and rolled the throttle back to flight idle for the required two-minute engine cooldown.

As the girls got out and headed for their packs in the baggage compartment, I pulled the logbook from under my seat and began filling it in for the day: where we'd been, time for each flight. Every year the paperwork became more a part of the job, which I resented. A lot of it seemed to be superficial and a waste of time.

From the baggage compartment at the other end of the helicopter, I heard Kathy say with mock civility, "Ooh, no, Chris. Let me get that for you. I insist."

"C'mon, Kat," Chris whined. "I'm tired." I couldn't see them from the cockpit, but Chris had probably left the extra gear, a shovel and the survival kit, for Kathy to carry.

Linda and Chris walked by, followed a moment later by Kathy, who was carrying the survival gear. "Thanks for the ride," Kathy said, flashing me a smile as she hurried off after the other two, a long blond ponytail waving beneath her well-worn cowboy hat.

Chris and Kathy were 20, Linda a few years older, and they were tough. They'd spent the last ten hours working their way through a muskeg swamp and a dense stand of black spruce. The frigid water was often knee deep, and the little trees grew so close together their rasp-like limbs interlocked. The only things the young women disliked more were the tussocks that grew in the thin layer of frozen ground that thawed briefly in the summer. The tall clumps of mounded grass twist and turn underfoot. It was like trying to walk on big hairy basketballs, as Kathy put it.

They preferred the alpine. The footing is better in the mountains. There are also endless vistas of Alaskan wilderness, and usually it's cool enough to keep the bugs down, but the mountains aren't necessarily easy. Most of them are steep, as steep as avalanche chutes, and often covered with alder thickets. Alders grow low to the ground in all directions with their limbs intertwined. The only way to get through them is to crawl. Even worse than the alders are the patches of Devil's Club, a truly wicked plant about five feet tall whose long thorns are unavoidable and easily penetrate anything short of body armor. The wounds they inflict stay sore for several days.

The girls worked hard in a demanding environment, and they were in great shape for their efforts. But as they walked away their backs bent under the weight of the heavy packs they carried, feet barely left the ground. They were obviously tired, but you wouldn't know it from the animated conversation they were having. Then Chris looked back and laughed. The thought crossed my mind that they'd been talking about me, what an idiot I was for putting them in a vertical dive down a cliff, and I felt a twinge of guilt.

I checked the clock in the cluster of gauges in front of me. The turbine engine had been cooling at flight idle for more than two minutes, so I rolled the throttle off, unbuckled my seatbelt and shoulder harness, then settled into my seat to wait for the heavy main rotor blades to come to a stop. It had been another long day. In the morning I had put out two crews of three and one of four between seven and nine, moved all of them around noon, then brought them home between six and eight. I'd been in the air for eight of those thirteen hours.

As the seconds ticked by I could feel my muscles relax and the tension drain from my body. From the time I opened the throttle in the morning until I walked away in the evening, I never really relaxed. It wasn't a big thing, but until everyone was back in camp I had no idea how my day was going to end. Sitting alone in the cockpit, knowing that things had gone well, was always a peaceful moment.

When the last rotor blade swung slowly overhead and stopped, I left my comfortable seat and tied the rear blade to the tail boom. Then I walked around the helicopter looking for anything out of the ordinary, something loose or leaking, bent or broken. Nothing looked out of place, so I climbed up on the fuel truck, another of Fred's good intentions.

On most jobs in field camps I fueled the helicopter out of 50-gallon drums with a hand pump. In an effort to make life easier, Fred bought a fuel truck, pre–World War II judging by the body style, with a 500-gallon tank and engine-driven pump. It wasn't a bad idea, but the pump broke the first day. After that, the only way to get the fuel out of the beast was to pump it by hand from the top of the tank, which was eight feet above the ground and often slippery.

The refueling done, I climbed down from the truck, lit a cigarette and sat in the thick bed of moss and lichen in front of Alice. The Talkeetna Mountains on the horizon were backlit by the soft glow of the setting sun. To my right I could hear Alpine Creek, bubbling and splashing as it dropped down the grassy slope of the Clearwater Mountains. The lingering warmth of the day felt good through my T-shirt as I lay back in the grass behind me. High above, a lone patch of altostratus clouds glowed red in the sun's last rays. With a sigh of contentment, I realized there was no place I'd rather be, that this was possibly the best job I'd had in Alaska.

Other field camps were good, by some standards better, in their own way. The Federal and State firefighting crews were the most basic when it came to living conditions, a length of Visqueen plastic to sleep under and military c-rations to eat, but the work was rewarding. Oil companies always had their act together, great food and a dependably comfortable environment. Specialty operations, like the mineral exploration companies, were more hedonistic, with hot tubs and imported wines. Even in field camps that were inaccessible by road. But none of them could provide the peace and tranquility I felt at that moment, and I couldn't help but reflect on my first season.

Five years earlier I took a summer job flying out of Cape Yakataga, a desolate stretch of the southern coast. I lived with Minnie and Erwin Eggabrotten. Other than a small military contingent manning a radio relay station farther down the coast, Minnie and Erwin were the only people in the area. They put me up in the claustrophobic attic of their smoky one-room log cabin. The book I brought to read was Dostoyevsky's Crime and Punishment, and like Raskolnikov I felt trapped in an untenable situation.

The job was to take a technician named Ed to service propane-powered radio transmitters strategically placed on the tops of mountains between Cordova and Yakutat. Ships off the coast used the transmitters for precision navigation. We took tanks of the propane to sites chosen for their prominence among the other peaks, so that the transmitters' signals would carry the maximum distance.

The landing sites were difficult, typically on pinnacles or steep, narrow ridges, no room for mistakes, and the weather was terrible—fog, low clouds, rain, and wind. I wasn't used to flying in winds that blew so hard the rain never hit the ground. There was turbulence everywhere. The flying was the worst I'd encountered, and the work was inherently dangerous.

Because the landing sites were so confined, I had to carry the propane tanks in cargo racks attached to the side of the helicopter. The tanks blocked the cockpit doors, limiting my ability to get out of the helicopter in an emergency. Which probably wouldn't be an issue if we crashed, because there was a good chance the propane would ignite. I was a flying bomb, trying to land at impossible sites in high winds. But it was taking off from a perfectly safe landing site on a windless day, without propane tanks, that almost got us killed.

We were on a shoulder of Heney Peak, not far from the fishing village of Cordova, where Ed was trying to fix an inoperative transmitter. It wasn't going well. We'd been there most of the day and hadn't gotten it on line. The sun was heading for the horizon when clouds began to build up on the slope below us. I told Ed it was time to go, but he ignored me and kept working on the transmitter. Less than an hour later I couldn't see the landing gear from the cockpit.

"Ready," Ed told me when he finally climbed into the copilot's seat beside me.

"For what?" I asked. "We aren't going anywhere."

We sat there for a least an hour before the cloud began to thin. At one point I could clearly make out the round orb of the sun not far from where the horizon would have been, indicating the cloud was quite thin and sunset wasn't far off. If we didn't get out of there soon we were going to spend the night on the top of that mountain.

Staying on top of that mountain in a cold damp cloud, trapped in the confines of the cockpit with a guy who was, judging by the smell of his breath, still metabolizing the alcohol he'd consumed the night before, wasn't the way I wanted to end the day. Less than a dozen miles away there was a hotel room with a hot shower and clean sheets waiting for me. So I decided to start the helicopter and fly out of the cloud, using the sun for a heading and relying on the helicopter's flight instruments to maintain straight and level flight.

In the console in front of me, along with the usual airspeed and altitude indicators, there was an artificial horizon and a vertical speed indicator. I had logged several hundred hours of IFR, flying on flight instruments alone, and was relatively certain that we'd be out of the cloud in seconds.

After letting the helicopter and its flight instruments warm up for five minutes, we lifted off into the cloud and headed for the glow of the sun. Seconds after we left the ridge the attitude indicator tilted to the right and rolled upside down.

In an instant I had lost my primary flight instrument, the one that let me know if I was flying level, in a climb, turning or diving.

Most of the same information was available from my other instruments, but not in one glance. I looked at the airspeed indicator. It was climbing. The vertical speed indicator showed us going down at 200 feet a minute. That was okay. We were accelerating into a dive, and I corrected for it. But my directional gyro showed we were turning slowly to the left. That wasn't good. We could be in a simple turn to the left; or, we could be rolling upside down to the left.

More than once I'd considered what would be the right thing to do in exactly that situation, in a cloud and not sure if the aircraft was under control. My conclusion was to reduce power, take all the lift out of the rotor system. That way the helicopter would be hanging from its rotor blades and less likely to roll upside down. So, I lowered the collective and held the airspeed at 60 mph. Seconds later we dropped from the bottom of the cloud several hundred feet above the raising slope of Heney Peak.

That tense evening on Heney Peak was five years ago, I recalled, lying in the moss in front of Alice. A lot had changed, as far as the work I did, and who I flew around, but not the close calls, I realized with a twinge of remorse. The cliff dive was less than an hour old in my memory. I could clearly hear Linda say, "You're crazy, Tom." She was laughing, probably joking. Truth of the matter was, what I'd done wasn't crazy. It was reckless and irresponsible.

Although I had thousands of hours in the cockpit I didn't consider myself a professional pilot, the type who lived and breathed flying, knew every page of the flight manual. Maybe that was part of the problem, I thought. I didn't want to be part of a regimented profession, I couldn't even recall ever wanting to be a pilot. I just liked to fly, likely as not because it had been a part of my life from an early age.

The first time I was in an airplane was with my father in his Luscombe, a two-seat airplane, when I was 18 months old.

About the only thing that stuck in my brain was looking down at our house as we flew over, seeing the chicken coop was in a different place than I thought it was. Later flights were more memorable, like the first time I got to steer the little airplane. I also remember feeling as comfortable bobbing around in the air as I did driving home in the car afterwards, and how I often missed the benefit of being able to see things from several hundred feet in the air.

After my parents died in a private airplane crash during a landing that went wrong, the idea of becoming a pilot never crossed my mind. That is, until I was suspended from college in the middle of the Vietnam War and received my draft notice. Then, through default, becoming a pilot became a lesser evil. Unless I did something else, like leave the country, I'd be carrying a rifle in the snake-infested jungles of Vietnam within a year. That's when my older brother, Norm, suggested I fly helicopters. His brother-in-law, Harry, was doing it, and reportedly having a good time. So I joined the Army as a flight school candidate.

Where I found flying around with my dad interesting, operating the controls of a helicopter was fascinating. Airplanes charge down a runway and climb away from the ground as fast as they can; helicopters simply rise off the ground and go exploring. Flying them came to me easily, and the training the Army gave me was second to none. We were taught everything from the gear ratio of the helicopters' main transmission to navigating by the stars. From flight school we went straight to Vietnam. I ended up flying for the 1st Cavalry Division Airmobile in a very active war zone northwest of Saigon. After the war I flew in Borneo and then southern California.

By the time I got to Alaska, I was well trained and had flown all around the world. While I didn't consider myself a professional pilot by any means, I knew I was good at what I did. I also knew that competency came from experience, learning one step at a time while never forgetting the limitations of the aircraft and the pilot. That was the problem with the cliff dive, I realized. I'd gone too far.

My introspection was interrupted by what sounded like someone in camp yelling my name. Probably the cook, I thought, sitting up and brushing pieces of lichen and moss off my clothes. It was almost eight, the time we usually had dinner. "Goodnight, Alice," I said to my helicopter, and followed the trail the girls had taken down the hill.

There were 12 of us living in tents among a stand of white spruce trees on the edge of Alpine Creek. Like most field camps in Alaska, the crew was a diverse group. This one had been brought together to work for FSL, the Forestry Sciences Lab, a department of the U.S. Forest Service.

Fred, the project leader, and Ken, his crew chief, were the only full-time FSL employees. They spent the summer in the field collecting data, then compiled, analyzed and distributed their findings from their office in Anchorage during the winter. It was a 10-year project that took in most of the state. The rest of us were part-time or on contract, hired for the length of the field season—in this case, three months.

Chris, Kathy, Will, Rocky, Tim and Paul were studying forestry or some other natural science in colleges in the lower 48 states. They were there for different reasons; however, they all wanted to spend a summer in Alaska, make a little money and find out what it was like to work for the government. Federal agencies were the largest employers in their fields.

For Linda the job was a chance to get out of Allakaket, a small Athabascan village in the middle of Alaska that was 50 miles from the nearest road. The cook, Bill, was a veteran hired on the preferential hiring program, a must-hire position. The last person on the crew was Dave. He was also a veteran and had spent time in Vietnam, but that was all I knew about him. I was employed by Tundra Copters and based in Fairbanks.

Dinner was almost over when I joined the crew. No one likes to miss meals in a field camp, especially dinner. When you work in the woods and live in a small tent, dinner is one of the few civilized rewards the day has to offer.

Bill was standing at the open fly of the canvas cook tent

with a big spoon in his hand, scowling at me. "Come on, Smith," he said. "Think I'm cooking for you?"

Cooking was a gross overstatement for what Bill did. The food he gave us was "prepackaged for individual use," "add water and stir," or it came from a can. I considered telling him what I thought about his cooking almost every day, but he was the type who'd spit in your soup.

"Just going over Alice, Bill," I told him. "Making sure she's okay to fly tomorrow."

"Sounds like a personal problem to me," the cook replied curtly.

"Well, if you get deathly ill, or shoot yourself in the foot with that big pistol on your hip, and have to be flown out of here to a hospital, you wouldn't want to crash and die, would you?" Bill was the only one of us who carried a gun in camp. Apparently he was afraid of bears.

The cook grunted and dropped a pile of instant mashed potatoes off the spoon onto a paper plate and handed it to me. A ladle of what appeared to be chili came next.

"Salad's on the table," he said, pointing with his spoon at a chopped up head of iceberg lettuce on the picnic table in front of the tent.

I might not have disliked Bill quite as much if he hadn't replaced Camille, our cook for the first month of the summer. Every meal she made was a delicious combination of meats, pastas, breads, fruits and vegetables, followed by an exceptional dessert. She worked at it all day. The cook tent became a social center where we'd sit around making small talk while waiting patiently for her next meal.

"How about that windsock?" Fred asked as I walked by on my way to the table.

"It's great, Fred. I shouldn't have any trouble landing into the wind with that there." Without waiting for a reply I kept going to the picnic table where Rocky, Paul and Tim were finishing their meals.

Paul looked at me and smiled. "This cliff dive," he asked, trying to sound serious. "You know. It's not something

15

you'd up and do. You'd ask us first. Right, man?"

I had to laugh, even though I'd have been happier if the girls hadn't said anything. "Okay, you guys," I said to the group at the table, hoping to put an end to it and get to my meal. "You're just jealous, and you know it."

"Why sure, we're jealous," Rocky joined in, his mischievous grin as subtle as his west Texas drawl. "We'd all like to be pretty girls and have you show off for us," he chuckled. Of the guys in camp, Rocky was my favorite. He had a way of looking at things that always turned out well. But he also liked to stir things up.

"Yeah, Smith," Tim joined in. "When do we get to do a cliff dive?"

Tim actually seemed upset. He was our resident conscience. It could easily be the principle of the thing that bothered him. The bias I'd shown the girls.

"Anytime, Tim," I replied, relatively sure he didn't really want to fly down the face of a cliff. "Let me eat first. Okay?"

"Seems to me…," Rocky began.

"Don't worry about it," I told him, annoyed that we were still talking about something that wouldn't happen again. I wasn't going to put Alice through that again. "I don't think I'm going to be doing any cliff dives for a while. But…"

"What's a cliff dive?" Fred asked from right behind me.

I cringed as all eyes turned to me. I had no idea that our self-appointed safety officer had joined the group around the table. However, judging by the smirks, Rocky and Paul had known. If Fred found out what a cliff dive was, he'd shit.

"Well, Fred, it's, uh…," I began. Rocky and Paul were trying to conceal their laughter. "Someone told me…" Nothing came to mind.

"Fred." It was Bill. "I'm closing up the kitchen. All right?"

When Fred turned his attention to the cook, I stood up, dumped my plate in the trash can and slipped into the woods beside the cook tent, mentioning something about coming right

16

back. I knew that there was a good chance he'd forget all about it if I weren't there to question. The guys at the table wouldn't tell him either. We liked to play games, but no one really wanted to get anyone in trouble.

The woods were dark and the temperature had dropped at least 15 degrees since sunset. It's never summer at night in the mountains. I didn't want to get chilled, so I continued on to my tent, crawled inside and pulled on a wool shirt. Over the years I'd grown to appreciate the itchy material. Quality wool can be wet against your skin, frozen on the outside, and you'll stay relatively comfortable if you don't stop moving. Wool also always smells like wool, even when you haven't bathed recently.

Outside again, I made myself comfortable in front of my tent and lit a cigarette. It was a great site. Perched in the open on a steep bank above Alpine Creek, the site got both morning and evening sun, and I had a view of the Talkeetna Mountains. When you live in a tent most of the summer, finding the right spot becomes important.

Behind me something large was making its way through the woods. Had to be a person. Nothing makes as much noise as a person. Probably Tim on the way to his tent, I thought. He was a good guy, sincere in his beliefs and one of the hardest workers on the crew.

High in the sky it was still twilight. Darkness had crept out of the woods and was closing in. I snuggled deeper into the tall grass, searching for the last of the day's warmth in the ground below. My first winter in Alaska had been so cold, and it hadn't been over anywhere near long enough to be forgotten.

2

THE NORTH SLOPE

Last winter had been tough, and would have been a lot worse if I hadn't spent some of it away from Alaska. Around November, when the temperature dropped well below freezing and there wasn't a lot of flying to do, I left for Southern California. Three years earlier I'd bought a house in Ventura. The tenants had recently moved and the place needed some work.

After everything was in good order, and I'd found a new tenant, there was no reason to hang around Ventura. I took advantage of an inter-airline agreement Tundra Copters had with Pan Am, and flew to Tahiti for less than a hundred dollars each way.

I spent the first week in a hotel near the quay in Papeete. It was nice, slow-turning ceiling fans, louvered doors that opened to a wood balcony with rattan chairs, nightlife, but I was going through my money faster than I intended. To lengthen my stay, I moved in with a fisherman and his family on the outskirts of town for the next few weeks. Ten dollars a day included three meals, which all tasted a lot like fish. With less than a hundred dollars left I got on the weekly ferry to Bora Bora, a place I'd always wanted to see.

The island was every bit as picturesque as it appeared in National Geographic, an emerald atoll in a royal blue sea. Several hundred people lived in the only town on the island, mostly in thatch and plywood huts. There also an expensive hotel on a point of land south of town. After renting a bicycle from a guy on the pier where the ferry landed, I pedaled past the expensive hotel to a little beach without a person in sight.

I had left my suitcase at the hotel in Papeete. In a small backpack I had a light Oaxacan hammock, some mosquito netting, a large bottle of water, a baguette of bread, and a paperback copy of James Clavell's Shogun. I strung the hammock between two palm trees, read, swam, lay in the sun and slept. I was glad I'd brought a hammock instead of a tent when the land crabs came out that night. They were all over the place, scooting around sideways with their claws in the air. Some of them were as big as cats.

On the third day thirst and hunger overcame the serenity I'd attained in my solitude, so I got back on my bike and continued my trip around the island. Not far from town I was stopped by the delicious smell of a hamburger being grilled. According to a hand-painted sign, the delicious smell was coming from the Bora Bora Yacht Club. The thatched hut that served as a bar and kitchen, and a dingy tied up at the small dock, was all there was to it; however, after quenching my thirst on Coca-Cola, and downing a thick, juicy burger, I told the bartender that I thought it was the best yacht club in the world.

Hearing my flattering words, the owner/cook came out of the kitchen and we recognized each other immediately. Ten years earlier, on my way to Vietnam, we had drunk a lot of beer together on an island in the Caribbean Sea. The last word I'd heard of him was that he'd left to sail around the world in a concrete sailboat.

"Like the burger, did you?" he asked.

"One of the best," I confirmed. "As good as the Stone Balloon's." I added, paying him the ultimate compliment. The bar in an old limestone building not far from the harbor in Christiansted had the tastiest hamburgers in the world.

"That's who I stole the receipt from," he laughed.

After catching up on our various adventures in the last decade, he asked how long I was going to be around. When I told him I was out of money and about to leave, he told me to string my hammock between two palm trees behind the bar for as long as I wanted. He also let me have burgers and beer at cost after I put in a little time behind the bar.

My hiatus from Alaska lasted nearly three months, well

into February. When I left Tahiti for Fairbanks, it seemed reasonable to expect the weather to be better than it was when I left. During the brief walk from the airplane to the terminal that expectation disappeared. It was four in the afternoon, 30 below zero, and pitch-dark. As I walked off the plane the frigid air found its way through my light jacket. The snow squeaked shrilly under my shoes. By the time I reached the terminal my cheeks were burning and nose hairs frozen solid. I couldn't get out of the cold fast enough, but I was glad to be back. Although I had the house in California, Fairbanks was my home.

Not long after I bought the house, Darcie left and ended our one-year marriage. A month or two later I called Craig. We had been best friends since the first days of flight school, where we met while walking penalty laps. There were obstacles, like understanding his southern drawl and irregular sentence construction; however, we had a lot in common, similar feelings and views.

Craig and his wife, Sheryl, had moved from Georgia to Alaska several years earlier when he got the job working for Tundra Copters. By the time I called, Craig was their general manager and didn't hesitate to offer me a job. He and Sheryl even put me up in their house for the first summer.

Fairbanks felt like home, and Tundra was the best company I'd worked for. It was small, operating four to six helicopters, and completely informal. The owner stayed in California where he had another helicopter company, leaving everything to Craig's discretion. Who we worked for, how we did the job, everything was entirely up to him.

When I got back from Tahiti, and spring was nowhere in sight, the only reason to go outside was for food and drink. The rest of the day I read a little and watched television a lot. Then I began spending an inordinate amount of time in bed.

I'd go to sleep at a normal time, ten o'clock or so, but sometimes wouldn't get up until noon. When six or seven came around, the normal time to get out of bed, I'd simply lie there and watch the bright little airport lights outside my bedroom window in the hangar.

Little blue ones lined the taxiways, and yellow the main runway. A strip of white lights ran down the centerline of the runway, bright red lights stretched across the approach ends, brilliant white strobe lights flashed in directional sequence for hundreds of feet along the approach axis, and above it all there was the rotating beacon on the top of the control tower, flashing green to white, green to white in a coal black sky. I'd lie there, watching the pretty lights and fall asleep without feeling a thing.

I didn't realize how much the quality of my life depended on the weather until ice fog settled over Fairbanks. The phenomenon occurs when water vapor in the air freezes, somewhere around 40 degrees below zero. Everything disappears in the leaden blanket of the frozen fog, color, light, even sound. Stepping outside the hangar was like dying, like being a zombie in a world void of sensation. At that point I began to sleep even more and stay inside as much as I could.

Around the middle of March, when the days had grown noticeably longer and the temperature was climbing, word got out about a streambed full of gold near the Nelchina Glacier, and the Great Nelchina Gold Rush was on. Prospectors from around the state, even a few from the lower 48 states, braved the elements to get a piece of the action. Other than Craig, I was the only other pilot available, so Craig sent me to the Nelchina for spot charters.

The only place to stay within 40 miles of the gold strike was the Eureka Roadhouse, a ten-room motel, restaurant and bar. It was a bizarre scene when I got there. Like going back in time. Canvas-wall tents, the kind used by miners on gold rushes for a hundred years, surrounded the place. And a small army of scruffy-looking men milled around fires built in the snow. There were even a few dog teams staked out.

For a week I flew cash customers 10 miles into the frozen Chugach Mountains, 200 bucks per person round trip to the strike area. It was cold, but the weather was good, crystal clear blue skies and no wind. The only demanding part of the job was landing in the fresh snow. Near the ground the force of the rotor blades blew the light snow into the air. For the last few seconds of every approach I couldn't see a thing.

The best part of the job was hanging out in the bar at the end of the day, listening to the men talk. A lot of it was bullshit, but some of them were the real thing, prospectors who went into the most rugged country in Alaska by themselves and survived for years at a time. Those guys were called "sourdoughs" after the starter they took along with their wheat to make bread. Most of them were a little odd, if not downright crazy, and their stories were amazing.

The Nelchina gold rush ended as quickly as it began. Once the available land was staked, the prospectors folded their tents and went home to wait for spring, which appeared to be getting closer. The days were noticeably longer, the sun warmer. I'd even heard the songs of a few migratory birds. Between Tahiti and an early spring, I was beginning to think winter in Fairbanks wasn't all that bad, until Craig called me into his office a few days after I got back in town.

"You about ready for another job?" he asked.

We didn't get two jobs a month that time of year, much less two a week. I thought he was joking and laughed, "No."

"How about up on the Slope?" he asked.

"You're kidding?" I said. Craig grinned, he wasn't. "No way, pal," I told him. "Absolutely not."

The North Slope is a great, flat, treeless plain on the edge of the Arctic Ocean, 500 miles long and 100 miles wide, the most northern part of Alaska. It is also one of the coldest places on earth. I was up there the year before and almost froze to death. And that was in the middle of May when the average high temperature was 15 degrees above zero. Craig wanted me to go up there in the beginning of March. When the average high temperature on the Slope is 15 degrees below zero and the average low is 30 below.

"Afraid so," Craig persisted.

"Come on," I whined. "It's your turn." He just laughed. "It's going to be too cold to get any work done," I told him, knowing I was going to the Slope.

"That's the way they want it. Nice an' cold," Craig added patiently. Then he went on to explain that the oil flowing through the pipeline was warm enough to keep some streams open that should be frozen solid. Fish were living year-round in places they normally couldn't. Some people from the Department of the Interior wanted to find out what kind of fish they were.

"I'd send Rusty," Craig said, finishing up. "But he's got that race comin' up."

Other than Craig and me, Rusty was the only other pilot on the payroll that time of year. In a few weeks he was going to run the Iditarod dogsled race, billed as the last great race on Earth. It began in Anchorage, on the south coast of the state, and ran northwest through mountain ranges, forests, across rivers, lakes, and every type of terrain imaginable, to Nome, over 1,000 miles away on the edge of the Bering Sea.

It isn't the length of the race, the time it takes, or even the rough terrain that makes the contest so tough. Those obstacles could be overcome with training and endurance. The biggest threat is the weather. When the temperature hits 50 below, and the windchill makes it a lot colder, both the musher and his dogs are risking their lives. Holing up in a cabin in that kind of weather is one thing, but hooking up your team and heading out into it is something entirely different.

Surprisingly, the race can be even more difficult when the temperature gets too high. The snow becomes slow and standing water ices up paws and the sled's runners, making it hard on the dogs. If the weather stays above freezing long enough, the streams and rivers open up or flood over the ice. Crossing them can be deadly.

As much as I respected what Rusty was doing, I really wished he could take the job on the Slope. He'd been up there in the winter a lot more than I and had more experience with the cold and whiteouts. Whiteouts occur anywhere the sky is uniformly overcast and there is complete snow cover, including all the vegetation. When the light is low and shadows disappear, the gray sky and white ground blend together.

Distance and depth are lost and vertigo overwhelms the senses. The North Slope was famous for its whiteouts in March, and crashes were not uncommon. I'd been on the edge of vertigo, felt its strength as it pulled me in, and feared it.

"It'll only be a week, maybe two," Craig assured me.

Two days later I took off for the North Slope with three fish biologists from the Department of the Interior. On the outskirts of Fairbanks we flew over Dredge Number Eight. Built around the turn of the century, Number Eight was a hundred-foot-long, 30-foot-wide wooden-hulled barge with a dredge on the deck. Using dragline and buckets, it had worked its way up Goldstream Creek. When the gold ran out in the '40s it was left weathering gracefully in its last pond, a vivid reminder of the past. It didn't take much imagination to see the old monster at work, black smoke billowing from the tall stack of its steam engine as bearded men in wool shirts and canvas pants moved mountains of dirt and rock for a sack full of precious gold.

A few miles later we picked up the "haul road," the dirt road that runs the length of the oil pipeline that bisects Alaska. Most of the time I navigated by dead reckoning, relating what I saw in front of me to a map. I flew too low to rely on the few electronic navigational aids available in the state. Even my simple magnetic compass couldn't be trusted because of our proximity to the magnetic north pole. Although I liked navigating by dead reckoning, following the haul road was too easy not to enjoy.

We followed the course of the road over the west end of the White Mountains, cruising along just high enough to clear the ridges. Below us there wasn't anything but low spruce trees and fresh snow. It was disturbing how quickly the few signs of spring around Fairbanks had disappeared as we flew north.

An hour and a half later my passengers and I stopped in the village of Bettles for fuel, then we began working our way through the Brooks Range. We flew up the Middle Fork of the Koyukuk River, following the valley into the south side of the mountain range. From the windswept peaks thousands of feet above us to the frozen streambed below, nothing moved. Not a sign of life anywhere.

After passing Mount Doonerak and the Frigid Crags, tall pinnacles of granite and shale, we climbed Atigun Pass, the portal to the North Slope. As we flew through the pass the sun grew dim in a hazy sky and the temperature dropped to 15 below. A few minutes later there was a vertical drop of 2,000 feet into a river valley flowing north, and we were out on the Slope. In front of us lay 50,000 square miles of undisturbed snow. Somewhere in the middle of the great expanse of frozen tundra, 130 miles away, was our destination, Deadhorse.

Less than an hour later the orange plumes of flares burning gas off the wellheads around Prudhoe Bay appeared in the haze ahead of us. It was the beginning of the four-foot-diameter pipe that carried two million barrels of crude a day from the oil fields along the northern coast of Alaska to Valdez, a seaport 800 miles away on the south coast. The oil field was an eyesore, but a welcome one. Since we'd crossed the Brooks Range, the temperature had steadily dropped to 25 below zero. The helicopter's heater was barely keeping up and my feet were cold.

We checked into the Happy Horse Hotel, a modular structure of large metal containers with small windows. It looked like something you'd find on the moon. The next day we were still there. The temperature never got above 30 below, my cutoff point for flying. Any colder than that, there is too much risk of freezing to death if anything goes wrong. That kind of weather is also hard on the helicopter. But the next day was clear, sunny and the temperature climbed to 10 degrees below zero by midmorning.

We followed the pipeline south until we found a frozen stream that crossed an underground stretch of the pipeline where, amazingly, there was open water. While the biologists mapped the stream and looked for fish, I took a walk. On a little rise not far from the helicopter, I paused, looking around at endless vistas of ice and snow. There's nothing out here but us, I thought, squinting off into the distance. Anything trying to live out here would freeze, I surmised. It was a strange feeling, like being on another planet. Then a small bird fluttered into sight, darted left and disappeared with the wind.

When I got back to the helicopter it was time for lunch, and a relatively warm eight degrees above zero. Nice enough for a picnic, I decided, climbing into the cockpit and opening my sack lunch. Sheltered from the wind it was almost pleasant. After lunch I settled into my seat and closed my eyes, until I heard one of my passengers yell, "Hey! Over there!"

On a rise less than a hundred yards behind the helicopter, standing shoulder-to-shoulder and staring at us, were ten or eleven musk ox. In their ankle-length coats of matted wool they looked like something out of a Star Wars movie. Although the size of a small horse, they looked more like enormous furry hamsters. They did, however, have some impressive sickle-shaped horns sticking out of the sides of their heads. While I stared in fascination, a strong gust of wind kicked up a wall of snow between us. It twisted and turned in wild abandon for a moment then settled down. The musk oxen were gone.

The third day Alice's generator went out on our way back to the hotel. After dropping my passengers off at the Happy Horse, I flew over to ERA's hangar, the only helicopter company with a base on the Slope. I found several pilots and mechanics in the break room, nice enough guys, who told me that they had a spare generator and could sell it to me. But when I asked if I could roll my helicopter inside their hangar to change it, they said no. It was against company policy to let other operators use their facilities. What a contrast to Tundra, I thought, where we didn't have company policy. We were pilots. When we weren't flying we were ourselves.

Before I began I knew that changing the generator outside was going to be painful. Because it was recessed well below the turbine engine, there wasn't a lot of room to work. I was going to have to take my gloves off. Back at the hotel I checked the temperature as I ran an extension cord to the helicopter, 27 degrees below zero and dropping.

26

With electricity to the aircraft I was able to wedge a small electric heater under the engine that would blow on my hands while I worked. The nuts came off the studs without incident. Although heavy, the generator was out and the new one in place within minutes. Then I had to put the nuts back on and my gloves came off.

It stung when I picked up the first nut, but I got it on the stud easily enough and secured it with my wrench. The second nut burned the tips of my fingers, actually hurt, and I had trouble twisting it onto the stud. I dropped the third one as soon as I picked it up. It hurt that much. The ache in the tips of my two fingers continued to grow, so I took a look and, sure enough, there were two little white patches of frostbite. I held the offended digits inches from the heater for a moment then back in my glove. Ten minutes later I came out of the Happy Horse and put the last bolt on with the other hand.

Craig told me the job would only last a week or two, but it was the end of March before we finally got out of Deadhorse. I wouldn't have described any of the days as pleasant, even though a lot of them were extremely sunny. Still, as cold as it seemed to be, life was returning to the North Slope.

While we'd been north of the Arctic Circle the hours of daylight had gone from eight to eleven. A few days before we left, a furry mouse-like creature scurried across the hard-packed snow in front of me. As I was wondered how the little guy could survive on top of the snow, he disappeared between two tufts of dead grass. On closer inspection I found that the brown stalks were absorbing the increasingly strong sunlight and melting perfectly round holes in the snow. Down the hole the furry creature had gone, I could see the beginnings of buds and shoots. The feast was about to begin.

The North Slope, contrary to its desolate appearance in the winter, is, during the summer, comparable to the plains of the Serengeti in Africa when it's raining. It was about to become a premier wildlife range. Millions of creatures, most of them birds, migrate to the Slope each summer to breed, and they need a lot eat. The vegetation coming to life under the snow was the beginning of the food chain that would feed them.

It was warming up fast on the Slope, but nothing like Fairbanks. The day we got back it was 55 degrees and felt like 70. The only snow left was hiding in the woods. Sitting behind the hangar, basking in the sun, I took in a long deep breath. It smelled like spring. Winter's wearisome grip was broken.

Three weeks later I hadn't done a lot other than sleep and lie around in the sun. Craig, Rusty and I split the few flights that came up. Rusty was back to work full time after a remarkable showing in the Iditarod. He didn't win, but had done well enough to be named Rookie of the Year, a prestigious award for an impressive accomplishment.

I had done so little in so long, when Craig told me my old friend Dan Hawkins wanted to go into the Horn Mountains for a few days with me, I couldn't think of anything I'd rather do. Dan was a professor at the University of Alaska, a geochemist and prominent figure in the small but influential field. He also sang lead in a local stage production of Die Fledermaus, and was the first guy I flew for when I went to work for Tundra. There had been a lot to learn back then, and Dan, a genuinely warm-hearted man, made it easy for me.

"What're we gonna be doing, Dan?" I asked as we headed south out of Fairbanks.

"Well, we're going to be looking for the most elusive zeolites," he said with a smile.

"Which are?" I asked.

"A naturally hydrous, aluminum silicate. Which, as we all know, is greatly appreciated for its ion exchange capacity and, of course, gas absorption properties."

"Appreciated by whom?" I inquired politely.

"Ah, my young friend," Dan exclaimed, visibly pleased by my interest. "Do you drink water?"

"No," I answered. "Pretty much stick to beer."

Dan chuckled appreciatively and continued, "Zeolites are used in water softeners and lots of other places. Even as a dietary supplement for cows."

"Oh," I said, sounding as impressed as I could.

The Horn Mountains were 200 miles south of Fairbanks. Where we were working on their exposed southern slopes, spring was even further along than in town. Sweet grass and wild flowers covered the mountainsides. There were also a lot of ground squirrels. At first the good-sized rodents were leery of me, but relaxed once they understood that I just wanted to lie in the sun on a warm rock like them

Birds' songs, sunshine and balmy breezes made for a pleasant week with Dan while he mapped out zeolite deposits. When we got back to Fairbanks, buds were forming on barren limbs in some stands of trees and on bushes. Slender green shoots were poking through last year's growth of grass. The days were nearly 14 hours long, and the snow was completely gone.

Seasons change fast that far north and I couldn't have been happier. Then, late one night, during a particularly invigorating game of pinball at the Midnight Mine, Craig looked at me and smiled for no apparent reason. That was the second clue something was up. All evening, every time my glass of whiskey got anywhere near empty, a fresh one appeared.

"This is a pretty good pinball machine," Craig said, casually enough. When I agreed, he added, "The best one I ever played was up in Barrow."

Barrow sits on a naked peninsula jutting out into the Arctic Ocean. It's the only place farther north in Alaska than Deadhorse, nothing but hundreds of miles of frozen ocean between it and the North Pole. A couple thousand residents, mostly native Americans, a small contingent of Air Force personnel, and a few arctic researchers lived in the isolated village. I'd never been there and couldn't think of any reason to go.

"Yeah," I said, not very interested.

"I think it was Star Trek or something." I didn't say anything, even though we both knew I was a fan of the television show. "They got all kinds of games up in that NARL camp. You know, that research camp up there in Barrow."

When I didn't react, he let it go, but on our way back to the hangar, out of the blue, he said, "We've been thinking about havin' the birthday this weekend." It was going to be the second annual party celebrating the end of winter and return of Tundra's summer employees. Craig and Sheryl put it on at their house. Last year it was on my birthday, so they called it a birthday party.

"Great," I said. Then I realized that my birthday wasn't until the next week, and Sheryl had mentioned that they were going to have the party on my birthday again this year. When I turned to tell Craig he was a couple days off, he was grinning. That's when I realized there was a pattern... free drinks, pinball in Barrow, party on a different day.

"Why, you son of a bitch," I almost laughed. "I can't believe it. You're tryin' to get me up on the Slope again. Aren't you?" He kept ginning. "No way, Craig! Absolutely no goddamned way."

"That's why we gotta have your birthday party early," he said.

"Forget it, man," I told him. "I'm not going back up there. It's still winter up there for Christ's sake." There wasn't a limb, branch or stem that didn't have a bud on it about to burst. The ice had gone out of the Tanana River. Spring was here, and I was so ready to enjoy it. "I've never been there, Craig. It's still winter, not the time to learn a new area."

"Just head towards the North Pole, and keep goin'," he said. "And don't worry about a new area. You're going to be workin' out over the ice."

That was something I'd never done. Fly over the polar ice, past the last land in North America.

"What's the job?" I asked, trying not to sound interested.

I was to meet my passengers at NARL, the Naval Arctic Research Lab in Barrow, and take them north, a hundred miles out onto the frozen ocean, where they were going to drill holes in the ice. The core samples they were after would be part of a database for research. In conclusion, he told me, "Don't forget your shotgun. They want you to watch out for polar bears, too." That definitely sounded cool. I'd never seen a polar bear in the wild before.

A few days later, along with a couple of pilots, mechanics, their wives and girlfriends, I found myself celebrating my birthday in a bar in downtown Fairbanks. The party had begun earlier in the day on Craig and Sheryl's porch, but when the sun went down and the temperature with it, we moved to Tommy's Elbow Room, where I met Andie, an attractive young lady who had never seen a polar bear in the wild either, or even flown in a helicopter.

3

WHITEOUT

The day after Tundra's annual spring party, Andie and I climbed in Alice and took off for Barrow. After we were out of the airport traffic area I pointed the helicopter's nose north and settled into my cruising altitude of 500 feet. I liked that altitude for a number of reasons. We were high enough to see where we were going but low enough to be out of the main flow of regional air traffic. Five hundred feet also gave me enough time to find a landing spot if I lost my engine, and was close enough to the ground to get there in a hurry if I had to. It was also a good altitude for watching what went on around me.

In flight school they taught us to stay at least 1,000 feet above the ground, primarily to give us more time to find a forced landing area in the event of an engine failure. It was true that the farther we were from the ground the more places we could glide to without our engine; however, I'd found that from 1,000 feet I couldn't see the potential landing spots as well as I could from 500 feet above the ground. When it came down to it, I preferred knowing where I was going, to having options that, upon closer inspection, might force me to look somewhere else at a critically low altitude.

Before we lost radio contact with Fairbanks, I switched frequencies to open a flight plan with the FAA's Flight Service Station, part of a network of radio transmitters and receivers around the state that kept track of aircraft.

"Fairbanks radio. Helicopter November five-eight-one-two-nine," I called.

"November five-eight-one-two-nine. Fairbanks," a guy came back.

"Roger, Fairbanks. One-two-nine, I'd like to open a flight plan," I told him, then proceeded to give him the pertinent information about our flight: type and color of aircraft, pilot's name, number of people on board, contact numbers, route of flight, fuel on board and a few other details, including our estimated time of arrival in Barrow. I always figured my time and added a half hour to be safe. It was embarrassing to underestimate and have them begin a search.

We stopped for fuel at Bettles. At the airstrip, which was also the center of town for its 50 or 60 residents, we had to wait awhile before a guy in his 80s came out of the hotel to pump the fuel for us. He glanced at me. Then took a closer look.

"Aren't you the young fella that helped George and Martha?" I was amazed the old man remembered. It had been awhile.

On a stopover in Bettles for fuel two years ago, I did a favor for a young couple. He was an airplane pilot, she was a concert pianist, and they were in the last stage of moving into a cabin way out in the woods. The story of what I did appeared in an edition of Alaska Magazine.

"Finally the last freight haul was made and a survey of George and Martha's room at the lodge revealed only one thing left: the piano. George spent a week uncomplainingly building a crate for it, and finally it was gently shoved inside and ready to go. After much discussion it was decided hauling it by snow machine and sled would be too tricky and the risk to the piano too great.

Back at the lodge, the crated piano sat forlornly in an outside shed. We accosted every helicopter pilot who traveled through. Finally, about breakup time, the time of year the rivers thaw and ice "breaks up," we lucked out and found a kindly man who didn't think airlifting a piano twenty-three miles was an odd request at all. Before he had a chance to refuse, we had the piano ensconced in a cargo net. In a flurry of snow, the crated Yamaha creaked off the ground and was whisked away. The pilot's fee a case of beer and the promise of a full concert by Martha just for him someday."

"They're real happy up there," he told me as he put Alice's fuel cap back on.

I appreciated the old man telling me that, but was still too hungover from our annual spring party to say anything more than, "That's nice."

Instead of using the Koyukuk River and Atigun Pass to get through the Brooks Range to the North Slope, as I had a month and a half earlier, we headed up the John River to Anaktuvuk Pass. Halfway up the John we passed Crevice Creek and the homestead of my friends Bill and Lil Fickus. We would have stopped in to say hello. Their nearest neighbor lived 40 miles away, so they always enjoyed company. But we were running and I wasn't feeling very social.

Because I wasn't feeling that well, Andie did most of the talking on our flight north. A lot of it was about a guy in Barrow. It turned out that an ex-boyfriend of hers worked for the town's fire department, and she was looking forward to seeing him. Which only deepened the depression of my hangover. I'd been hoping she might keep me company in Barrow. From what I'd heard the place wasn't known for its social life.

Flying up the gentle slope of Anaktuvuk Pass, we went by the village of Anaktuvuk. The residents, not more than 200 people, were the Nunamiuts, some of the last nomadic Eskimos in North America. However, it looked like they spent most of the time right there in Anaktuvuk eating their favorite food, caribou. Not far from the village was a pile of bones at least 20 feet high and 60 feet long. The sun-bleached tangled mass of ribs, leg bones, spines, skulls and antlers was a sculpture of sorts, open, light, and macabre.

Until we got to Anaktuvuk the weather had been relatively nice, in the 50s with very little snow on the ground. But when we dropped down out of the mountains onto the North Slope, the ground was covered in snow and there was a layer of haze in the sky ahead of us. As I turned northwest towards Barrow, we ran into a little snowstorm. There was room to go around but I didn't bother because I could see through it, and they can be fun. Spring snowflakes are large, maybe five times the size of normal snow.

As we closed on the snow at 120 mph, I checked the outside air temperature. It was well below 45 degrees, so I switched on the engine anti-ice and pressed the caution light for the particle separator to make sure it was working. I also gave the flight instruments a quick check. I doubted I would need the artificial horizon, or any of the other instruments that helped me fly without being able to see outside the cockpit, but if the bubble iced up or something, I knew I'd be awfully glad they were there and in working order.

At first the large flakes appeared to be drifting lazily, almost lighter than air. But as we got closer, a hundred yards or so, they began to move in our direction. It was as if they'd suddenly noticed us and were coming to investigate. The closer we got to the enormous white flakes, the faster they came until, at a phenomenal rate of speed, they raced up over Alice's nose and flashed across the windshield of the cockpit.

"Cool," Andy murmured into the microphone of her headset.

"Like punching into a meteor shower at warp speed," I concurred.

Halfway to Barrow we stopped at Umiat for fuel. There are only two sizable communities on the North Slope, Deadhorse and Barrow. Umiat is somewhere in between, an outpost in the middle of nowhere with one function, to sell fuel to aircraft like us. A handful of people lived beside the airstrip on the banks of the Colville River to man the Flight Service Station and sell fuel. The price I paid for jet fuel was nearly twice what I'd paid in Fairbanks, way more than it cost to get it there, but I couldn't blame them for overcharging. Umiat was flat and gray. It got above 60 for a few days in the middle of the summer and went down to a hundred below in the winter. I'd need to be making a lot of money to live in a place like that.

When we left Umiat the weather began to deteriorate. The temperature dropped to ten above zero and the overcast thickened. Before long I had to slow down to 100 miles an hour. The light was fading and it was getting difficult to see the flat, snow-covered ground below us. Finally the horizon between the sky and ground disappeared. By then we were down to 60 mph and 20 feet above the ground. Without a horizon, the only reference I had was the little thaw ponds that dotted the tundra. The dim shadows along their banks gave me enough ground reference to keep going. It wasn't easy because there were lots of open areas, so I kept flying slower and slower.

When the visibility dropped to the length of the helicopter, I told Andie, "This isn't worth it."

It was time to turn around. The conditions were bad and getting terrible. Besides, by then we were only going 30 or 40 mph. At that speed, along with the erratic course we were flying from pond to pond, there was a good chance we'd run out of fuel before we reached Barrow. Reflexively, I glanced out my side window to clear the turn I was about to make. What I saw was a total whiteout, one drab color all around us. It was like stepping inside a Ping-Pong ball and closing the door. My sense of balance reeled out of control as I whipped my head around, searching the snow in front of us for whatever it was I saw last. But it wasn't there. All that I saw was gray, nothing else.

While my eyes searched, my mind raced. I knew I was losing control of the aircraft... had to be. We were still moving forward, but were we also tilting? Which way? I could feel the adrenaline pumping in my veins, pounding in my head, but my hands wouldn't move. They didn't know what to do. Instruments, I thought in a panic, glancing at the artificial horizon in front of me. The little bar showed we were level but climbing at thirty degrees. That didn't seem possible. I couldn't trust it. Time was running out. A wave of nausea swept over me and I froze.

In that split second of indecision my peripheral vision

caught movement to the left. A large animal was there long enough for me to see it was a caribou. Then it simply disappeared, became a seamless part of the void.

The caribou was gone but I'd seen enough. Fixating on the spot where it had been, holding that picture in my mind, I rolled the helicopter to the left, then level again, and lowered the collective. To make sure we weren't going in nose-low, I brought the cyclic back even more. Then I noticed a dark patch on the ground ahead of us. It was dirt, exposed when the animal had pawed through the snow to feed. Gambling that the strip of tundra was level ground, I straightened Alice up a few degrees to the right and pushed the nose down a lot, then brought the collective up some to cushion the landing, and cringed... waiting to hit the ground and hear the traumatizing sound of a main rotor blade slicing into the tail boom and ripping it off, or feel the aircraft jerk violently as the tail rotor tore into the ground. But nothing happened.

When I realized we weren't moving, that we were on the ground, in the snow, I rolled the throttle off. After a short dying whistle from the turbine as it spooled down, all was quiet. Only the main rotor blades moved, slowing down with each revolution. I flipped the generator and battery switches to the off position and looked at Andie.

"What happened?" she asked.

I didn't answer right away. I wasn't sure what part she'd missed. "I don't know. I mean, a whiteout, but I..."

The intensity of the situation left me a bit confused, but one thing I knew was that we'd been lucky. If that caribou hadn't exposed the tundra we would have hit tail-low, possibly hard enough to flex the advancing rotor blade down and into the cockpit. That didn't happen often, but it had killed people.

As soon as the rotor blades came to a stop, still unable to believe the helicopter was all right, I turned the handle of my door and pushed, then pushed harder. The snow was up to the window. A few more attempts and I was outside in a steady wind blowing from the north. Icy snowflakes peppered my cheeks, and I shivered as the chill cut through my jacket. A quick look was all it took to see the aircraft was fine. In fact, all I had to do was crank it up and we could take off. Instead I grabbed two of the sleeping bags, part of our winter survival kit, from the baggage compartment and climbed back into the cockpit.

"Is Alice okay?" Andie asked.

"Amazingly enough, yes," I told her.

"Are we going to be here awhile?" she asked as I handed her a sleeping bag.

"Maybe," I told her. "At least until the weather changes. But we're going to need these things anyhow. It's going to get cold in here real soon." I checked the outside air temperature, 22 degrees, below freezing but definitely survivable, I thought. As we sat there in silence, I felt the tension in my body give way to depression, or possibly the hangover. Anyway, I felt horrible.

"Could you see anything? I mean right before we, ah, landed?" I finally asked Andie.

"No... you mean you couldn't see anything either? God, I haven't seen anything but snow since we left Umiat," she told me.

"We're awfully lucky. I mean, if that caribou..."

"What caribou?"

I told her about the caribou I'd used as a landing site, and then apologized for not turning around sooner. I also told her why I chose to land in the snow rather than switch to my flight instruments, explaining that I wasn't sure the artificial horizon was working.

"It's not that I think it's broken. I just had to decide quickly, and at the time I didn't want to trust our lives to something I wasn't a hundred percent sure was working correctly."

While we talked, what light there was began to fade. The sun was going down. The chance of us spending the night there was getting better by the moment. Checking the outside air temperature again it read 19 degrees, a three-degree drop in as many minutes. Before getting into my sleeping bag I remembered the flight plan I'd opened as we were leaving Fairbanks. If we weren't in Barrow within the hour, they'd start searching for us.

I doubted that I would reach Barrow, but I might get an aircraft in the area, so I turned off everything electrical except the primary VHF radio and flipped the battery switch on. It was already tuned to 122.4, the frequency for Barrow's Flight Service Station, so I pressed the transmit switch on the cyclic.

"Barrow radio. Helicopter November five-eight-one-two-nine. Do you copy?"

A friendly female voice filled my headset. "November five-eight-one-two-nine, Barrow. I read you five by five." Radio contact was one nice thing about flying on the Slope. If there had been hills or even a lot of trees between us, I wouldn't have been able to reach them as far away as we were.

"Roger that, Barrow. We're down in zero visibility approximately six zero miles southeast of your location. I would like to close my flight plan."

"Roger, one-two-nine. Understand close your flight plan at this time."

"That's affirmative, Barrow. And could you say your weather and anything you've got for this area?"

She gave me the current weather for Barrow, Umiat, Deadhorse and Camp Lonely, the only places on the Slope that reported weather. All of the stations except Camp Lonely were reporting winds from the northwest, several thousand feet overcast, and decent visibility. Camp Lonely, an oil camp about 20 miles to the north, was reporting several thousand feet overcast and less than a quarter mile visibility in blowing ice and snow from the north.

"Barrow, one-two-nine, thanks a lot. I've got a pretty good idea what's going on. We'll be here until the weather changes, I guess." The prospects of that happening any time soon weren't great. A friend who worked at Camp Lonely for a year told me the wind never stopped blowing there.

"Roger, one-two-nine," Barrow came back. "Understand, no damage and on the ground in whiteout."

I sat there for a moment thinking, not wanting to break contact with our only link to the rest of the world. But there was nothing left to say and I had to save the battery to start the helicopter in the morning. We had our sleeping bags and the shell of the helicopter to keep the wind off of us. It wouldn't be that bad. As I reached over to turn the radio off, it came to life.

"One-two-nine, Barrow, you still there?"

"Sure am," I replied.

"Come up one-two-six-point-three." I dialed the frequency into the radio, keyed the mike and identified myself.

"Roger, one-two-nine, this is Sergeant Wills. I've got you on a true heading of one-four-seven degrees, approximately seventy-three-point-two statute miles from Barrow. You're in a band of blowing ice crystals. The tops are five hundred feet above you. It's about four miles wide and you're right in the middle of it. Got a solid copy?"

"You bet, Sergeant. Thanks a lot. Certainly do appreciate the info," I told him, completely surprised. Although the man didn't say who he was, he had to be at the DEW, Defense Early Warning, site. Who else had radar that could pick up a helicopter sitting on the ground in a whiteout 70 miles away?

The little Air Force base at Barrow maintained a low profile, keeping an eye on Russia for signs of aggression. I'd never heard of them talking to a civilian aircraft before. Regardless, it was reassuring to know that someone knew where we were. If the weather didn't change in a day or two, with our exact location, they could send someone to pick us up on snow-machines.

"Hey! Look at that," Andie exclaimed.

I followed her gaze. There was something off to the west, a faint rosy glow. The sun was setting. It had dropped below the overcast sky above us on its way down. The orange ball was barely visible through the blowing snow and ice, but as we watched it grew brighter and spread out horizontally in a thin scarlet ribbon. In a few seconds it was going to be below the horizon.

"This isn't going to last long," I said, reaching up to make sure the battery was on. Then I pushed the starter button on the end of the collective. "And, according to the guy on the radio, we got two miles to go before we're out of this."

As the starter whined and the jet fuel ignited, I breathed a sigh of relief. We were on our way to dinner and a warm bed. But I wasn't relaxing. As soon as I pulled up on the collective the rotor blades were going to dig into the air and a dense cloud of snow was going to envelope the helicopter. For a few seconds we'd lose sight of the ground and the sun, be in a total whiteout again.

I also had to be careful not to climb into the overcast above us. We'd really be screwed then. So I set the altimeter to zero, figuring I'd stay between 50 and 75 feet. My maps showed nothing over 50 feet tall between where we were and Barrow. I also checked my flight instruments again, just in case I needed them. The attitude indicator appeared to be working. Then I brought the turbine up to operating RPM and took off fast in a nose-low climb. The snow must have been compacted by the wind because hardly any blew into the air. We never lost sight of the ground or the sunset, and were safely in Barrow less than an hour later.

In addition to being the northern-most town on the North American continent, Barrow is one of the coldest and darkest places on earth. For three months the sun doesn't shine. The average high temperature for the entire year is 15 degrees above zero, 17 degrees below freezing. Not the kind of place I would visit.

We left the helicopter at the airstrip and wandered through the little town on the edge of the Arctic Ocean. There wasn't much to see. A few metal-sided commercial and public buildings, nothing over one story tall, and hundreds of same size box-shaped homes as plain and unadorned as the terrain around them. They were designed to stay warm, we decided, not look good.

I left Andie at the fire station with her ex-boyfriend and checked in with the people I was going to work for. They were pleasant enough, and the accommodations at the Naval Arctic Research Lab weren't bad. I went to bed that night feeling good about being warm and secure, but a little apprehensive about the next day. If the whiteouts were bad out on the Slope, flying over a perfectly flat ocean covered with ice and snow could only be worse.

We took off heading north the next morning, out over the Arctic Ocean under a clear blue sky, where my fears proved to be unfounded. Even if it were overcast I would have been able to see the surface. Large ridges of broken ice, some piled 10 feet high, ran across the frozen sea in every direction. It was all the reference I'd need to fly in almost any weather conditions.

"What's going on down there?" I asked the scientist in the copilot seat. When he gave me a blank look, I pointed at the broken ice below.

He laughed. "Those are pressure ridges... wind, tides, the ocean's currents, unequal heating all work together to break up the ice and keep it moving. The ridges are what happens when it's pushed together."

"They're formed by water pressure?"

"Pretty amazing, huh?"

A hundred miles later it was time to land. Although I knew the ice below us was thick enough to support a bulldozer, landing that far out on the ocean made me nervous. Shutting down even more so. Frozen or not, we were still over thousands of feet of water and way too far away from land.

While the scientists set up their equipment, I wandered towards the closest pressure ridge. Long ribbons of snow came out of nowhere, twisting and hissing as they raced across the ice. The ridges were massive. Some of the blocks piled on top of each other were the size of cars, the deep recesses between them backlit in a pale blue light. It was hard to imagine how the movement of water underneath the ice could exert so much pressure.

When I was almost to the ridge I crossed fresh polar bear tracks. Instantly my cavalier attitude towards seeing one of the large white bears changed. The tracks were enormous. As my imagination realized the size of the creature that had made them, I felt uncomfortably out of place. When I looked up at the jumble of ice in front of me, it dawned on me how many places there were for a bear to lie in wait for something like me. So I went back to see what the scientists were doing, appreciating the fact that there is security in numbers.

By midafternoon they had the core samples they wanted. While they were packing it for transportation, I wandered over and peered into the hole the core came out of. The water was closer than I thought, only a few feet down, and it was black, its depth unfathomable. To me it was a small window to a big world more intimidating than the one on top of the ice.

When the scientists were done I took off and turned to the back azimuth of the heading we'd followed out that morning, but nothing looked familiar. I turned on the ADF. The Automatic Direction Finder is a flight instrument that homes in on a selected radio signal. It said that Barrow was straight ahead, right where it was supposed to be, so I held my course.

A couple of minutes later we came to an island of ice that I remembered well. The pressure ridges around its edges formed an arrow, and it had been pointing south, the way back to land. Now, according to my compass, it was pointing southwest. I was about to check the ADF again when the guy in the copilot seat asked me what was up.

"My ADF and compass say Barrow's that way," I told him, pointing straight ahead. "But we flew across that piece of ice below us from that direction." I pointed to the right. "Look. It's shaped like an arrow."

He laughed again, "That's because the currents underneath the ice turned it."

It wasn't bad work, flying around drilling holes in the ice, but it was cold, and all the while I kept thinking about my friends at Tundra. While I was bundled up in wool, they were walking around in shorts and T-shirts, sunbathing behind the hangar and drinking beer instead of getting chilled to the bone day after day.

By the time the job was done I couldn't wait to leave, and neither could Andie. I hadn't seen her since we got to Barrow, but several days before I was going back to Fairbanks she showed up and asked if she could come with me. How could I refuse? She had to be desperate to get back in a helicopter with me.

As Barrow faded into the distance we were both in good spirits. Apparently things hadn't worked out with her ex-boyfriend, but she didn't seem too upset. The weather was nice, high overcast, and we were on our way back to town. However, a half hour later the weather began to change. "Deja vu," Andie said as the visibility began to drop.

It did look a lot like the stuff we'd run into on the way to Barrow, and it was in the same vicinity. Chances are, like before, it will be 500 feet thick and four or five miles wide, I thought. I don't like to fly above bad weather in a single engine helicopter. If the engine quits you have nowhere to go. But the alternative was to fly under it, most likely into a whiteout again, or go back to Barrow and wait for the weather to change, which could be days.

"What do you say we go over it this time," I suggested, beginning a climb to a thousand feet. If we couldn't see a clear path to the other side, I was going to turn around.

Fifty miles later we were still on top of the clouds. We'd even climbed a couple hundred feet to stay above the weather. I would have been concerned that it didn't end in five miles like I'd thought, maybe even turned back, but where we were wasn't bad. The clouds above and below us were thin. There was plenty of light. Every once in a while I saw what looked like it might be the ground, but it was hard to be certain with everything covered in snow. Also, I had my ADF to follow. Its needle was pointing straight ahead, right where Umiat should be.

When we were about halfway to Umiat, within radio range, I dialed in their Flight Service Station to check the weather. At the time we left Barrow, they were reporting broken clouds at 400 feet, tops at 600, and overcast skies at 2,000.

"Umiat, helicopter November five-eight-one-two-nine."

"Helicopter November five-eight-one-two-nine, Umiat."

"Roger, Umiat. Please say your weather."

"One-two-nine, current weather is wind three-zero-zero degrees at eight, visibility two miles, ceilings three hundred feet."

"Roger, Umiat. Understand three hundred, is that broken or overcast?"

"One-two-nine, Umiat. There are a few holes, but we can't see the tops."

Umiat's weather had deteriorated since we left Barrow, but it was encouraging to hear that the clouds were still broken and they could see two miles. They probably couldn't see the tops because of the overcast layer that was above us. Anyway, it didn't sound any worse than where we were, and we could always turn around and go back to Barrow.

Half an hour later, by multiplying our airspeed by our flight time, I figured we should be at Umiat. But the clouds below us were still too thick to see the ground, so I called flight service again. They told me that now they couldn't see any breaks in the low overcast either. If we hadn't been so close to Umiat I might have turned around. But we were there, and even if we couldn't see the landing strip we'd get a needle reversal on the ADF when we flew over their transmitter. Then we could look around for a way down.

Five minutes later we should have been well past Umiat, but the ADF needle was still pointing straight ahead. That didn't make sense. I'd never been that far off my estimated time of arrival on such a short flight; however, by making a slow turn I'd be able to tell how far away we were. If the ADF station was close, the needle would move quickly. A slower deflection would mean we still had a way to go. So I rolled Alice to the left and watched the needle. It didn't move.

What the hell, I thought, and gave the instrument a sharp rap with my knuckles. The ADF needle stayed right where it was, pointing straight ahead of the aircraft. Shit, I said to myself. It wasn't working. But the big question was... how long had the damn thing been inoperative? Since Barrow, I had to figure.

"What's happening now?" Andie asked.

"Wait one," I told her, needing some time.

We could be miles off course, I realized, nowhere near Umiat. Because I couldn't navigate by dead reckoning in the clouds, I'd been holding a compass heading since Barrow, periodically checking the ADF to confirm that we were still on course. Which it did, pointing straight ahead of us the entire flight. So I hadn't bothered to compensate for wind drift because the ADF needle always lined up with our compass heading, indicating drift wasn't an issue. But Umiat said the wind was eight knots from the northwest. That would put us south and as much as 20 miles past Umiat. We'd never find it without the ADF.

I looked southeast towards Anaktuvuk Pass and Fairbanks. It looked bad. Not knowing where we were, I didn't see how we could find the pass in that weather. Next I checked the fuel gauge. We had more than enough to get back to Barrow, so I turned to a heading that would take us back. Even without an Automatic Direction Finder we could find the town because it was on the edge of the ocean. All we'd have to do is get to the beach and follow it.

"The ADF isn't working," I told Andie. "We're heading back."

Once we were established on our new heading I took care of a few things I wanted to do before we left the area. I called flight service and made sure I had the right frequency on the ADF. It was. I reset it. Next came the avionics circuit breakers. None of them had popped, but I reset them anyway. Finally I turned the instrument itself off, then back on again, and gave the glass cover of the ADF head a few more taps with my knuckles, but the needle stayed glued in place.

By that time we should have been near Umiat again,

passing on our way to Barrow. "Umiat, one-two-nine, say Barrow's weather please," I called out of habit. We were heading that way.

"One-two-nine, Umiat, Barrow's current is... wait one. Wind three-one-zero at ten, obscured in fog, overcast estimated at two hundred feet."

Unfuckin' believable, I said under my breath. How could the weather have gotten that bad in one hour? We weren't going back to Barrow. That was for sure. We couldn't find the shoreline in that weather.

"Umiat, how about Deadhorse?"

"One-two-nine, Deadhorse is eight hundred overcast, visibility one mile in light snow."

That was it. We were stuck. I couldn't see anything but clouds to the south, the way home. We'd never find Umiat, Barrow or Deadhorse because we were above the overcast level of all three.

Then I remembered the Air Force's DEW site in Barrow. But decided that wouldn't help either. I couldn't reach them by radio from where we were. Even if we had radio contact and they got me on their radar, we still had to get down and their weather was the worst, zero visibility all the way to the ground. No matter where we went it would be the same or worse.

It might have been funny, getting trapped that easily, if I didn't know how much trouble we were in. I glanced at Andie. She'd been listening to what had been said on the radio and was staring at me wide-eyed.

"That's not good, is it?" she asked.

"We could be in deep doo-doo," I told her, and rolled the helicopter into a slow turn to the right.

Flying a standard rate turn would be the best way to stay in one spot while I went over our options, which didn't take long. There was only one. We were going down. I knew we were somewhere near Umiat—their radio was coming in so strong—and that the clouds had bottoms 300 feet above the ground with relatively good visibility underneath, which was the best weather on the Slope at the time. If we tried to go anywhere else we would simply become more lost in worse weather.

The only thing left to do was make sure the flight instruments were working properly, and pick a spot to begin our descent. Between the airspeed and vertical speed indicators, altimeter and artificial horizon, I could make a controlled descent through the cloud cover below us. The big question was... would we see the ground before running into it?

We would probably break out of the bottom of the clouds in plenty of time. Unfortunately, it would most likely be into whiteout conditions, not a lot of difference than being in the cloud. But even if we never saw the ground, if I kept our rate of descent to a couple hundred feet a minute and our airspeed below 30, I figured we'd probably survive the crash. Once again, though, I didn't know where we were. If we did crash, we might die from our injuries and exposure before anyone found us.

"Umiat, one-two-nine, ah... we're at twelve hundred, in between layers, and our ADF is inop." I explained what the problem was and what I was planning on doing, finally asking the controller, "You don't have any search and rescue capabilities there, do you?"

"That's a negative, one-two-nine," he said. "I can notify Barrow."

I brought Alice's nose into the wind and brought the airspeed back, getting ready to lower the collective and begin to descend. Then I thought of something else. "Umiat, are you in contact with other aircraft in the vicinity of Umiat?"

"Negative again, one-two-nine" he replied. "Sorry."

This just isn't working out, I thought. "Umiat, one-two-nine. I'm going up one twenty three point five." I dialed in the frequency used by pilots when they fly up and down the pipeline, and keyed my mike. "Any aircraft on the Slope, this is helicopter one-two-nine, do you copy?" A long, painful minute went by. "This is helicopter one-two-nine, in the vicinity of

Umiat with a PAN [in trouble but not life threatening—not as serious as a 'Mayday' call]. Any aircraft flying the pipeline, or receiving this transmission, please respond."

"Roger one-two-nine, this is ERA two-four. We got you." My heart leapt at the sound. As welcome as the person somewhere out there was the noise in the background. Judging by the sound his engines were making, the pilot who answered my call was flying a turboprop airplane. Anything expensive enough to have a turbine in it would definitely have a full complement of flight instruments. Regardless of the weather, he could probably make it to Umiat.

"Two-four, one-two-nine. Please say your location," I asked, unable to control the relief in my voice.

"Presently thirty south of Deadhorse, en route Coldfoot. What's the problem?" I explained that we were lost somewhere around Umiat, trapped between layers with no navigational aids and that our alternate landing sites were weathered in. "Roger, one-two-nine. This is a VIP flight." The pilot sounded annoyed.

"Two-four, one-two-nine, sorry to hassle you with this. Could you deviate to Umiat to pick us up visually? Let us follow you anyplace we can see the ground." When he didn't come back right away, I added, "At least give us heading and distance to Umiat… or mark the spot where we were last seen." The radio remained silent. What an asshole, I thought, and waited.

Some airplane pilots in Alaska resent helicopter pilots. We came in and took over some of their work; however, as important, we are less restricted, don't have to play by the same rules, and that makes some think we aren't as professional. It makes others jealous. As I was about to key my mike and beg the airplane pilot for help, he was on the radio.

"One-two-nine, two-four, roger, just got off the phone with flight ops. They've approved your request. Estimating Umiat in two-zero minutes. Got a solid copy?"

"We'll be waiting, two-four," I called back. "And thanks for saving my ass."

"No problem," he laughed.

Andie and I kept flying in a wide circle, talking, until something out my side window caught my attention. For an instant, below us there had been a discernable dark spot. It wasn't a shadow in the convoluted surface of the cloud, much darker.

I rolled the helicopter in that direction and saw it again, a distinct dark smudge. Whatever it was, it had to be on the ground, and I wasn't going to let it get away. After a quick check of my flight instruments, I lowered the collective, brought the airspeed back to 40 mph, and began descending in a 30 degree banking turn to the right at 200 feet a minute. As we sank into the gray mess below us, I felt a twinge of fear. I'm flying into another whiteout, I thought. But the feeling of apprehension disappeared as quickly as it came. I felt comfortable in the controlled descent, using the flight instruments for reference, and there was definitely something down there.

The dark spot often grew faint, even disappeared once in a wisp of cloud, which was tense. I knew that if I lost sight of the ground for more than 10 or 15 seconds I'd have to level the helicopter and be prepared to fly it into the ground. But the spot kept getting darker.

We dropped out of the cloud directly above a cut-bank in the middle of a big bend on the Colville River, only a few miles south of the landing strip at Umiat. It was the exposed dark soil on the south facing side of the steep slope that caught my attention. I took in a deep breath and exhaled slowly, then radioed the airplane pilot, told him that we were on the ground, and thanked him again for coming to our rescue. Then I landed at Umiat for fuel. While I pumped Jet A into Alice, Andie went inside the closest building. When she got back, she seemed upset.

"Was there a problem in there?" I asked.

"No. Well, yes. The toilet..."

When I began to laugh she shot me a nasty look. "I'm sorry, Andie. I honestly forgot all about the toilets, or I would've told you. Really." To "flush" the toilets at Umiat you step on a little pedal near the floor. When you do, an enormous flame shoots into the bowl and incinerates the waste. If you are sitting down it's quite a surprise.

"Were you sitting down?" I had to ask.

"Completely unaware," she confided.

Andie and I took off and flew under the clouds until we were well into the Brooks Range. As we flew over Anaktuvuk Pass the weather improved, the sun came out and the temperature began to rise. Fifty miles down the John River from Anaktuvuk we came to Bill and Lil's homestead. This time we weren't in a hurry, so I landed beside their two-story log home. Alice's outside air temperature gauge was reading 42 degrees. Andie and I smiled at each other as we stripped off a layer of clothes.

When Lil, Andie and I were seated around the table in the kitchen, along with a couple of their dogs and the remains of a moose Lil was butchering, Bill got out a bottle of Canadian whiskey.

"You want some?" he asked.

"Jesus, Bill. It's the middle of the day," I told him.

"That didn't stop you last time you were here," he said, winking at Andie.

"Yeah, but I've got to fly..."

"That didn't stop you last time, either," he laughed.

"That's not fair at all, Bill," I laughed too. "That was a matter of life and death... yours, I might add."

I dropped in on Bill and Lil at the end of a job in the Brooks Range late last fall. It was early in the day, and like Bill said, I didn't turn down the glass of whiskey he put in front of me because I wasn't planning on going anywhere until the next day. While we drank, it began to snow, wet and heavy.

An hour later, when three or four inches had accumulated, Bill told me that he had a group of hunters staying with him. They had gone out in their airplane to hunt moose that morning and were supposed to have been back well before dark, which was coming early because of the snow. He

51

also told me that his guests were weekend pilots, guys who barely flew enough to stay current, much less competent.

"I'm gonna have to go look for those guys pretty soon," Bill said. "With all this wet snow and it droppin' below freezing, their wings might've iced up. Good chance they've wrecked that little plane of theirs."

Bill was right. It was dark. If they were with their plane they weren't going anywhere. And if the hunters had crashed and were injured, someone had to go get them. It was going to be a tough night to stay alive in the woods.

Telling Bill I was going outside to pee, I got in my helicopter and took off. As I flew by his house the door flew open and I could make out Bill shaking his fist at me. I knew he would be mad, but it made more sense for me to go. Even if he found them with his airplane, which would be so much harder, he wouldn't be able to land and pick them up.

I found their airplane undamaged on a sandbar in the river. The hunters weren't there, so I went looking for them. By flying in increasingly larger circles around the plane, I found their tracks less than a quarter mile away. Minutes later I had them back at Bill's, and it was a good thing I'd found them. They were completely lost, soaked through with sweat, and getting tired. One guy was already showing signs of hypothermia. Later Bill agreed my helicopter was the tool for the job.

That was one of the perks of flying helicopters in Alaska. From rescuing hunters to airlifting a piano, I got to do things I felt good about. Surprisingly, of those two incidents, helping out with the piano was more rewarding than saving the hunters.

Several days after I found them wandering around lost in the woods, I was checking out of a liquor store on the outskirts of Fairbanks with a six-pack of beer. The guy ahead of me in line was one of the hunters. Fairbanks isn't that big, and there's only one liquor store in the Goldstream area.

"How'd the hunt go?" the guy at the cash register asked him.

"Real fine," the hunter said. "Got ma moose."

As he picked up his package he turned enough to see me and, judging by the sudden look of embarrassment on his face, recognize me. Instead of saying, hey, or thanks, or maybe buying my six-pack, he turned and walked out to his car. The people I moved the piano for gave me a whole case of beer.

As Andie and I headed south, I told her that we had one more stop to make. A friend of Craig's had staked a claim beside a hot spring in the Ray Mountains. The only way to get to it was by foot or helicopter. When he heard that I was going to be in the area, he asked Craig if I could take a few supplies out to his cabin.

We found the stuff cached on the side of the pipeline haul road, all kinds of building materials, including a long steel tube, which had to be strapped across the landing gear. And the load was so heavy we barely got into the air. However, the hassle was worth it once we got to the hot spring. Unlike most natural hot springs, this one didn't smell like sulfur or have an odor of any kind. The boiling water simply seeped out of a boulder field on the side of a hill and drained into a series of small pools.

As we stepped naked into the first and coolest pool, thick, slimy algae slithered around our ankles. It was a little weird as we slid deeper into the water and the long gelatinous leaves enveloped our bodies, but the soothing effect of the steaming bath spread quickly. By the time I was up to my neck everything felt fine. Considering how cold I'd been for so long, it was just one, long delicious moment.

For quite a while we lay there, relaxing. Then, like two albino alligators, we worked our way through slime-covered channels in the rocks from one pool to the next. In the second to last pool the water was too hot to go farther. In a shallow part, on a luxuriously soft bed of algae, we made love.

The fun wasn't over for Andie and I. Because I refueled in Umiat instead of Bettles, we didn't have a lot of extra fuel when we picked up the load to take to the hot spring. With the added weight, drag of the tube across the landing gear and reduction in airspeed, we almost ran out of fuel on the last leg of our flight.

But it didn't matter. I was back in Fairbanks with my friends, and it was full-on spring. The winter had been long, stretched to its limits by the extension in Barrow; however, summer in Fairbanks was fair compensation. Like nowhere else I'd been, summer is green and in constant motion. Water flows, grass grows, lifeless trees sprout leaves and bend in the wind, while all day and through the night, birds sing. And the transition is fast.

The same thing happened at Tundra Copters, rapid change in the spring. The mechanics came back well before the field season began to get the helicopters ready for the jobs Craig had been lining up all winter. They were going to have to fly for four straight months and needed to be gone over thoroughly.

Ray England, our head of maintenance, and Sparky, the most senior mechanic, had been there through the winter. Recently Mike Parker, who lived outside of town in a house shaped like a light bulb, and Dan Baldini, our best field mechanic, joined them. The other seasonal mechanics would be coming back a little later. They were mostly field mechanics, guys who went into the bush with the tools and parts they could carry, and kept their helicopters running for months. Most field mechanics got paid more in the bush, so they didn't come back until it was time to leave town.

The pilots who'd previously flown for Tundra also came back in the spring, earlier than necessary. Some employers brought pilots and mechanics back in the spring so they wouldn't be tempted to work for someone else that summer. Craig did it because they were friends. To him it was like a family reunion.

Ken Brunner came back from Louisiana talking about putting together a revolutionary golf magazine. I'm not a fan of the sport, not enough patience, but after a couple beers together he had me convinced he could make his idea work. Almost every pilot I knew had a get-rich-quick plan that didn't involve flying. Ernie Lonas showed up next, bringing his endless charm and savoir faire. A few days later John Russell returned from wintering in the deserts of Africa, which he advised against no matter how tempting it sounded. Then Johnny Burns got in from Kansas with his guitar.

Alaska and Tundra Copters came to life in the spring, and so did I, staying up much later almost every night, mostly in bars, and rising earlier and earlier each day. Often as not, I went for a run when I got up. Ostensibly, I did it for my health, but the real motivation was to get outside.

From our hangar the airport perimeter road went into the woods along a meander of the Tanana River. The beaver that lived at the east end never got used to my morning routine and slapped his tail repeatedly at my intrusion. From there the dirt road followed the higher ground between muskeg and the river, winding around the end of the airport. In all, the run was three miles, but it usually took the better part of an hour because I walked now and then, mostly to enjoy the day.

One of the nice things about being a pilot is that, if you aren't flying, you are usually free to entertain yourself. There was a fair amount of busywork, but when the weather was nice, which was most of the time, I found something to do outside. In the evening we usually got together for a few beers behind the hangar, our favorite spot to watch the sun go down.

Lying in the grass outside my tent on Alpine Creek, reminiscing about the long cold winter and how nice summers were, I noticed that the damp, cold air coming down the Clearwater Mountains carried the smell of smoke. Someone had finally lit the campfire.

- 4 -

DEVILS CANYON

On my way to the campfire I passed by Chris and Kathy's tent. The small North Face the two friends shared was set up halfway between my tent and the campfire.

"Hey," I called as I went by.

"Hey, yourself," Kathy answered.

"Wait for us," Chris added.

Together we followed a path worn in the thick moss on the forest floor. Ahead of us the campfire flickered between tall limbless trees, growing brighter with every step. We could hear guitar music and singing, which is just as important as beer and friends for an enjoyable evening around a fire. Our musician was the amiable, boyishly handsome Will. He played the guitar and was planning on performing for a living. We all thought he could do it if he worked on a few things, like his repertoire. Will only knew one song, "Tennessee Stud." Fortunately, we all liked it.

We passed unnoticed by Fred and Ken working away in their office, an enclosed ten-by-six-foot metal trailer. Fred pulled it around to camps that could be accessed by road, no matter how rough, behind his vintage, powder-blue Dodge Power Wagon, which, he would enthusiastically tell you, had 12 forward gears and three in reverse. The office was one of Fred's most useful creations. After a couple days of rain everything but the office got wet, especially our clammy little tents, so it was nice to have one dry place in camp.

The fire was going well. Bright sparks rose above it, flickering as they disappeared into the dark sky. The regulars were there, Rocky, Tim, Paul, Will, and Linda. Fred and Ken usually came by when their work was done, but the other two guys in camp, Dave and Bill, never showed up. With Bill, we figured he knew no one liked him. The jury was still out on

Dave.

As Kathy, Chris and I walked into the circle of light thrown by the fire, Rocky handed each of us a cold bottle of Pabst Blue Ribbon beer. It was his night to buy. In camp we took turns providing the evening's refreshments, a case or two of beer and the occasional bottle of sipping whiskey. Wild Turkey was the favorite. The rotating bartender system eliminated confusion, suppressed hoarding and avoided the inevitable problem of someone feeling that they were the only one buying.

"Will," Rocky laughed. "Play 'Tennessee Stud' for these nice folks."

Obligingly, Will sang: "The Tennessee stud was long and lean, the color of the sun and his eyes were green. He had the nerve and he had the blood. There never was a horse like the Tennessee stud..."

Paul sauntered over from a conversation with Linda. "What's happening, my man?" he asked us. Paul's scraggly and unkempt looks were deceiving. Underneath the earthy exterior was the soul of a very hip individual, innately smooth and relaxed. "Hey, Rocky. You got any of that there chewin' teebackee?" he asked his friend. Half of the guys in camp were chewing. I didn't like the taste or the spitting involved. Besides, the two packs of Lucky Strikes I smoked each day took care of my nicotine needs.

After handing his can of Skoal to Paul, Rocky turned to me. "Now, Tom, tell me about this cliff dive y'all did this afternoon."

"Give me a break, will ya, Rocky?" I asked, tired of the subject.

"Yeah, but Chris said...," he tried again.

"Don't be an asshole, Rocky," I muttered.

"Ohh, Tom," Rocky cooed. "You haven't called me 'asshole' in weeks."

Paul joined in. "Yeah, Smith. You never call me asshole anymore either. What's up, man?"

"I've learned your names... assholes," I told them,

almost keeping a straight face.

It was true. I had the habit of using that indelicate word; however, in my defense, I used it out of necessity, not malice. Working around helicopters is dangerous, especially in the mountains where decent landing sites are few and we often ended up doing things like "toe-ins."

If the slope of a mountain is too steep to land, and there's no other place to drop off my passengers, I often put the tips of the skid-type landing gear against the side of the mountain and hold the helicopter there at a hover. When I tell them to get out, my passengers open their doors, step down on the landing gear and off onto the mountain. If the slope is really steep, it gets tougher. They have to drop their packs on the side of the mountain, carefully so they don't roll, close their doors, then slide their feet forward along the landing gear, clinging to anything they can find on the side of the helicopter, until they are close enough to the mountain to step off.

While they are doing the balancing act on the landing gear, which is only four inches wide, the aircraft is in constant motion. The wind from rotor blades hitting the uneven slope makes it difficult to keep the aircraft steady. It doesn't move around a lot, but it moves in every direction. The down drafts from the rotor blades buffet the crew with gusts up to 50 miles per hour. There's also the 500 horsepower turbine engine above their heads screaming like a banshee, and the three-foot-wide tail rotor humming away behind them like a gigantic buzz saw.

With all that going on, people get distracted and make mistakes. Because of the helicopter's precarious position on the side of the mountain, little things can be disastrous. It's part of my job to let my passengers know when they are about to do something that might get us all in trouble. That's where "asshole" comes in. I'd found that when I yelled, "Watch out for the tail rotor," no one paid attention. But when I yelled, "Watch out for the tail rotor, asshole!" everyone looked up.

"Anyway," I told Rocky, "it's only an expression."

Actually, most of the people I took into the mountains

were intelligent and pleasant to be around, and the young men and women on the FSL crew were anything but assholes or incompetent. They were so capable around the helicopter I felt comfortable letting them do things I hadn't let anyone else do, like take the tops off of trees so we could get into spots otherwise inaccessible.

On the flatter and wetter terrain the crews sometimes had to spend hours getting to their plot because I couldn't land nearby. Often the problem was black spruce trees. They were short, usually less than 20 feet high, but grew in thickets for miles. Often I could get to within a few feet of the ground, right at the plot, before my rotor blades began taking the new growth off the top of the trees.

Frustrated by such a small distance, I told the crews that if they didn't tell Fred, it was all right with me if they cut the tops off of a few trees so we could land. The idea worked well. I'd hover up against the tree while one of them leaned out the door and cut off the top five feet with a handsaw, then we'd land.

"You guys aren't assholes," I told the group around the fire. "As far as you know."

Turning my back on the barrage of insults that ensued, I walked over to where Kathy and Chris were sitting on a log, talking. As I sat down beside Kathy, Chris stopped in midsentence. They turned and looked at me for a moment, then went right back to their conversation.

"No, it's ridiculous. I don't think Fred knows what's going on, but someone's got to do something about it," Chris said, visibly upset.

"Who are you talking about?" I asked. They turned and looked at me again. "You guys talk about everyone behind their backs. Come on, admit it. You're wicked harpies," I teased.

Kathy laughed and Chris relaxed a little. "We were talking about Paul doing the plots by himself," Kathy told me.

"Plots" are what the FSL crews called their survey areas. Every morning I dropped the crews off in groups of two or three at a new plot, where they did an inventory of the one-acre sites. They recorded the type, number, size, density and condition of the trees. They also evaluated the soils and understory vegetation, and wrote down what signs they saw of wildlife. Kathy had put together an impressive scat collection over the course of the summer.

"It's Dave," Chris sighed. "He's not doing anything. The guy just sits there. Or walks off into the woods. Paul's doing all the work." She picked a piece of bark off the log underneath us and began picking it apart. "You know what I think? I think Paul's too nice a guy."

I looked at Kathy. "I guess Dave's talking to himself and stuff. Looking pretty weird too," she added.

Dave was a decent guy, maybe a little distracted at times but not a bad person. He was also a Vietnam vet, in the infantry, I thought. Other than a few pilots and mechanics, I didn't know many veterans and wasn't interested in their affairs, but I thought that they were getting unjustly blamed for all kinds of things. So, feeling a little defensive, I didn't feel like dumping on Dave. Then I remembered how weird he'd been one evening only days before, and had a change of heart.

"You guys know I won't let him ride in the front seat anymore," I joined in.

I was bringing Dave, Paul and Tim back from a plot near the Maclaren Glacier. The terrain, rolling hills covered with low alders and brush, was perfect for contour flying, so we were cruising along at 120 mph, less than 20 feet above the ground. Dave was sitting in the copilot seat to my left. In between our seats was the collective. Because the control is very sensitive, moving it a fraction of an inch will make the helicopter climb or descend, I always keep my hand on it when I am that close to the ground.

We were leaving a shallow valley not far from, coincidentally, Crazy Notch, when out of the corner of my eye I noticed Dave staring at me. I ignored him, but he just sat there, two feet away, looking straight at the side of my head. Finally I turned and looked. Dave was smiling. His eyes were bright, fixed on mine, and the expression he wore was one of affection, almost adoration. Still looking directly at me, he picked up his right hand and put it on top of mine on the collective. "I love you," he said, and pushed down, not very hard, but with enough pressure to drop Alice halfway to the ground before I pulled the collective back up.

"What the hell are you doing?" I yelled into my mike. Dave turned and looked straight ahead, a silly grin on his face, but he'd heard me. I saw him flinch when I yelled at him. "Keep your goddamned hands off the controls, Dave!" I scolded him.

I'd been mad, but I knew that if Dave really wanted to kill us, he could've done it. Most likely I was as angry, if not more so, with myself. I should have suspected something. The look he gave me was strange enough to make anyone think twice, and I knew he didn't really love me.

Chris clapped her hands in excitement as she remembered what she heard about the incident. "Oh, that's right. You guys almost crashed, right?"

While we were talking, Fred and Ken joined us. Fred, for all his exuberance and intrusive ways, was a very good boss, as helpful as anyone I'd worked with. Ken, tall and relaxed, was the antithesis of short, fidgety Fred, and every bit as much of a good guy to work with. He never bothered anyone, just got the job done. They made a good team.

Ken stopped to get a beer from Rocky, but Fred didn't drink in camp. Instead, he played cribbage, and he was heading straight for me. I was the only one in camp who would play with him. Everyone else had a ready excuse, or claimed not to know how the game was played.

The problem was, Fred couldn't control himself when he was winning. His expressions of glee often assumed embarrassing, even disturbing proportions. I really didn't like playing with him either, but I liked the game and he was pretty good at it. So I played and put up with his being Fred.

"Well, Smith, are you ready for another sound beating?" Fred asked when he got to me. He was doing his best to appear at ease, but his eyes revealed what was really going on. They were focused one second, then darting here and there the next, a sure sign of cribbage lust.

"Wouldn't that be the first time, Fred?" I couldn't help myself.

"Yeah, right!" He leapt at the bait. "What about last night? Why I..."

An hour later, around ten o'clock, Fred got up and announced that he was going to his tent. He did that every night, tried to let all of us know that it was time for bed, that we should put down our beers and get some sleep. But everyone just said, "Good night, Fred," and went back to what they were doing.

Fred didn't care. He understood the people he had working for him. They were an energetic, well-educated, independent group, idealistic enough to believe they could do everything. And they went out of their way to prove it. Besides, Fred could go to his tent feeling great about coming from behind to beat me, again.

Still smarting from the defeat that everyone within shouting distance knew about, I joined the others by the fire. Ken got up from where he was sitting, came over and stood beside me. Checking to see no one was listening, he leaned closer and said, "Funny thing about that cliff dive and your middle name."

"Cliff dive? What do you... How'd you know my middle name?" I asked.

Like most people, I rarely used my middle name. It came from my mother's side of the family and didn't have a lot of practical use, other than its oddity. My middle name is Leming, one "m" short of the mouse-like creatures, lemmings, known for periodic en masse migrations. Legend has it they will even leap off cliffs in their need to move on, earning them the undeserved reputation of being suicidal.

Ken was right, though. My middle name being so close in spelling to a reputedly self-destructive animal, and my plunge down a 3,000-foot cliff were an interesting, though whimsical, coincidence.

"It's on your pilot's license. Tundra sent a copy of it along with your qualifications for the job," he told me. "And don't worry. I'm the only one who knows you're a suicidal rodent masquerading as a helicopter pilot," Ken told me, laughing as he walked off towards his tent.

I didn't think it was that funny. However, many years later, on an Alaska Fish and Game site, I read that a native name for Alaska's lemmings is "kilangmiutak," which means "one-who-falls-from-the-sky."

In between Will's last performance of "Tennessee Stud" and his next performance of "Tennessee Stud," I heard strands of flute music coming from the direction of Tim's tent.

"I gotta get a little control," I told Rocky, who was sitting not far away. "I mean, flying down that cliff was pretty stupid. Or at best extremely impulsive. And I should have..."

"I know what ya mean," he replied.

"Yeah, it's not that I really...," I began again, but stopped when I realized Rocky wasn't listening.

"Dang thing," he said, turning his log stool around, trying to get it level. The short section of log Rocky was using for a seat had distracted him.

Our campfire was on sloped ground because it was the only opening in the tall trees wide enough for a fire. There was one level spot, but that was Will's because he provided the entertainment. Everyone else was forced to deal with the terrain. It really wasn't a problem because we'd taken the lengths of logs we sat on and cut the bottoms to match the angle of the slope. However, when it got late, some angles didn't seem to match up anymore.

"There! That's got the gall-darn thing," Rocky said, grinning, happy with his handiwork. "Now, what was it you were sayin', Tom?"

Before I could answer, Rocky took a big sip of his beer. As he did, he began to lean downhill. "Hold on, Rocky," I warned. He almost went down, but caught himself at the last moment, cursed, and went back to adjusting his stump.

Sitting around the campfire with friends after 12 hours of work was more than being social or a substitute for friends and families thousands of miles away. It was a place to relax, stand by the fire and get warm, the reward for making it through another day in the mountains. It was also a place to enjoy where we were, living outdoors in the middle of the Alaska Range. Even when it was raining, we came to the fire, put our backs to the weather and had a cold beer.

"I loved that girl with the golden hair. The way the Tennessee stud loved the Tennessee mare," Will sang, giving his six string one last strum for the night. "See you guys in the morning," he said, as he left the light of the flames and disappeared into the woods.

A few minutes later Kathy and I left Linda, the last one, at the fire. "Spirit of the Night," Kathy called her. Long after everyone else was in their sleeping bags, she would be alone by the glow of the fire, enjoying the end of another long summer day. Like many native Alaskans, Linda relished the soft summer nights, often until morning.

"Winter is for sleeping," she said with a broad smile. "Not the summer."

As I stumbled along behind Kathy through the pitch-black woods, I was glad she had a flashlight. On my own on a similarly dark night, I walked straight into the trunk of a spruce tree. It almost knocked me out. Surprisingly, though, the next morning I didn't even have a bruise.

Outside her tent, Kathy paused. "Thanks for another good day in Alice, Tom."

"Thanks for getting me halfway home," I replied, as a flood of moonlight broke through the clouds and turned everything around us a ghostly white.

Kathy was looking at me, her head tilted to one side, smiling. "By the way," she said. "How have you managed to stay alive so long?" She knew how old I was. One night she pointed out that she was nine while I was in Vietnam.

"What?" Oh, the cliff dive again, I thought. "To be honest, I don't usually do stuff like that." One of her eyebrows

64

rose slightly, so I added, "I admit I've done some radical things in a helicopter, but not showing off like that."

Kathy reached up, took off her cowboy hat and began brushing the rim of it with the tips of her fingers. The moonlight was fading, but I could see she was smiling.

"What about Devils Canyon?" she asked, the smile becoming a grin.

Where the Susitna River runs through the Talkeetna Mountains, there is a canyon that's a thousand feet deep in places. In 10 miles the water drops over 400 feet, mostly in a few treacherous stretches. Often the raging water fills the narrow canyon from wall to wall. Although its inaccessibility has kept most people off the river, of the few enthusiasts who have kayaked Devils Canyon, a number of them have drowned.

I could see why. From above the canyon, almost a quarter of a mile away, the ferocity of the torrent twisting and turning below was spellbinding. The river never stopped changing shape. I couldn't keep my eyes off of it, nor help but be intimidated. Even from the relative security of Alice's cockpit there was little doubt what that water would do to a person.

The canyon was a unique place and, rumor was, it might soon be gone. There were two helicopters in the area doing preliminary survey work for a dam. The story going around the field camps was that the State of Alaska and a large utility company were going to dam the canyon to power a hydroelectric plant. In turn, they could offer inexpensive energy to attract business to the area.

One day I decided Devils Canyon had to be flown before it became a lake. Not without risk, I knew. There could be things down there, old mining cables, wires, things that couldn't be seen from above. In some spots the canyon appeared to be narrower than the diameter of Alice's rotor blades. But most concerning, if anything went wrong there was nowhere to go but in the water.

Nevertheless, after a few weeks in the area I'd mapped out a course I thought would be safe enough, except for one or two spots. When I told Kathy and Chris what I was thinking, they were skeptical.

"Will Alice even fit down there?" Chris wanted to know. "I mean, some of those turns are pretty tight, Tom."

"I think so. There may be one or two tricky spots, but that won't be a problem," I said.

"Why not?" Kathy wanted to know.

"If I have to, I'll climb up to where it's wider," I told them.

"Sounds fun," Chris exclaimed.

Kathy agreed, and so did Linda.

For the record, I didn't ask the guys if they wanted to fly the canyon because Ken was management and couldn't, Will and Tim would decline for safety reasons, and Dave was too crazy, which left Rocky. Unfortunately for him, the canyon trip would have to be part of a flight to or from a plot, and crews never consisted of less than two people.

A few days later, while dropping the girls off at their plot, I mentioned that it looked like a good day to fly Devils Canyon. By the time I was ready to pick them up the day had warmed up enough to take Alice's doors off. Not having doors would be good for the trip. Low-level flight without doors is surprisingly different than with them.

Without doors everything seems to be closer, more real. A moose with a mouth full of pondweeds, a duck herding its ducklings into the reeds, a waterfall cascading into a crystalline pool, all become larger than life with the doors off. However, I couldn't fly as fast without doors. Above 80 mph the wind whips around the cockpit like a cyclone, picking up anything that isn't strapped down. But we would be flying down the canyon relatively slow.

Three minutes away from the girls' plot, about the time they could hear the sound of Alice's rotor blades, Kathy came on the radio.

"Tom, this is Kat, do you copy?"

"Roger that. I hear you fine. How about me?"

"Yeah, Tom. Hear you okay too." The radio went dead

for a moment, then she said, "We had a bear scare."

"How long ago?" I asked, genuinely concerned.

"Couple hours, anyhow," she told me. That wasn't anything to worry about, I thought, wondering why she'd bother to tell me about a bear that had left hours ago. "Yeah, Tom," she continued. "He headed east. Keep an eye out for him. Large furry guy about five feet tall."

Kathy wasn't worried about the bear. She was worried about Alice. The purpose of the radio call was to let me know where the bear was, so that I wouldn't chase it into them. Bears run from helicopters, especially low-flying ones.

Not knowing if the bear was still east of them or had moved around, I pulled the nose up and climbed to 1,000 feet. At that altitude I wouldn't spook the bear. When I was directly over the crew, I bottomed the collective and pushed in some right pedal. A fraction of a second later I rolled the cyclic to the right and pushed it forward, only a little, putting the aircraft into a spiraling dive.

In the army we called this type of approach a "high-overhead." When we had to get to troops in contact with the enemy, we came in at three thousand feet and spiraled down over them. That way, we were harder to hit. And if we got shot down we could crash in a relatively safe spot.

A hundred feet above the trees I pulled the power back in and brought the nose up, opening the spiral into a slow, wide turn around the clearing the girls were in, before rolling out level and landing.

"That looked like fun," Kathy said, climbing into the copilot seat.

"I love it," I told her.

"Hey, I like the no-doors look!" Chris exclaimed from the back.

It was obvious all three of them were looking forward to the trip down the canyon. Kathy was smiling, Chris was giddy and Linda had that twinkle in her eyes.

Several minutes later we dropped down a gentle slope to the Susitna River and turned downstream towards Devils

Canyon, our skids almost touching the calm, dark water of the wide river. We flew south for a few miles then turned 90 degrees to the right, following the river straight into the heart of the Talkeetna Mountains.

Grassy slopes gave way to rock outcrops and cliffs. The water picked up speed the deeper we flew, mounding over submerged rocks as it rushed along. In the middle of a tight turn to the left, Devil Creek joined the Susitna through a deep cleft in the north wall.

Up to that point the flight had been a cruise. Alice effortlessly handled the four or five sharp turns we'd gone through, rolling smoothly into 40-degree banks. But not far from where Devil Creek came in, the cliffs began to close in. Before long solid rock walls rose hundreds of feet above us, no more than 70 feet apart.

The diameter of our rotor blades was 33 feet and inches, so there was plenty of room; however, in the corners I had to slow down so Alice wouldn't slide sideways. Before long we were below 60 mph, the minimum speed I wanted in case we lost our engine. Above 60 I could trade altitude for airspeed and probably reach a landing spot somewhere above us. Below that speed, we would probably end up in the fast moving water.

The sun disappeared as the cliffs grew taller and closer, and the river began to move faster. Ledges protruding from the walls gored the dark water, churning it into a frothing mass. Enormous waves built against the faces of the few boulders large enough to resist the powerful current, while holes that could swallow our helicopter formed on the downstream side.

While I was taking it all in, the canyon took a sharp drop. The water turned a deathly gray and came unglued as it rolled off unseen cliffs, falling in huge, writhing cords from one ledge to the next. Great blasts of spray shot from the cascades, filling the air with a cold mist that coated Alice and whipped through the door-less helicopter. We could taste the river.

Quickly I did a cross-check of my instruments. If we

had to go into the water below us, we were dead. I nosed Alice over to pick up some airspeed, but had to slow down for a sharp corner. As we banked into the turn I decided it was time to climb out. We'd been in a risky situation for too long. Then I changed my mind. Around the corner the river was flat. The only reminders of the torture it had been through were small ridges of standing water dancing between the canyon walls. I looked at my passengers.

"You guys doing okay?" I asked. Chris glanced at me, but no one replied. Apparently they hadn't heard me. For a moment I thought the intercom might have quit working. Then I recognized the look... eyes shining, smiles. They were completely digging it.

I was glad to see them enjoying the trip, and relaxed a bit myself, until I looked down at the river. The water was still calm but moving faster, almost as fast as we were flying. It looked like it was racing us. How could that much water be going that fast in such rugged terrain? Then my hands reflexively tightened on the controls.

The bed of the river dropped so quickly, it literally left the water behind. The entire river, 40 feet wide and five feet deep, went airborne, arcing smoothly before slamming back into its bedrock cradle. Twenty feet later the river rose into a gigantic standing wave so steep, large sections of water constantly caved back into the trough. Its top undulated back and forth in an apparent effort to overcome gravity.

I pulled back on the cyclic, slowing down to almost a hover, to take it all in. The heaving water was so powerful, like a contained beast. We were only feet away. Realizing how vulnerable we were, I pulled in power and nosed Alice over.

As we cleared the top of the wave the helicopter shuddered from nose to tail and leapt a foot in the air. My heart stopped. I scanned my instruments. It wasn't the aircraft, I ascertained, about the same time I realized the jolt must have been a blast of air displaced by water impacting on the downstream side of the wave. After that the river leveled out. For the second time I considered climbing out of the canyon.

The next part of the flight was going to be difficult. Less than a mile ahead there was a radical S-turn followed by the tightest part of the canyon.

Looking down at the turn from above the canyon, it appeared that the switchback was so sharp, actually cutting back into itself, we might have to come to a hover to get around it. And the turn wasn't the kind of place we wanted to be low on airspeed. The river ran straight into a cliff, reeled backwards in great, rolling waves, then dropped off to the left in more than a 90-degree turn. Less than a hundred yards later the river swept 90 degrees to the right, back to its original heading.

The switchback really messed up the water, forming rapids no one could survive. But as we closed in on the first bend it dawned on me that there was another way to get through. So I continued to fly into the turn without slowing down, heading straight towards the cliff on the far side.

When Kathy looked over at me, obviously wondering what was going on, I pulled Alice up into a steep climb. Hugging the near-vertical slope to our left, we quickly rose 300 feet to the top of the ridge that jutted into the turn. The second we cleared the crest, I pushed the cyclic forward and Alice shot straight down the other side.

Halfway to the water below, I remembered where we were and looked up. Directly ahead was the tightest part of the canyon. The walls on either side of the river closed in and, as I'd speculated from above, at water level the distance between the 300-foot cliffs appeared to be close to the width of our rotor blades.

Reflexively I brought Alice's nose up and pulled in a lot of power. My initial assessment was that we weren't slowing down fast enough to stop before we ran into the cliffs. If we couldn't fit between them or come to a stop, we had to get out of there. The only way I could do that would be to turn upstream into the S-turn.

While that was going through my mind, our rate of descent changed. There was a light wind blowing upstream.

Possibly we got some additional lift from that, so I kept Alice's nose pointed downstream. As we closed in on the gorge it began to look as if we might fit. With a dependable wind on our nose, I could afford to take my time and slip slowly between the cliffs. Also, the water below us was calm.

More than once the rock faces closed to within four or five feet of the tips of the rotor blades. When they got that close I imagined a line snaking dead center between the cliffs, and followed it, with periodic checks left and right to be certain. In that particular lighting I could set the edge of the rotor disc quite well.

The narrow gorge didn't last long, and it was the end of Devils Canyon. Opening up ahead of us was a wide green valley. That was great, I thought, and nosed Alice over to build airspeed for a grand finale, a cyclic climb. A cyclic climb is the opposite of a cliff dive. You start out fast in normal flight. Then pull the nose up further and further, slowing down as the helicopter climbs.

Usually I would get going 120 mph or better; however, with the wind whipping through the open doors it began to get uncomfortable around 90. As I began to pull back on the cyclic to initiate the climb Alice began to shake in an odd way. The abnormal shudder dissipated as the nose came up and I lowered the collective, which made the maneuver smoother. Within seconds we were climbing at a 30-degree angle and 200 feet above the river. Bright, warm sunshine filled the cockpit. I pulled the cyclic back further and the nose climbed to 40 degrees above the horizon. Then I raised the collective, pulling the aircraft into the climb, pointing us even higher.

Pushed back in our seats by the force of the climb, the only thing in front of us was the great expanse of a bright blue sky. It seemed as if we were going straight up. At 400 feet we were getting really slow, almost out of momentum. At the last second, just before the stall, I brought the nose down to the right, leaving us parallel to the ground on our right side. For a moment we paused, hanging between the positive and negative forces of gravity. Hands, feet, intestines, all registering the sublime sensation of weightlessness… a perfect moment. What flying feels like in my dreams.

As we began to fall I rolled Alice level and pushed her nose over, diving towards the river below. In seconds we had our airspeed back, and I finished the maneuver by gently bringing the nose up to straight and level flight.

I glanced over at Kathy, and asked, "What do you think?"

"How about one more time?" she replied.

The flight down Devils Canyon had indeed been wild and, standing there in the middle of the night outside her tent, Kathy was right to call me on the "safe pilot" bullshit I was giving her.

I was about to change the subject when she bent down, unzipped the fly to her tent, and said, "Goodnight, little lemming."

"Goddamn it," I protested. "Ken was whispering. You weren't supposed to hear that."

"Who said that's how I knew. Goodnight," she laughed, as the sharp sound of the tent's zipper brought the evening to an end.

Bad day for looking good, I decided as I felt my way through the dark forest to my tent. No doubt I'd been showing off, and exposed my passengers to unnecessary risk, but I exposed them to risk every day, for Christ's sake. Flying in unforgiving terrain, high winds, severe turbulence and bad weather at maximum weight. Landing among tall trees with inches to spare, or on steep slopes with no place to go if something goes wrong. That was my job… to deal with those things, at any given moment.

Why, I reasoned, shouldn't some of that skill be applied to the pursuit of new and interesting experiences? Especially when you factor in the helicopter's versatility. That they can do almost anything imaginable, or at least physically possible, as I'd learned time after time.

Off to my right I could hear the sound of Alpine Creek growing louder and figured my tent couldn't be too far away.

Moments later another hole opened in the clouds and moonlight's glow filled the forest. Surprisingly, my tent was right in front of me.

Later, in my sleeping bag on the verge of sleep, I smiled when I thought about Kathy and how we interacted. She was quick witted and liked to laugh, independent and confident, and also attractive. Slim hips, nice firm breasts, a strong back and square shoulders; there wasn't an ounce of fat on her. I also liked the way she dressed. How she tucked her long blond hair into that old cowboy hat to keep it out of the way, the baggy flannel shirts and green fire-resistant pants the Forest Service handed out. Kathy was as natural as she could be, and honest, which was something I could appreciate in a woman after Darcie.

I met Darcie at a wedding in New York. A year later we were in California. I was flying offshore and had bought a house in Ventura near the beach. Not much later we got married. Less than a year after that I was flying down the coast past Rincon after a prolonged period of rain and noticed an odd colored mud flowing down the only street in Seaside, one of the small communities along the coast.

That evening I noticed that the same mud was on the sides of Darcie's car. When I found her in the kitchen, thinking I'd be clever, I asked, "So you spent the day in Seaside?" She didn't move, just stood there staring at me. "Don't you want to know how I know?" I asked.

"No," she finally said, in a firm and level voice tinged with malice. "You're right, I was in Seaside because I'm balling Rick, and I want a divorce!" Then she turned on her heal and left. Rick was a coach at the tennis club we belonged to, and I'd just found out he lived in Sea Cliff.

I had no idea what had been going on, which was hard for most of my friends to believe. It turned out that Rick was the latest lover on a long list, including bag boys at the market, a car salesman, the guy who installed the outdoor Jacuzzi, quite a few of my friends and one brother. All in less than the year we'd been married. I found it hard to believe how naïve I'd been.

With the house, two cars, the tennis club, and a sailboat to pay for, I was strapped for cash to begin with, but paying legal fees and the bills Darcie ran up after she moved out was the reason I ended up in Alaska. The pay was twice as much as I could make in California. Even with the better pay, it took two years to pay off the expenses of divorce. Which is why I had so little money for my trip to Tahiti in the beginning of last winter.

The girl I'd been living with on and off for the past two summers was a lot nicer person than Darcie but wasn't a long-term relationship. I met Sara through a mutual friend at Tundra. Although we got along well, I didn't fit into her world. Sara was also a topless dancer at the Runway Lounge, and her friends, a loosely knit group of misfits, treated me like an outsider. Which was okay with me. I'm not a huge fan of vicarious participation. Sara was way into Buddha, whom I liked, but not enough to get involved.

Sara didn't fit that well into my world either. She was a little crazier than I was used to. Sometimes she was so removed I couldn't get her attention, and other times so intense it was unnerving. Sara could also be indifferent, answering idle questions with "coocoo ka choo" or some other catch phrase from cinema or song. She could also work herself into passionate stances on ridiculous matters.

The more I thought about Sara, I realized it was time to bring that relationship to an end. I hadn't seen her in weeks, but some of her things were still in my room at the hangar and rumor had it she was sleeping there when I was off flying. No big deal, I thought, but definitely time to move on.

Who knows, I mused, Kathy seemed to like me, and hadn't shown more than passing interest in anyone else in camp... then I remembered her telling someone that she was going to Anchorage when she finished work to meet a boyfriend from Montana, a bear biologist. They were going to travel around Alaska for a few weeks. Besides, when the contract with FSL ended in September I had another job lined up for at least a month, then I was thinking about taking a trip to Australia or New Zealand. And from what Kathy had said around the campfire, she was going to graduate school somewhere.

Outside my tent Alpine Creek splashed and gurgled as I slipped into a deep, dreamless sleep.

5

THE GREAT TANANA RIVER RAFT RACE

The first thing I heard in the morning was Bill, yelling, "Kitchen's closing. I'm puttin' the food away in ten minutes. Smith, you better get your ass up here if you want breakfast." Then I heard the patter of rain on my nylon tent and groaned. The days were always long when it rained.

As I lay there mustering the energy to get up, I took a guess at what I'd see when I stuck my head outside. The rain had a steady beat with a wide pattern, so it was light, I thought, and there wasn't any wind because the sound never wavered.

In most environments people learn to tune noise out. In field camps sounds are a part of the social fabric, a form of communication, a public address system of sorts that lets you know what other people are doing. The sound of a zipper announces a coming or going. Kitchen noise is unique and of interest to everyone. It was also nice to know when a bear was in camp.

I pulled on my clothes, already damp, unzipped my tent and crawled out headfirst. The rain was even lighter than I thought, and the bottoms of the clouds were only 200 feet above the trees. But the overcast appeared to be thin, as I'd thought. We'd be able to get out of camp, I decided.

Most of the people in camp would rather go out in the rain than sit in a soggy tent all day, knowing that they'd have to make the work up later. But if it was pouring rain or the clouds were in the tops of the trees, we didn't fly because it just wasn't worth it. Too little work got done and the chance of spending the night in the helicopter increased exponentially.

"Hey!" Chris exclaimed, when I joined the stragglers at the cook tent. "Look what the cat dragged in." When I got closer she added, "You look terrible, Tom."

Not having seen a mirror in several days I couldn't be

certain, but there was a good chance she was right. Both my hair and beard were long. After a sound night's sleep they often ended up heading in several different directions. I ignored Chris, but as I walked by Kathy she reached out and, grimacing, began putting my beard back in place with her plastic spoon.

"Gross," she said.

Personal appearance was seldom a priority of mine, even less so in field camps. There was a pot of coffee on one burner of the little gas stove in the cook tent and oatmeal on the other. Coffee cranked me up too much, and oatmeal triggered my gag reflex, so I had my usual breakfast of an orange and a bowl of Cheerios. We seldom had fresh milk, and the canned stuff tasted terrible, so I usually ate dry cereal or just had an orange.

After breakfast, I packed a can of tuna, two pieces of bread, a Coke and another orange in a lunch bag. Then it was up the hill to preflight Alice. On the way, I stopped by the office on wheels to check in with Fred and Ken. Spread out on the table between them was a map of the plots.

"You can't get there from here," I told them.

Ken laughed. Fred grunted and said, "We're just trying to find some plots you can get to in this weather."

"What've you got along the river?" I asked him.

I wanted to stay along the river because it's easy to get lost in the mountains when the weather is bad. Maps don't work very well when the clouds are low. Everything looks the same, especially when it's raining. The compass isn't of any use because you never fly in a straight line long enough to figure out where you are. And there's always the risk of running into something. Cliffs and trees come out of nowhere.

About the only thing that works reliably is following rivers or streams large enough to be depicted on the map. There is a lot more detail in streams. Every turn and confluence is depicted. Whereas, an open valley above tree line has only contour lines. Also, over water you don't have to worry about running into as many things.

"Well, there's thirty-nine here," Fred said, referring to one of the plots on the map in front of him. "And forty-seven over..."

"Let's see, Fred," I interrupted.

Generally I didn't have a problem with Fred planning the day for us. It was part of his job. Also, he flew airplanes and knew something about a helicopter's capabilities. But on days when the weather was low I liked to pick the plots myself. Getting the crews to work in bad weather was one thing, but getting them back in was another. If the weather got worse during the day, as it often did, I wanted them in places I could find even if the clouds were down to the ground.

After agreeing on three plots, with alternates in case we couldn't get to them, I made my way through the wet brush to Alice. One nice thing about rain in the morning is the dead bugs on the windshield come off easily. Once the bugs were gone, I sprayed the Plexiglas with Lemon Fresh Pledge. Because most helicopters don't have wipers, we used furniture polish to help water roll off at slower speeds, like during final approaches and at a hover.

The windscreen clean, I began the daily preflight. I checked the air pressure sensors, the pitot tube and static ports in Alice's nose. Next I checked the battery, chin bubbles, external antennas, landing gear and undercarriage, cargo hook, door hinges, latches, fuel cap, engine and engine mounts, exhaust cones, drive shafts, gearboxes, transmission and transmission mounts, oil levels, grease fittings, rotor mast, swash plates, drive link, push-pull tubes, rod end bearings, rotor head, pillow boxes, droop stops, rotor blades, fuselage, tail boom, stabilizers, tail rotor pitch change links, blades and bushings. Lastly, I drained the water from the fuel tank sumps. Then I climbed in the cockpit, slouched back in my seat and closed my eyes.

"Get up, ya lazy bum," Chris yelled as she, Kathy and Ken walked up the knoll.

When they were closer, I sat up and gave Chris a look of disgust and asked, "What's that hanging out of your nose,

78

Christina?"

Chris stopped dead in her tracks and wiped a sleeve across the tip of her nose. She was a very likable person, and attractive. Like Kathy, Chris was in extremely good shape, and her long raven black hair was always brushed and shiny.

"Where?" she asked, as the tops of her ears began to turn red. When she saw the grin on my face, she laughed, "You turkey."

"Where's Linda?" I asked as they put their packs in the baggage compartment. Linda usually worked with Kathy and Chris.

"She's with Rocky and Will," Kathy said. "Ken's helping us today because Tim's going to work with Paul and Dave."

"They're getting behind," Chris added, giving me a knowing look as she climbed into the copilot seat.

I kept my door propped open with my foot while my passengers got in and put on their seatbelts. If I didn't, their warm, wet bodies would fog every piece of Plexiglas in the aircraft. The only ventilation in a Jet Ranger is a small sliding window in each of the doors and two forced-air vents on the windscreen, which only work well when the helicopter is moving.

Door closed, seatbelt and shoulder harness buckled, I reached down and removed the note hanging from the emergency fuel shutoff. It read, "Untie the ROTOR BLADES dummy." Already did that, I said to myself then glanced up at the rotor system to be certain. Starting with the blade tied down doesn't hurt anything if the engine is shut down right away, but it's very embarrassing.

"Everybody ready?" I asked without the benefit of the intercom.

Nobody replied, so I reached up and flipped the battery switch on, checked my voltmeter for 24 volts and depressed the starter button on the control head of the cyclic. From the engine compartment behind us I could hear the clicking of the igniter and the metallic whine of the turbine's compressor section spooling up. When the compressor reached 15 percent, around 10,000 rpm, and the engine oil pressure gauge indicated a slight rise, I opened the throttle. Start fuel poured into the burner can and ignited. A deep, resonate moan came from the exhaust cones as the rotor blade above me moved slowly to the left... then the second blade swept by. Within seconds, the rotor blades were a blur, their tips moving close to the speed of sound.

Once the engine was turning at operating rpm, I did a cross-check of my engine instruments and picked Alice up to a two-foot hover. After a clearing check around the helicopter and another cross-check, I eased the cyclic forward. The nose dropped a few degrees and we began to move. With full fuel, three passengers and their gear, we were heavy. It was all Alice could do to hover, and going to forward flight took even more power.

As the helicopter slid smoothly off the cushion of air it had been riding on, we dropped to within inches of the ground, but Alice struggled forward, wallowing in her own rotor wash, trying to reach 20 mph. At that speed the dynamics of the airflow through the rotor system would change, and she'd begin to fly. Then I'd be able to reduce power by as much as 30 percent, taking the strain off both of us.

I didn't need to see the airspeed indicator to let me know when we hit 20 mph. There was the shudder, a tremble from somewhere in the rotor system that came down the rotor mast and shook the whole helicopter. It was mild, lasted only a second, and when it was over Alice was flying, pulling away from the ground and rising into the gray sky above us.

No sooner had we picked up Alpine Creek on our way to the Susitna River than we flew into light rain. The visibility dropped to a hundred feet as wisps of cloud flew by our windows. It was going to be a long day flying in this stuff, I thought, banking around the clouds in an effort to keep Alpine Creek in sight. But once we reached the Susitna River the ceiling went up and the rain ended as quickly as it had begun. Within minutes it lightened up so much I had to put on my sunglasses. By the time the last crew was out, the skies were blue and there was only one thing left to do, find a pleasant place to spend the rest of the day.

The primary consideration was always mosquitoes. They were everywhere, voracious and inescapable. The only dependable places to get away from them were mountaintops, where it was too cold or windy for the nasty little buggers, and the sandbars in the middle of wide rivers, where it was too hot and dry. The closest one of the two that day was a rocky little island in the middle of the Susitna.

Within minutes of dropping off the last crew I had my clothes laid out neatly in the shape of a beach blanket. Perfect, I thought as I lay down, except for the twinge of guilt. While I was lying in sun, Paul, Tim and Dave were walking around the woods sopping wet. I could still hear Paul's voice on the radio, "Goddamn it, Smith. You shithead!" There was guilt, but it had been an accident, and pretty funny.

We found the plot easily enough near a wide bend in the river, but the area was heavily wooded. As far as I could see there weren't any openings large enough for Alice. However, on a second turn around, almost dead center in their survey area, there was a large hole in the trees. Feeling fortunate, I went straight in and brought Alice to a hover. When we touched down I could feel the ground was soft. Helicopters are tail heavy, so I kept a little power in to keep the helicopter light and the tail rotor safe. Then I told the crew it was all right to get out.

I heard the right rear door open, and looked over my shoulder to see Tim climb out onto the cargo rack. Everything was perfectly normal, his pack over one shoulder, clipboard in hand, as he took the short step from the cargo rack to the ground. Then, quickly, and incredibly smoothly, he sank chest deep into the ground. For a second, not a muscle moved, not even the placid expression on his face, then he looked really surprised. I had landed on a small pond covered with a mat of sphagnum moss so thick, it could almost support the weight of a person.

Seconds later Paul pulled Tim back into the helicopter and I hovered over as close as I could to the edge of the clearing. It was still wet, but not as deep. After discussing their options the crew stepped into the knee-deep water rather than have to hike a long way in. Not wanting to add to their discomfort by buffeting them with the wind from the rotor blades, I took off as soon as they were out. That's when Paul, who thought it was funny up to that point, got upset.

While I'd been holding the helicopter steady in the moss, the hollow landing gear had filled with water. When I took off, climbing straight up out of the hole in the trees, the water poured back out of the skid tubes, drenching all three of them.

Around noon an eagle woke me from my nap. Its high-pitched screeching and chirping always seemed uncharacteristically wimpy for a bird of such stature. After stretching muscles stiffened by sleeping on rocks, I gave Alice a bath. I always brought along some laundry soap when I worked out of field camps. It cut the turbine soot. Then, recalling what Chris and Kathy had said about my appearance at breakfast, I took a very quick rinse in the 50 degree water. Later that day, when I picked up Tim, Paul and Dave, they weren't wet anymore, but they were still mad.

"I'm sorry, Tim," I said when he had his headset on. "I had no idea that was a bog. Or that the skids were full of water," I apologized. "But you should've seen your expression!" Paul and I laughed, but Tim and Dave didn't.

About 10 minutes into the flight one of the master caution lights on the panel above my instruments illuminated. Paul was in the copilot seat and noticed the bright red light. "Are we gonna die?" he asked nonchalantly.

"Not immediately," I told him. "But I don't like to see that one come on." It was wired to a chip plug in the engine.

A magnet in the tip of the chip plug picks up anything metal floating in the engine oil. When enough metal accumulates to bridge the gap between the magnet and the metal housing of the plug (about one-sixteenth of an inch) a caution light in the cockpit comes on. Usually it came on because of metal "dust" accumulation, part of normal engine wear, but I had to land as soon as possible to check it out. If it wasn't normal wear it could be the beginning of an engine failure. Turning at 50,000 rpm, turbine engines come apart fast.

The closest landing spot was a mosquito-ridden bog, but I didn't know when I'd find something better. The chip plug came out of the engine in record time, a minute or two, because I was being eaten alive by mosquitoes. I would have had it back in just as fast, but there was a good-sized piece of stainless steel stuck to the magnet. It was large enough for me to see that one side was polished, like a bearing or a piece of a gear tooth. The engine would have to be replaced.

All I had to do was fly to Fairbanks, about two hours away, and have the mechanics put in a new turbine. But I couldn't take passengers with me. If the engine quit and we crashed, I would be in a lot of trouble with the Federal Aviation Administration.

"This engine's shot," I told the crew. "I've got to take Alice back to Fairbanks and get a new one put in and, unfortunately, I can't take you guys with me. Too much of a chance it will quit." I went on to tell them that once I was in the air, I could contact a Flight Service Station and have them phone Tundra. "Then they'll send someone to get you," I concluded.

"How long will that take?" Paul asked.

"If they have a helicopter ready to go. Three hours from now, around nine or ten. Hopefully before dark," I told him.

"And if they don't have one ready to go?" Tim inquired.

"Could be awhile. At least tomorrow morning," I admitted.

"You dumped water all over us this morning. Now you're going to leave us in this mosquito-infested hellhole for who knows how long? I don't think so," Paul put in, as upset as I'd ever seen him.

"I can't take you up with the engine making metal," I

explained.

"What if we won't get out of the helicopter?" Tim asked.

"Well," I said.

For all I knew there wasn't another helicopter in the hangar. In which case Tundra would have to charter one. It might be late the next day before they got picked up, possibly the next. Besides, if the engine was coming apart it would turn on the chip light again and we could land, possibly after reaching a Flight Service Station and Tundra. And I did owe them.

"I guess I could take you to the nearest road and drop you off. But it's got to be your choice."

The crew voted unanimously to go with me. I wiped off the chip-plug, put it back in, and ran the engine for a few minutes, waiting for the caution light to come on again. It didn't, so we took off. Twenty minutes later we were over the Parks Highway and it was time for another decision. I could drop them off and they could hitchhike back to camp on an almost-never-traveled dirt road while I flew on to Fairbanks. Or they could come with me and have a good time in town while Alice had her engine replaced. Once again it was unanimous.

Just south of Windy Pass we landed at a pay phone on the side of the road and called the state troopers. I asked if one of their men could stop at Alpine Creek to let Fred know we were all right. Then I called Tundra Copters and left a message that we were on our way in and needed a new engine. The company tried to keep a spare on hand, but the last time I was in the parts room I didn't notice one. I also hoped there would be a mechanic or two around. It was getting late.

My fears were unfounded. The moment we landed the tall hangar doors rolled open and two mechanics, Sparky and Otter, came out to attach the ground handling wheels to Alice's landing gear. Through the opening doors I could see a turbine engine on a workbench.

While Paul, Tim and Dave went into the office to find a

ride to town, I helped push Alice into the hangar.

"So, she's makin' metal," Otter commented as we rolled the helicopter along on its temporary wheels.

"Big chunks, Otter. Biggest darned chunks I've ever seen," I told him.

"Far out," he said.

I always exaggerated things for Otter. He was a great mechanic but quite spacey. Only extremes seemed to get his attention.

"Remember that trip we took around Denali a few months ago?" I asked him as we parked Alice beside the replacement engine.

"That was amazing," Otter replied, rewarding me with a great big smile.

Early in the summer, Otter showed up at our camp in Hurricane with a battery strapped on the back of his motorcycle. Tundra had a helicopter working at Chelatna Lake and its battery was dead. The only way to get to Chelatna during the summer was by air, and I had the closest company aircraft.

After the last crew was back in camp, he and I took off in Alice. As we flew over the Chulitna River, heading into the evening sun, Otter slouched back in the copilot seat, almost hidden in his long scraggly hair. He looked as if he hadn't taken a shower or been to bed in days. His thick wire-rimmed glasses were so smudged I couldn't tell if his eyes were open or closed. But all of a sudden he sat up and looked out his side window, trying to see behind us.

"Hey, I thought we were going to Chelatna," he exclaimed.

"Relax, Otter!" I told him and grinned. "We're taking the scenic route."

The normal way to fly to Chelatna Lake, located 75 miles southwest of Hurricane, was a straight line: down the Parks Highway for a while, then across the Chulitna River and both meanders of the Tokositna River, through the 2,000-foot pass between Dutch and Peters Hills, and across the Kahiltna

River Valley. But it was a pleasant midsummer's day. The winds were calm and the sky incredibly blue. With weather like that, I decided we might as well take a look at Denali. It wasn't far out of the way, and the southern exposures of the incredible mountain are something you don't get to see often.

A few minutes later we were flying up Hidden River, following it into the labyrinth of mountains that surrounded Denali. Climbing the narrow valley to its headwaters at the Buckskin Glacier, we were going back in time. Summer became spring as we passed through 3,000 feet. Leaves shrank and became buds as the temperature dropped. At 4,000 feet the grasses and other low-lying vegetation began to turn brown and then disappeared, leaving a barren streambed littered with broken rock and other glacial debris. At 5,000 feet we were over the Buckskin Glacier and it was winter.

Ice and snow covered everything. The only signs of the warm weather just a few miles away were small, brightly colored melt pools scattered around the glacier's surface. Some were bluer than the clearest winter sky, others a soft emerald green. Set in the glacier's gleaming white mantel, they were mesmerizing.

Rock walls thousands of feet high and miles long rose around us. On top of their gray-black faces, ice and snow clung precariously to sharp ridges and pointed peaks. To our right a small glacier hung in space from the top of a cliff.

"Whoa," Otter exclaimed, his mouth agape.

"No shit," I agreed. It was one of those extraordinary moments. Overwhelmed by the extremes surrounding me, I was part of it.

Nearing the head of the Buckskin Glacier, the Mooses Tooth on our left, a monolith of granite, rose almost a mile from the glacier below. Ahead, and several thousand feet above us was the pass we were looking for, so I pulled in some power and began to climb.

The glacier bent and cracked as we followed it up the mountainside. Wide crevasses, hundreds of feet deep, opened below us. Reflexively I checked the engine instruments for any indications of trouble.

A few minutes later we shot through the pass, only a few feet above its dark rock saddle, out into the Ruth Amphitheater, a dazzling sea of snow in a citadel of granite. Ahead of us and to our right three white rivers, different forks of the Ruth Glacier, flowed into the valley filling the three-by-five mile bowl with thousands of feet of ice. To our left, Mount Barrille and Huntington formed a 10,000 foot wall of rock and ice broken only by the outlet of the amphitheater, a deep gorge between the Mooses Tooth and Mount Dickey. On the right, Explorers Peak, Mount Dan Beard and the Southeast Spur of Denali rose between the forks of the Ruth Glacier. Above the Southeast Spur we could see the top of the East Buttress at 15,000 feet; however, at 7,000 feet, we were too deep in the valley to see Denali.

We continued across the amphitheater and up the West Fork on the other side, into the shadow of Denali's South Buttress. It was still more than a mile above us, and we were at 9,000 feet. At the head of the West Fork we had to go through an 11,000-foot pass to get to the Kahiltna Glacier and Chelatna Lake, so we began to climb again.

As we crept up the side of South Buttress, the top of Denali began to appear. At 20,320 feet, its South Peak is the highest spot in North America. When we reached 10,000 feet we could clearly see the mile-wide cornice of ice and snow that formed the summit. At 12,000 we could see the entire south side of the great mountain. Its vertical rock faces rose from the Kahiltna Glacier, unimpeded for 10,000 thousand feet. As I watched, a large plume of snow lifted off a cornice close to the summit. Rising in a graceful wave on the wind, curling and flowing like a banner, it drifted off into space.

That flight along the south side of Denali had been perfect.

As Otter took the ground handling wheels off Alice, and Sparky began unfastening the engine cowling, I headed for the door to the front offices. On the way I noticed that the red and blue helicopter against the wall, tail number N 59387, didn't have an engine.

The secretary was gone for the day but Craig was in his office busy with paperwork, so I slouched in the chair in front of his desk. The overstuffed armchair was covered in hair because Garp, Craig's dog, was usually in it. I didn't have much use for the spotted bird dog, fetch the ball and sleep were about all he could do, but I had to give him credit. He was the only dog I knew that was getting along well with a bullet in his brain.

Craig and Sheryl believed that their neighbor shot Garp in the mouth with a .22. That's the size of the bullet that showed up on an X-ray of his head. Garp probably got shot when he brought his slimy tennis ball over and dropped it at the neighbor's feet. The dog invariably stood around waiting for the ball to be thrown, looking up, mouth open and panting, twitching his stumpy tail. Craig and Sheryl weren't happy their neighbor shot their dog, but they knew how obnoxious Garp could be with his ball.

I had to give Craig credit, too. He managed a multimillion-dollar company with the worst kind of problems: complicated and demanding government contracts, pressing timetables, seasonal hiring, finicky pilots and mechanics, along with a secretary who kept rearranging his files. "She does it for job security," he complained, "I can't ever find anything without askin' her." Through it all he was calm and rational, but never predictable.

When Craig looked up from his paperwork, I asked, "Who else is in town?"

It was the height of the season. The hangar was usually empty but there were two helicopters parked on the apron.

"Russell and Burns are around. But I think they're playin' tennis." With the sun up 20 hours in Fairbanks, you can play tennis all night if you want to. "Or they're out drinking." A moment later he added, "Maybe both."

Like Craig and I, John Russell and Johnny Burns had both flown in Vietnam and were good friends. They were also the most dynamic pilots at Tundra. Burns grew up in a small town in Kansas and left with an irrepressible sense of humor and an inexhaustible desire to have as much fun as possible. Russell had a unique ability to keep the world and life in perspective simultaneously, with preference to the world, and get the most out of both. Between the two of them they had more energy than the rest of Tundra combined.

Russell was also our new chief pilot, having replaced Peter Jutras, one of the more intelligent and less sane pilots I knew. John was a good choice, especially with respect to organizational skills and general neatness. Craig often compared his work to mine. "See any difference?" he'd ask, holding up a copy of my paperwork next to Russell's. Unlike mine, John's was legible, with nothing crossed out or written over. His work was also always accurate and complete.

"Anyone else around?" I queried.

"Nope," Craig said.

"How many pilots we up to?" I asked, trying to get my friend away from his paperwork.

I knew that Rusty, our Iditarod champion of sorts, was somewhere in western Alaska, and the other regular summer pilots were also on contract scattered around the state, but when I left we were still several pilots short.

"Lynch got in and out on contract already," he told me.

"How's Tom doing?" I asked. We'd flown together in Indonesia several years earlier.

"Doin' fine. And we got a new guy named Norm," he said without looking up, but then paused and put what he'd been reading on the desk. "Real nice guy... a lot older than us."

"How old?" I asked.

Other than a few guys in the Army, I couldn't think of any pilots I knew who weren't in their early 20s. In fact, the only old ones I knew were airplane pilots, guys like Craig's dad, Buzz. He flew P-51s in World War II, an incredibly fast and heavily armed fighter plane, and one of my personal favorites. After the war he went to work for Eastern Airlines and was still flying DC-9s. Buzz was a professional. Flying was his life.

There was also "Pop," a white-haired guy who managed the parts room for one of the first helicopter companies I flew for. He flew B-52s over Germany in WWII and then worked for American Airlines for 25 years. He'd even flown Ford Tri-Motors all over the world. They were the first metal passenger airplanes. When he told his stories, he sounded like one of us. Along with a certain feeling of accomplishment, there was always irony, humor, and an undeniable sense of wonder.

They were the only older pilots I knew.

"Thirty-six, I think that's what he put on his resume. A civilian pilot," Craig added.

"No shit," I exclaimed.

Guys who got their helicopter licenses on their own were not only rare, they were also a curiosity to me. After Vietnam there were a lot of helicopter pilots vying for a limited number of jobs. Civilian pilots had to pay for their own flight training, which cost a fortune, and they had to compete with us. Their dedication was impressive.

Craig reached for the pages on his desk again.

"I see three-eight-seven's officially the hangar queen," I interjected before he could get back to what he was doing.

I was referring to the red and blue helicopter in the hangar whose engine was missing. A "hangar queen" is the helicopter that gets cannibalized during the busy season to keep the others flying. It begins innocently enough. An aircraft is grounded for something relatively minor like an inoperative rotating beacon or something. Then, while it's waiting for a new part to be shipped from California, another part disappears. Although all the scavenged parts are reordered, the time lag in shipping from the lower 48 states keeps the queen in the hangar.

"She was the hangar queen," Craig said, with emphasis on "was." "But she's gonna be on a job in two weeks." Optimism is a great thing, but what Craig said wasn't going to happen. Along with an engine, 387 needed a major structural component repaired before she could fly again.

In the beginning of the summer, while showing a new mechanic how to clean out the engine-deck drain tube with compressed air, Sparky encountered a plug. Following standard procedure, he crawled underneath the helicopter to blow it clear from the other end. A few seconds later, a loud bang resounded through the hangar. Sparky had plugged the air hose into the wrong tube and ruptured the fuel cell bulkhead. In his defense, the two tubes are right beside each other and look a lot alike, but repairing the bulkhead was a major job.

"Two weeks," I said. "I guess Otter can do it if nothing else comes up to distract him." Which was almost always the case.

"Otter's going out with Burns in a few days… be gone the rest of the summer almost. Moranville's gonna take care of it," Craig said with confidence.

"Who's Moranville?" I asked.

"Hired him last month." At least half of the mechanics were new this year. "Good guy. Saved my life," Craig added, grinning broadly.

This is going to be a good one, I said to myself. "What are you talking about?" I asked.

"Sheeit, didn't I tell you about that?"

"I've been out working," I reminded him.

"You know about the raft race, right?" Craig asked cautiously.

A few weeks earlier, Craig and several Tundroids, as some of Tundra Helicopters' employees were known, floated the Tanana River in The Great Tanana River Raft Race. They worked on their raft for a month or more. It floated on empty 50-gallon fuel drums fastened together, and had a wood deck complete with railing, aluminum lawn furniture, barbecue, crow's nest, and, in a surprisingly far-thinking move, an outhouse.

It was the first running of the race in over 15 years. Fairbanks officials canceled it back in the '60s because so many rafters were drowning, about eight people in three years, mostly from getting too drunk and falling in the cold, silty river. But people missed the annual event and rules were now in place that the town believed would make the race safe. The new rules required rafters to register with the race committee, pay an entry fee, and wear life jackets. Most of the entrants complied with the first two.

"I heard a few stories," I told Craig. "But nothing about Moranville saving your life."

"You know about us goin' down the slough, don't ya?" he asked, looking sheepish for a moment.

"No," I replied.

Craig went on to tell me that they'd made a wrong turn and ended up on one of the Tanana's many meanders. It led back to the main course of the river eventually, but sloughs run slow and often have a lot of snags. As it turned out, getting lost was their excuse for crossing the finish line almost one day after the winning time of six hours.

"Right after we got on the slough, we hit a snag. Big ole tree with its top broken off, stickin' out of the bank just a bit off the water," Craig went on.

"Is that when you lost the crow's nest?" I asked, having heard about that.

"Nope, we lost that before. That's the reason we went down the slough. Couldn't get up high enough to see which channel to take. Anyway, when we caught the snag I was asleep in the shitter."

"You what?"

"It was the only place with a roof. Went in there to get out of the rain, ended up takin' a nap. Next thing I knew we hit the snag. It stopped the damn raft dead in its tracks. And I woke up about halfway to the water.

"You went into the river?" I asked, amazed.

"Yeah. The door just flew open an' I went flyin' out. Just as good I did, though. When the snag broke loose, it tore off the barbecue an' then demolished the shitter. If I'd been in there it would've killed me for sure."

Going in the river could have killed him almost as quickly. The water is so cold it's hard to think much less swim.

And, like most Alaskan rivers, the Tanana was permeated with glacial silt washed down from the mountains. It doesn't take long for the fine silt to saturate a person's clothes, making it almost impossible to stay afloat.

"Jesus, Craig! What happened?"

"I thought I'd be clear of the raft, but the damn thing ran over me."

"The raft ran over you?"

"That's how Moranville ended up savin' my life," he told me, as if I were having trouble understanding English. I wanted to laugh but couldn't. What he was describing was pretty scary. "Bonked my head on one of the barrels an' went under. Thought I was gonna die right there, but Moranville saw me as I went by. He just reached down through the hole cut for the shitter an' pulled me right up like a little wet puppy. Pretty amazing when you think about it. He only weighs about a hundred an' fifty."

"Well, I guess you're right," I agreed. "Moranville probably can fix three-eight-seven's bulkhead." We sat in silence for a while. "What do you think? Time for a beer at the Mine?"

"Can't do it. Gotta stick around." Then Craig's tone changed. "How the hell you gonna go drink beer? Aren't you goin' back out when that engine's in?"

"Man, talk about force of habit," I laughed.

Craig began thumbing through the paperwork on his desk.

"How's the FSL job going?" he asked without putting down the letter he'd been reading.

Craig had been FSL's pilot for four years, and was the main reason it was such a good job. He taught Fred and Ken how to utilize the helicopter and interact with the pilot. He was also responsible for so many women being on the crew.

When the job began, Fred asked Craig if he would be able to hover in and out of holes in the woods with four people, the maximum number of passengers for a Jet Ranger. Most pilots would have said no, that in a lot of conditions the helicopter wouldn't have enough power to hover out of ground effect. And they would have been right. But Craig thought about it for a while, and then said, "Sure. If the passengers don't weigh more than a hundred and twenty or so."

That's how the crew ended up being half women. Unfortunately, Craig's cleverness was also responsible for his losing the job. He and Sheryl were working on a baby. She indulged him whenever possible, but Craig's being away all summer with a bunch of girls, while she was home pregnant, didn't seem like a good idea to her.

"I'm having a great time with FSL," I told him. "But they might think I'm a little wacko. Especially Kathy."

I told him about the infamous cliff dive, and that she was in the front seat. He listened to the details of the stunt with moderate interest until I told him about how close I'd come to VNE, velocity never exceed. Then he got upset again.

"You're kiddin', aren't you? You think VNE's a hundred an' fifty?" he asked incredulously.

"Yeah. Of course it is. It's marked on the airspeed indicator with a little red line," I said sarcastically.

The long scar down Craig's left temple began to darken. He'd gotten the nasty cut a long time ago when he went through the windshield of a friend's car after they went off the road and hit a house. One of the kids was killed.

"What about your damn cargo racks?" he demanded.

For a moment I just sat there. Then I dimly recalled a question on our annual recurrent training test. There was a separate airspeed for the cargo racks, the little one-by-four-foot flat racks attached to the top of the landing gear for carrying extra cargo.

"Oh shit," I said, sheepishly. "There is a different VNE for the cargo racks, isn't there? I forgot about that."

Craig groaned. "For a two-o-six equipped with cargo racks, it's one-twenty." He stared at me for a moment. "Are you trying to kill yourself?"

"Must be the lemming in me," I muttered.

"What?" Craig asked, still uncharacteristically upset.

"Why the hell would they make cargo racks that can't go as fast as the helicopter? That's pretty dumb," I said, taking the offensive. Before Craig could respond, I changed the subject. "Hey, what are you doing this weekend?" We worked a ten-days-on, four-days-off schedule with FSL, and our next break coincided with the weekend, when Craig might have some time off.

"Going to float the Chena," he said, his anger gone.

"No kidding? Cool. From where to where?" I asked.

"You know that sharp bend in the Hot Springs Road, where it turns north? From there to town," he told me. "If we can get that far in a couple of days."

"Who's going with you?" I loved to float rivers. It's such a comfortable way to see otherwise inaccessible parts of the world.

"Dave and the twins, mostly people from the team." Craig was the pitcher for the Sandkings, a B-league softball team that was, coincidentally, co-sponsored by Tundra Copters. "You know the twins, don't you? Those two good-lookin' blond girls Dave hangs around with."

"Yeah, they're pretty," I agreed. The trip sounded like it might be fun. "Mind if I come along?"

"Sure, but if you do we'll need another canoe... and something to put it in. We only got the company truck, and that has three in it already."

Mildly disappointed, I was about to move on to something else, when I remembered that Kathy drove a pickup truck. She said she'd left it in town when she went to work.

"Kat's got a truck. Right here in Fairbanks somewhere."

"You just told me she thinks you're nuts," Craig reminded me.

"That's true," I admitted. "But that might not be a bad thing. She's not all that sane herself." When he gave me a doubtful look, I added, "Didn't I tell you what she did to me on Keshgi Ridge?"

"Nope," Craig said.

"We were looking for some snow for ice cream," I told him. "And we stopped on Keshgi Ridge down by Hurricane."

On the way back from their plot one pleasant afternoon, Kathy, Chris, Paul, and I landed on a snowfield. We were on a mission for Will. He not only entertained us with his guitar pickin', he also made great blueberry ice cream in his hand-cranked ice-cream maker. All he needed was something to chill it.

While the others packed a pail with snow, Kathy and I walked to the edge of the snowfield's cornice, not far from Alice, and peered over. After a short vertical drop the snowfield ran down the steep mountain for at least a hundred yards. "Wish I had my skis," Kathy said as we stood there. "Too bad you don't," I said as, rather impulsively, I gave her a little shove.

"You pushed her over the edge?" Craig asked, amazed.

"Yeah. It wasn't that far, five, maybe eight feet. The snow was pretty soft, and it was steep, so I knew she wasn't going to get hurt when she landed." Craig just sat there looking perplexed. Kathy was on the FSL crew the year before, when he was their pilot, and he thought a lot of her. "It seemed like the right thing to do at the time," I said in my defense.

Finally he asked, "Well, aren't you gonna tell me what happened?"

"It was really funny," I said, laughing at the vivid memory. "She didn't scream or anything, just turned in midair, smiled, and grabbed my arm." Craig began to chuckle. "I'm not kidding, she was quick, yanked me right off my feet by my sleeve." We were both laughing. "Then, it was amazing, somehow she twisted around and landed on top of me. Almost knocked my wind out when we hit the snow, which wasn't that soft, by the way. And then, you're not going to believe this, she rode me down the snowfield like a sled, right into the rocks and shit at the bottom. My arms got all scratched up and I had a bunch of sore spots the next day."

After he stopped laughing, Craig said with a grin, "Sounds like you two were flirtin'." When I took the job, he'd predicted Kathy and I would get along.

I ignored his remark and got back to the point. "Anyway, maybe she'll let me borrow her truck. Or maybe she'll want to go too. That would be great. I'll ask her when I get back to camp."

It had been an hour or two, and I was anxious to see how Alice's engine replacement was going, so Craig and I left his office. The old turbine was out and Otter had the control for the overhead hoist in his hand, lifting the new engine into place. Sparky was perched on top of Alice ready to help. Sparky was a regular mechanic, but his specialty was working on the helicopter's electronics. That's how he got his nickname.

"They got that engine out fast enough," I commented.

"Yep," Craig agreed. "They're pretty good at taking 'em apart. It's puttin' them back together that worries me."

As we watched, the electric motor in the hoist whined and the turbine began moving towards the engine compartment. As it cleared the top of the helicopter, the slack chain hanging down from the hoist hit Alice just behind the passenger door. With a loud rattle and rasping sound the chain dragged across her side. Craig and I winced as Sparky, reaching for the chain, slipped. Fortunately, he was holding onto the rotor mast and didn't fall, but the chain slapped the thin skin of the helicopter a few more times before he got control of it.

"Let's go play some foosball," Craig said with a smile. "I think we make them nervous."

6

GOOD FRIENDS AND EX-WIVES

Above the offices at Tundra there was an apartment used primarily by pilots and mechanics that had no place to stay while they were in town. It had a kitchen, living room, several bedrooms, bathrooms and, in a large storage room, the foosball table. The walls of the room were bare, other than one poster. It depicted two seagulls in flight. Beneath them an inscription read, "Why? Because They Think They Can."

The lack of décor and unpretentious location of the room belied the import of what went on there. Foosball had recently replaced Ping-Pong as our favorite indoor sport. Most of Tundra's pilots liked the fast, tactile games and played them intently. Not only to win, but to show off. Quick reflexes are important to us. They are incorporated into almost everything we do in helicopters. From cross-checks to engine failures, speed is essential, which I had proven beyond a doubt to myself several years earlier.

It happened at Bornite, a hard-rock mine in the western Brooks Range. Most of the miners north of Fairbanks, especially the old timers, used a gold pan or sluice box and worked the smaller streams. The bigger operations went with the open-pit method, removing the overburden with bulldozers and excavators to get at the gold. Bornite was the only operation I knew of in northern Alaska the tunneled into the ground.

That day at Bornite I was sitting in the cockpit of a Hughes 500D, on the ground in the heavy equipment parking area, and all I wanted to do was finish the day and get some sleep. I'd been working 12-hour shifts seven days a week for more than a month, and the job was demanding.

Joe Parker, the head driller, and I were talking about where he wanted the next load of drill pipe dropped off. The aircraft was at full rpm and he was standing right beside the open cockpit door so we could hear each other. "Take this to Arctic Camp," he yelled over din. As Joe stepped back from the helicopter, I reached down with my left hand to close the door. As I pulled up on the handle to latch it, the engine screamed and the helicopter leapt into the air.

What had happened was the band on my watch was loose and hung off my wrist just enough to catch the collective as I pulled up on the door latch. Because I was moving heavy loads every day, I had it rigged light. Subsequently, when the wristwatch caught on the collective, the rotor blades went to full pitch. It happened so fast the only thing I was aware of was the look on Joe's face. The left skid had come up directly between his legs, about a foot short of his groin. It's not often you see the look on someone's face who thinks they are already dead.

The helicopter shot straight up, nose high and moving backwards. I didn't know what was going on, but my hands did. They moved quickly and were so smooth I didn't even feel them get on the controls. My right hand, which had been in my lap, got the cyclic and brought it forward just enough to stop the backward flight, while my left hand let go of the door handle and brought the collective down to stop the climb. They worked perfectly together, doing exactly what they had to do and nothing more.

Since I was already in the air I circled the parking area, checking over the aircraft and composing myself. The near disaster had shaken me up. I also took off my watch. When I landed next to Joe to apologize for almost killing him, I was surprised to see that he wasn't upset. "What the hell happened? Did you see how close you got to the ground?" he asked excitedly. "I was sure your tail hit. Never seen anything like it," he continued. "You should've seen the expression on your face."

After I shut down the helicopter I got out and we walked back to check the tail rotor, to make sure it hadn't been dinged. What we found defied belief. The tail had hit the ground. The hollow metal tube below the tail rotor was packed with dirt. When the helicopter reared backwards, it had driven the tube into the ground. For confirmation there were two perfect little gouges in the hard-packed surface of the parking lot.

What surprised me was that there was virtually no damage to the aircraft. The odds of catching the 3,000-pound machine at the exact moment it dug its tail into the ground, twice, were astronomical.

That was the first time I really knew how fast, and independent of conscious thought, my reflexes were. After that incident I looked at games like Ping-Pong and foosball differently. They were entertaining, but also an opportunity to work on those hidden reflexes. I only wished that mine were as reliably fast and accurate at foosball as they were that afternoon at Bornite.

Craig and I did a few wrist-loosening exercises, then got down to business. We only took points for clean shots, ones that were planned and resounded with a loud crack when the ball slammed into the back of the goal box. I liked the offensive part of the game, which requires skill, speed and patience. But it was on defense my reflexes really came into play. Nothing else could consistently block goals against a worthy opponent like Craig.

We were tied at three games apiece when John Russell and Johnny Burns walked in.

"So, it's the big guys against the little guys," Burns said. Both of them were a half-foot taller than Craig and I.

"We have our ways," Craig cautioned him.

The four of us got along well. Beside being the same age and sharing similar outlooks on life, we were members of a small group. We'd made it through flight school, a defining accomplishment, and from there we went to war together to pioneer the helicopter's use in combat. Quite a few of us died, and a large percent retired after they left the Army.

Of the remaining pilots only a few went to Alaska, where we did what we'd done in combat, develop the use of the helicopter in a hostile environment. Once again there were casualties, and the majority of the pilots that came to the 49th state left after their first summer and didn't come back.

We were a small faction of a unique group of pilots, and proud of it.

Competition at the foosball table was always welcome if they were any good at the game, which both Burns and Russell were. Johnny Burns liked a good laugh too much to be a real threat, too easily distracted, but John Russell was a different story. He had natural ability and could focus better than any of us.

"Aren't you supposed to be mountaineering on Denali?" I asked Russell. He and a friend from Seattle were going to climb the tallest peak in North America.

"Next week," Russell laughed. "Which gives me plenty of time to kick your foosball butt."

Russell and I had something else in common. We flew scouts in Vietnam. Like scouts through history, our job was to go out and find the enemy. One pilot and one door gunner methodically tracking armed men who wanted to kill us. We flew fast, maneuverable little helicopters, keeping as close to the tops of trees as possible to limit our exposure. When we caught up to them they were always waiting, hiding in the jungle below, so close we could see their eyes when they began shooting. John and I were in an even smaller group. The mortality rate in scouts was around 50 percent.

Craig and I stopped playing and moved to the same side of the table. Burns took defense and Russell lined up across from me on offense. If I'd known I was going to have to defend against John, I would have switched with Craig. Russell was incredibly fast and he never let up. As I bent over the table to give myself a better perspective on the ball and other players, I could feel the adrenalin begin to flow. Remember to breathe, I reminded myself, drawing in a deep breath and exhaling slowly.

The games were long and hard fought. Finally, it was match point, theirs, and Russell had the ball. Only my goalie stood between defeat and us.

"Smith, you short and somewhat undernourished...," Russell began.

"Sniveling half-man," I finished for him. "It's not going to work Joh..."

CRACK! While I was responding to his taunt, he blasted the ball past my goalie at an angle of at least 30 degrees and still made it resound like a direct shot.

After the games, Craig and Burns left for the television in the living room, while Russell and I went down the back stairs to the hangar. John was going to work on his climbing gear, and I wanted to see how Alice was doing.

The replacement engine was in its mounts. Sparky was coupling an electrical harness while Otter connected the transmission drive shaft. "Another hour," Sparky told me, so I wandered over to the corner of the hangar where Russell was packing a large expedition pack. It was amazing how much stuff he was going to have to take along.

When John saw me coming he stopped what he was doing and sat down on his pack.

"Because it's there. Right, John," I said, referring to the overused adage... why people climb difficult mountains.

"Exactly, Smith," he said.

"But why such a cold, forbidding place?" I had to ask.

Denali is a little less than four miles high. The temperature was always below zero up there, and the winds howled. They would also have to contend with intense sun exposure, ice climbs, crevasses, avalanches, and oxygen deprivation. I really didn't understand why people would go to such lengths to be so uncomfortable.

"No choice, my friend. You know how it is. One step leads to the next, and there you are on top of the highest peak in North America," he replied.

"Some guys got to be on top, right, John? Mountains, women..." I thought my remark was clever enough, John was a good-looking guy and women liked him, but instead of laughing he was visibly upset. "You worried about something?" I asked.

"Not really," he said.

Russell obviously wasn't interested in talking any longer. "Well, good luck," I said, turning to leave.

"How's Darcie?" he asked before I'd gone two steps.

I stopped and turned. His voice was strained. "What?" I asked. I hadn't talked to my ex-wife in over a year, longer than we'd been married. "I guess she's okay." He was staring at me intently.

"I take it she never said anything about... but, you knew. Right?"

I stopped breathing. In a flash I saw the guestroom door ajar, Darcie sitting on the foot of his bed. She was giddy and... goddamn, I said to myself. What an idiot. Russell had gotten it on with Darcie when he stopped by our house in California.

He kept playing with the climbing rope. I had to leave. "No, I didn't know," I muttered, as Russell swore to himself.

Upstairs, I joined Craig and Johnny Burns on the well-worn couch in front of the television. I couldn't help but think about Russell and Darcie. They'd been together for three days. What a sucker, I thought, for letting her get away with it right under my nose. And, Russell... at that point I decided to think about it later.

Around 10 p.m. Otter came upstairs. The replacement engine was in Alice and the FSL crew was back from town. After a quick test flight, Paul, Tim and Dave got in and we took off for Alpine Creek. As we climbed out of Fairbanks the sun was low on the northern horizon, poised to slip below the edge for a few hours before rising again. Seventy miles south of us, across the broad expanse of the Tanana flats, the 10,000-foot mountains of the Alaska Range stretched across the horizon. In the middle, Mount Deborah, Hess and Hayes rose thousands of feet above the others. While everything else on earth was fading into darkness, their snow-covered summits were still brilliantly lit by the sun.

I don't like to fly at night. Engine failure is something that happens, and most often at the worst time. It didn't make sense to complicate the situation by not being able to see the ground very well. Mountains make it even worse. However, my concerns about not flying at night didn't apply in the middle of an Alaskan summer. Some of the deeper valleys get quite dark, but even in the dead of night the sun is so close to the horizon there is at least a subtle glow in the northern sky. Just enough light to make out important terrain features.

Another reason I like to fly at night in the summer is the lack of wind. When you fly in the mountains you always have to know what the wind is doing. Its strength, where it is coming from, how it is interacting with the terrain, and what that means to your plans. If you want to fly up a valley the wind is blowing across, generally the air on one side will be rising while the other side has a downdraft, and the middle will be turbulent. If the wind is really strong, the side the updraft is on can change, but the middle will always be turbulent. Air moving down converging drainages can create wicked turbulence, but when it's moving up there's little to none.

Flying in the mountains at night when the air is calm is like dream flying, go wherever you want without a bump in the air. Because you don't have to think as much, be on guard, the flying is more relaxed. And, oddly enough, because there's less to see, it's easier to just look around and appreciate where you are.

Half an hour later the FSL crew and I were in the Alaska Range heading up the Wood River drainage past the site of the infamous cliff dive. We were on the same flight path we'd used that day... up the Wood River to Grizzly Creek and through the pass, the easiest route through the mountains to Alpine Creek. However, at Anderson Mountain, right before Grizzly Creek, the Wood River made a sharp turn to the east, towards Mount Deborah.

Two thousand feet below us a light at the Wood River Lodge shone dimly in the dark void of the deep valley. It was the middle of the night down there, but to our left the massive expanse of Deborah's northwest snowfield glowed scarlet in the last traces of the sun. I looked up Grizzly Creek towards the pass somewhere in front of us, then back at Deborah. Without even thinking about it, I rolled Alice into a smooth turn towards the mountain and began to climb.

At 6,000 feet we reached the lingering rays of the still setting sun. In its light the cockpit began to softly glow. In front of us, still several miles away, Deborah was all we could see. Framed by dark ridges, the shear snowfield on her left flank dropped nearly a mile to the head of a glacier. At 11,000 feet we could see the summit clearly, a pale island of rock, ice and snow high in the darkening sky.

We flew to within a few hundred feet of the peak, then turned southeast along the cold cliffs of its west face and began to descend. As we approached the southwest buttress, the last rays of the sun disappeared behind Deborah's summit. For a few minutes we flew in relative darkness, but as my eyes adjusted to the loss of light there seemed to be a pearly sheen on the mountain. In fact, the unearthly glow seemed to envelop us.

As we flew on, the light grew steadily stronger. Apparently it was coming from something in front of us. When it became obvious the light was indeed emanating from a spot somewhere around the side of the mountain, I also realized that it was at approximately the same altitude as us, and that it was incredibly powerful. About then my curiosity turned to caution. What could possibly be that powerful? And how the hell did it get to such an extremely remote location?

Then, as we rounded the southwest buttress, resting in the saddle of a ridge less than a mile in front of us was the biggest, brightest moon I'd ever seen. The ebony flanks of the mountain glowed ghostly in its frigid sheen.

I glanced around to see if my passengers were as impressed by the incredible sight as I was. When I looked at Dave in the seat behind me, I noticed that his window was covered with moisture, which was odd. The air outside wasn't that cold, and no one else's window had condensation on it. Dave had to be breathing really heavy, even hyperventilating, to put out moisture like that. Then I looked at Paul, who was sitting beside Dave. He smiled grimly, obviously thinking the same thing. Whatever was bothering Dave was not far below the surface.

The next morning, while I was going over the day's plots with Fred and Ken, I brought up the subject of Dave. "He's losing it," I told them.

Ken studied me for a few seconds. "Me too," he said matter-of-factly.

"First, Ken, you have to have something to lose," Fred came back, visibly pleased.

"You two might not be so glib if you'd been with us last night," I interrupted. Then I told them how Dave had been hyperventilating as we flew past Mount Deborah, and about the incident in Crazy Notch a few weeks earlier when we were flying low level and he pushed down on the collective. "I'm a little worried about him," I continued. "You know, he might try to screw around with the controls again or something. And crazy people can be incredibly strong."

"You really think there might be a problem with him flying with you?" Fred asked cautiously. "That's pretty serious."

"I don't want to get him in trouble, screw up his record or something, but I've got to err on the side of caution." Fred looked at Ken, who shrugged. "How about this," I said, knowing it was up to me. "He can only sit in the left rear seat. And the person next to him has to be one of the guys. I'd prefer Rocky. That way, if he loses it, he can't get to me, or the controls, without going through him first."

"That's okay with me," Fred said quickly. "And our break is in a few days. Maybe some time off will make a difference."

That night, sitting around the campfire, I told Kathy and Chris about the helicopter seating arrangement.

"You're kidding?" Chris said. "God. Poor Dave. Does he know you think he's crazy?"

Before I could answer, Kathy looked at me and said, "You were in Vietnam. Do you think this might have something to do with that? I mean he was over there. And on the news there's stories about guys freaking out," she continued. "Do you think he might be having flashbacks or something?"

"Well...," I began.

"Do you get them?" she interrupted, more curious than rude.

Chris looked at her friend and laughed in dismay. "What kind of question is that to ask a guy... do you get flashbacks? Why don't you just ask him if he's crazy too?"

"I'm sorry. I didn't mean that you...," Kathy tried to apologize.

"Don't worry. It's no big deal," I told her. After a moment's thought, I added, "Maybe Vietnam has something to do with the way Dave's behaving. I mean, I don't like loud noise or being surprised. Firecrackers, cars backfiring, the usual stuff like that makes me go for cover. But that really isn't surprising, considering."

"Considering what?" Chris asked.

"Well, that I've been shot at a lot. Actually got hit once," I told her. Getting back to Kathy's question, I added, "But as far as flashbacks? Sometimes I'll smell something, or see something, and it'll bring back a memory of Vietnam, but it's usually not much different than any other memory. I just sort of remember it and move on. But maybe it's different for Dave. I mean, I'm sure a lot of guys have more intense memories than I do."

"If he is having flashbacks," Kathy said. "Flying around in a helicopter probably isn't doing him any good."

"You got shot?" Chris interjected, not about to let me go until I told her the story.

"Well, the bullet hit me. But didn't do any damage," I told them.

Both the girls broke out laughing. "You mean bullets don't hurt you?" Kathy asked.

"Yeah," I chuckled. "No, it was just a really unusual situation."

My door gunner and I were on the way back to our base, very low on fuel, when I got a call to go help some ARVNs, South Vietnamese soldiers, who were about to be slaughtered by the NVA, North Vietnamese soldiers. It wasn't that far away, so we changed course.

When we got there, a young Special Forces captain was ARVN's adviser. He told me that the enemy had them pinned in the tree line along the side of the field I was circling. He wanted help getting back into the jungle where they could maneuver. I asked what he thought was the weakest spot in the NVA's position. The captain gave me a heading from his position and asked if I could take out as many of them as possible in that area.

I told him we were almost out of fuel, but we'd see what we could do. Then I asked him to pop smoke, set off a smoke grenade, so I'd know exactly where he and his men were. Once I knew that, I could fly the heading he'd given me and hose down the area with the Minigun attached to the side of the helicopter.

The Minigun was controlled by a trigger on the cyclic and shot 4,000 rounds a minute. With only 1,000 bullets remaining, our help wouldn't last long, but that many bullets in the right place could make a lot of difference. Plus, my door gunner had a couple hundred rounds left for his M60 machine gun.

"What happened?" Chris asked.

"Well," I began, and told them how I was working with the ARVNs. "And when I was about done, the American adviser got shot. That left me talking to some Vietnamese guy who only knew a few words in English."

Until then I had been keeping my speed up around 60 mph to avoid being an easy target; however, while struggling with the language barrier, I began to fly slower and move in closer to the ARVN's position. Before long I was hovering directly overhead at about 20 feet, trying to use hand signals to communicate.

As chance would have it, I glanced off to my right front

just in time to see a North Vietnamese soldier stand up from behind a fallen tree with his rifle pointed at me. At the same time the weapon kicked in his hands and my right foot flew off the tail rotor pedal. The bullet had gone through the belly of the helicopter and lodged in my boot, bruising but not breaking the skin of my heel.

"Must've scared the poop out of you," Chris said reverently when I'd finished. "Probably not the scariest thing that happened to you over there, though."

I was in a storytelling mood, about three or four beers worth, and decided to indulge Chris's curiosity. "Actually, it happened so fast I didn't really have time to be scared. It wasn't nearly as bad as the time I got shot down on fire."

"What?" Kathy asked.

"You're kidding?" Chris added. "On fire?"

Both of them seemed genuinely interested, so I told them about the time my door gunner and I were flying along low level at the end of another long day. We were both pretty relaxed as we headed straight into the setting sun, right into the middle of a helicopter trap, three heavy machine guns set up in a triangle several hundred feet apart.

Some of the first bullets hit the engine. I could hear it coming apart as the red "engine out" lit up on my instrument console and a warning horn began to blare inside my flight helmet. We had been trained to enter autorotation the second we knew our engine was gone, put down the collective and establish the desired descent speed; otherwise, our rotor rpm would rapidly decay and we'd fall out of the sky.

But I didn't want to lower the collective. We were over tall trees whose limbs would tear off the rotor blades. We'd end up freefalling a hundred feet or more. So I held the collective up, searching for an opening. Then more bullets hit. There was a muffled explosion and the stricken helicopter shuddered.

"The helicopter blew up?" Kathy asked, truly impressed.

"Yeah," I confirmed. "A bullet went through the fuel cell and the damn thing exploded. Blew the whole side of the helicopter off. The flames came all the way into the cockpit. I actually saw the fire come over the bulkhead at me."

Reflexively my eyes closed, but the flash fire that enveloped me consumed the oxygen in my open mouth. The expanding gasses reminded me of warm angel food cake. Then the smell of scorched hair filled my nostrils as my mustache cooked to a crisp. At the same time there was a searing pain in the back of my neck where the nylon nape-strap of my flight helmet was melting into my skin.

Before the fuel cell exploded, I didn't want to go into the trees. With the helicopter on fire, I couldn't. If we hit the trees the ruptured fuel cell would send jet fuel everywhere, turning us into a fireball. So I held the collective up and frantically scanned the treetops for an opening, but all that I could see was a tangle of sun-bleached limbs. A couple more red lights lit up on the instrument console. One of them was the low rotor rpm. That was not good. We'd be losing effective lift soon.

Around then it became obvious that we were going to crash into the trees whether I wanted to or not. Instinctively, I pulled back into my armored seat, wanting to distance myself from what was going to happen next. In the same instant something flashed between the trees in front of us. It didn't mean anything to me, but I couldn't help but glance in that direction. I saw it again, a shimmering sliver of silver... sunlight reflecting off water only a couple hundred feet away. I knew what I had to do.

"Luckily, there was a little pond in front of us," I told the young women.

As our bullet-ridden helicopter closed on the trees that separated us from the water, I knew that we weren't going to clear them. And with our rotor rpm so low, pulling up on the collective wasn't going to get us over their outstretched limbs either. We'd just lose what little lift we had and fall. The only thing the helicopter had left was a little airspeed. About 50 feet from the trees I brought the cyclic back, slowing us down, prolonging the agony, but it gave us enough lift to clear the trees.

"We ditched in the pond, but that wasn't the end of it," I told my small but attentive audience. "I almost drowned."

Just before we hit the water my door gunner jumped, then I landed the helicopter on its belly. When the blades stopped turning I crawled out of the cockpit, did a little dive from the landing gear sticking out of the water, and went straight to the bottom of the swamp.

"Yeah, when I went into the water the goddamned metal chest protector I was wearing pulled me down like an anchor," I continued. "It was really weird. I could feel each stroke getting weaker as I ran out of air. I was pretty burned out by that time, not thinking clearly, but I remember realizing I was going to die. Actually, it was more like ... so this is it. Like I'd run out of things to do."

"Jesus," Chris said. "What happened?"

"I stood up," I told her. "Didn't think about it, just stood up. The water was only four feet deep. So," I concluded, "if I had to say... that was probably the scariest time I had in Vietnam. Mainly because it went on for so damned long."

"No shit," Chris agreed.

"How did you get out of there?" Kathy wanted to know.

"My wingman saw us getting shot up and flew around the helicopter trap. He came in and picked us up," I told her. "Anyone want another beer?" I asked, standing up.

"Sure," Kathy said.

"Not me," Chris groaned, getting up too. "I'm hittin' the hay." And she wandered off into the night.

Kathy took her beer and we sat staring into the fire. After a couple of minutes she turned and looked at me.

"You sure fly a lot different than Craig. He...," she began.

Not the cliff dive again, I said to myself. "Look," I interrupted. "That cliff dive wasn't as crazy as it seems. I mean, we did things like that in scouts all the time, even crazier." It was true. To stay out of the enemy's sights we put the aircraft in some unusual configurations, like turning them on their side to fly between trees that would have otherwise knocked the rotor blades off.

"But...," Kathy tried.

"The point is," I continued resolutely, "in flight school they taught us how to get the helicopter from point A to point B, but they didn't teach us how to dodge bullets. We learned that on our own. And we didn't consult the flight manual when we were trying to get our machines to do the impossible. I mean, that's how you find out what a helicopter can do. That's where flying down the damned cliff wasn't much different."

Kathy laughed. "That's awfully nice, but I wasn't talking about the cliff dive. You guys land completely differently. He circles around, checks things out and takes his time. You just come straight in and land. Why the different approach? If you don't mind the pun," she said, grinning.

"Oh, sorry," I began, feeling relieved and a little sheepish. "Yeah, I do come in different. Actually, Craig does it the way most pilots do, the way we were taught, circle around, check out the landing spot... that works fine. But you miss a lot of things up there. I think the way I do it is better, especially in the mountains."

"By better, do you mean safer?" Kathy asked with a smile.

I ignored her question. "Other than obstacles, which you really can't see until you're almost on the ground, the main thing you're looking for when you set up your approach is wind direction. You've got to land into the wind. At a high altitude you can circle as long as you want above a mountaintop or ridge and never know where the wind is. It shifts and gusts and there's nothing on the ground but rocks to give you a clue."

"I've seen that," Kathy agreed.

"Don't get me wrong," I continued. "There are some indicators, updrafts, downdrafts, pressure on the tail rotor pedals, but most of the time you don't really know where the wind is until you are on short final. And it's dangerous to think you do. So, instead of wasting time circling around, I make my

112

best guess on the wind and set up the approach. Along the way I watch what's going on, for signs I guessed the wind wrong. If my rate of closure looks different than my airspeed, I go around. If the tail feels like it's being pushed, I go around. Anyway, instead of thinking I got it figured out, I watch for things to tell me I'm wrong." I paused, but when Kathy didn't respond, I added, "And, to answer your earlier question. Yes. I think it's safer."

"Like the cliff dive," she laughed.

"That's completely different," I replied, but then thought about it. My go, no-go approach to flying—do it until things look bad—did lead to uncharted territory... like the cliff dive.

"If your way is better, how come Craig doesn't do it?" she asked.

"Don't know," I replied. "Not sure we've ever talked about it." After a moment's thought, I added, "But maybe it's got something to do with the way we learned to fly. Craig flew gunships, you know, a pretty big helicopter loaded with machine guns and rockets, really heavy. He had to plan things out, set up everything he did or he'd crash. I was right down in the trees in my fast little machine, reacting to things before I knew what I was thinking. Like I've said before. We were the first guys to use helicopters in combat, teaching ourselves, so it makes sense that no two of us fly the same."

"I guess that makes sense," Kathy agreed. "If you don't think about it too long."

"But you don't have to worry," I assured her. "I don't think I'll try a cliff dive again for..."

"Oh, no," she exclaimed. "I thought it was great."

"Goddamn," I said, amazed. "Weren't you just asking me if the stuff I did was dangerous? And now..."

"I'm not saying it wasn't dangerous," she explained. "I'm saying it was a hell of a lot of fun."

"Speaking of fun things to do," I said, and went on to tell her about the canoe trip Craig was planning. "Think you might want to go with us?" I asked.

Kathy frowned. "I told Rocky I might tag along with him and Will. They're going to Anchorage, then maybe down to Homer to do some fishing."

"But you do like canoeing?" I asked.

"Spent some the best summers of my life paddling around the Boundary Waters in Minnesota," she told me. "What river are you doing?"

"The Chena," I told her.

Her eyebrows went up, and she asked speculatively, "You mean you're going to float through town?" Where the Chena runs through Fairbanks it isn't all that inspiring.

"No," I laughed, "farther up towards the hot springs. Below Tors Mountain. You know, the mountain with the big rock columns sticking out of it. Should be a decent trip. Some of it's out on the flats, but..."

"For how long?" she asked, beginning to show interest.

"Craig was saying three days." Seeing her hesitate at that, I added. "It's not the most exciting river in the world, but it sure beats Anchorage." She laughed. "And driving to Homer in all that weekend traffic isn't much better." Then, without thinking, I added, "And I can't go unless there's another truck to carry the other canoe."

Kathy took off her hat and hit me with it. "Why you conniving... is that the only reason you asked me to come along? My truck?"

"No, I promise." She wasn't buying that at all. "Okay, maybe just a little. But it would be great to have you come along too."

She looked at me for a long moment. "Let me see what I told Rocky. Make sure I didn't make any promises."

The next morning at breakfast Kathy told me she had talked to Rocky and that we were on for the Chena River trip.

7

WHITE WATER AND KATHY

When our four-day break began, Kathy and I climbed into Alice and left for Fairbanks. A couple hours later we were at Pikes Landing, a bar on a wide bend in the Chena River just west of the airport. Most of the Pikes' patrons were in some way related to the oil business on the Slope, and to each other it seemed, but it was a nice place to drink beer and watch the river flow—until the summer weekends. That's when the good old boys got out on the water.

Usually they just drove up and down the river fishing or taking their dogs for a ride, like they'd do back home. But there were always a few who'd made too much money on the Slope and had to buy a fancy speedboat. The more expensive, it seemed, the harder they tried to impress the crowd on the riverbank in front of the bar.

One guy in particular always went out of his way to give us a show. His boat barely fit on the river. It looked like something from Wide World of Sports, long, flat and pointy, and it roared like a dragster. He would come flying around the bend, a big rooster tail of water behind him, and race straight at the picnic tables along the bank. At the last moment he'd crank it over in a tight turn, spraying water at the spectators. The crowd loved it.

I saw him do it a bunch of times, but I wasn't there for his final show. Evidently he came around the corner and did his thing, then cut the engine to slow down a little too soon. The wave of water following in his wake caught up to him, rolled over the transom, and sank him on the spot.

Pikes also had good pool tables. Towards the end of the night, Kathy and I challenged Craig and Otter to a game. By the third game we were beating them so soundly that interest in the game was beginning to wane, except for Otter. He'd just recently figured out they were losing and had decided to do something about it.

"No, really, Kat. I'm not so sure that's a scratch," he argued lamely.

"Bullshit, Otter," Kathy said calmly. "It looked like the ball moved to me."

"Hey, I'll admit the ball moved, but that doesn't mean I hit it."

Kathy laughed and took her shot while Otter watched, a dazed expression on his face. I knew that look. He was working on a rebuttal, which could take a while, so I went back to my conversation with Craig.

"Anyway, we got to get going by eight if we want to get anywhere the first day," I told him.

"What about Kathy's truck?" he asked.

"No problem. She's coming by the hangar early. Oh, but I'll need your car to take her to the university tonight."

FSL had an arrangement with the University of Alaska to provide dormitory rooms for crewmembers staying in town on their days off. Free rooms helped offset the crews' meager salaries. And I needed Craig's car to get her there because mine was where it had been all winter, out behind the hangar with a cracked engine block. I forgot to check the antifreeze when I went to Tahiti. Somewhere around 40 below zero the engine froze solid and cracked. I hadn't fixed it because I wasn't sure it was worth repairing. I'd only paid 200 dollars for the retired taxi.

"I'll give you a ride when you're ready," Craig told me. He had a new Subaru and wasn't about to let me use it after I'd been drinking most of the night.

An hour or so later Kathy and I were ready to go and went outside to wait while Craig finished his drink.

"That was some pretty good pool we played tonight," I said as we sat down at a picnic table on the edge of the river. We'd gone undefeated.

"I think the competition had something to do with it," Kathy laughed.

"Yeah, Otter made it easy," I agreed. "It's hard to imagine that the spacey guy you were playing pool with is a really great mechanic."

"You certainly meet some unusual people up here."

"Well," I reasoned. "It is a pretty transient place. And being a dead end of sorts, it's not too surprising a lot of people who don't fit in anywhere else end up here."

"So, is that your story? Stuck at the end of the road?" Kathy asked.

I had to laugh. And think for a moment. "Well, I won't know if I'm stuck here until I leave," I told her. "But it was the end of a road of sorts." I told her about Darcie, the divorce, and having to pay off debts.

"That's the only reason you came to Alaska? Make money?"

"Do you question all the guys you drink with like this?" I replied.

"Just the guys I take canoe trips with," she said. The Chena burbled as it ran along the bank below us. "No, actually, I just wanted to know why you came to Alaska. For me it was a little more romantic."

"Yeah?"

"It began when I was eight or nine," she replied. "My dad brought us here on vacation. We traveled all over, from Sitka to Kotzebue, and I knew right away this was the kinda place for me."

"Love at first sight?"

"More like awe at first. What got me the most was the green everywhere, the deep forests and tall spruce trees of Southeast Alaska. And the endless horizon on the ocean, the rugged coastline, waterfalls, glaciers... and so few people. I'd never seen anything like it and I wanted to see more. When this job with FSL was advertised on the board at school, I jumped on it."

"I think that's great," I told her. "Getting in your truck and driving up here by yourself. Pretty gutsy thing to do."

"For some, I guess," Kathy agreed. "But I grew up

117

traveling. We moved to Venezuela when I was five. Lived there till I was ten and traveled all over South America in our little VW."

"No kidding. We traveled a lot too. Mostly summers." We talked for an hour or more. Both of us grew up in large families. She had three brothers, and I had three brothers and a sister. We had a lot in common and enjoyed talking to each other.

When Craig finally came out of the bar, we got in his car and drove to the university. Kathy directed him to the dorm she was staying in, finishing with, "My truck's parked out front."

It was a little after one in the morning. The sun was still below the horizon but there was enough light to make out the dozen vehicles parked in front of the dormitory where Kathy said she wanted to be dropped off. Only one of them was a pickup truck.

"That's you're truck?" I asked.

Standing at least a foot above everything else in the parking lot, it was big and red with a wide, white stripe running down the side. As we got closer, I could see that the windshield was cracked, the rocker panels were crushed, the eight-foot bed had several large dents and lots of little ones, the chrome was peeling off the front bumper, and the rear bumper, a big, homemade steel thing, was hanging several inches lower on the driver's side.

"That's Spot," she said fondly.

"Nice truck," I said sarcastically. There was still enough trim to see that it was once a top-of-the-line truck, a Super Cheyenne according to the western-style logo on the quarter panel, but it had definitely seen better days. "Does it run as good as it looks?"

Kathy shot me a nasty look. "He runs great. Got the three-fifty with a Rochester Quadrajet, and headers. Used to be a beer delivery truck in Missoula."

"Probably only gets country music on the radio," Craig remarked.

I had to admit that, although Spot was pretty beat up, it was a serious truck. The large tires, with their heavy tread and massive locking hubs for the four-wheel drive, made it look unstoppable. "After I pay my dad another fifteen hundred bucks, he's all mine."

"Your father is making you pay off a loan on that?" I was amazed. During our talk at the picnic table she told me a little about her father, an executive for an oil company, and the home she left behind in Lake Forest, on the lake, complete with tennis court and swimming pool.

"You'd have to know my dad," she laughed.

"Who did the paint job?" Craig asked. There were 20 or 30 black spots of all shapes and sizes scattered around the sides of the truck, obviously the product of an amateur with a can of spray paint.

"Me," Kathy admitted. "That's primer. Those are rust spots. Get it? Spots…"

"Sure do," I told her, then asked, "What's under there?" A plywood deck covered the bed of the truck.

"Everything I own," Kathy told me. "Mostly books and my stuff from school."

The setup reminded me of a Ford Bronco I bought to travel in Mexico when I was living in Denver. It had a canvas roof and doors, so there was no locking it up. Consequently I put a steel deck across the back to store my stuff like Kathy had. It kept everything safe and, with a four-inch foam pad, doubled as a bed.

"We'll have to take the plywood off to carry the canoe. You can stash your things in my room at the hangar, if you want." Craig said it was time to go. "See you tomorrow," I told her, getting back into his car.

When Kathy showed up the next morning I had to tell her that Craig wasn't going on the trip. Around four in the morning Golden Valley Electric had gotten him out of bed to check out lightning damage to a power line somewhere southwest of Fairbanks. He might not be back until the next day. Because there were so many other people involved in the canoe trip, Kathy and I decided to go along anyway.

Other than losing Craig everything went fairly well, and by midafternoon we were heading down the Chena, excited and ready for a good time. Kathy and I were out front, followed by Dave and the twins. Behind them were two more canoes with four more members of Craig's softball team.

The river wasn't much where we put in, around 30 feet wide and two feet deep, but within a mile it narrowed down and the water began to move. The first rapids we came to didn't look like much; however, when the bow dropped into the trough and the canoe began bucking up and down in the little waves, we were having a great time.

When the river flattened out again, Kathy called over her shoulder, "Hey, all that bumping up and down made me have to pee."

The Chena was moving right along where we were. No rapids, but fast enough to undercut the banks as it swept from one turn to the next. There were very few places that weren't steep slopes of three or four feet.

"How about there?" Kathy pointed to a low bank where we might be able to get off the water, but we were already past it. "There's a place," she said a few moments later.

"A little steep," I observed.

Less than a minute later, Kathy exclaimed, "You missed another one, Yo-Yo! Look, there's one up there. Come on, Tom. I'm serious, goddamn it." Then she began paddling wildly, turning the bow towards shore.

"What are you doing?" I yelled, laughing. The water was moving faster and the bank she was heading for was as steep as all the rest.

"I'm gonna ram the bank!"

"Okay," I said, knowing I had little choice. "Let's do it." And we began paddling as hard as we could, chanting, "Ram the bank! Ram the bank!"

The bow squished into soft dirt and Kathy was out of the canoe, up the bank and into the bushes in a flash. Not long after we got back on the river it slowed down again and the stretches of white water became farther apart. Before long we were getting bored.

As I was passing Kathy a bottle of inexpensive wine, she froze. "Listen," she said, in a hushed voice.

Kathy was staring downstream, but I couldn't see or hear anything. "Quit screwin' around," I complained. My arm was getting tired from holding out the half-gallon bottle.

"Don't you hear it?" she asked.

Then I heard something that sounded like wind in the trees. But the tops of the alders and spruce that lined the river were still. Then I heard it distinctly... the sound of rushing water. We picked up our paddles and went to work, anxious for the feel of rapids. However, as we rounded a sharp bend in the river, bow wake curling in front of us, it wasn't white water we saw but a logjam that blocked three quarters of the river. The sound of rushing water we mistook for rapids came from turbulence created by the river being forced into the mess of logs and limbs.

With our good head of speed we easily maneuvered around the logjam, but we were disappointed it hadn't been something more challenging. We had left the mountains behind and were out on the flats. We knew that the farther we got from the steeper terrain, the less likely we were to find white water.

After an hour or two on the meandering river without a ripple, I was sure the best of the trip was over. Then we heard the familiar sound of fast moving water. As we came around a wide bend, we saw what looked like the most challenging rapids so far.

The river swept to the right and took us with it, dropping quickly, kicking up spray and good-sized waves everywhere as we shot down the center, laughing and shouting in delight. When we got to the end I cut a hard sharp turn, bringing the canoe around into the calmer water of an exceptionally long backwater inside the curve of the rapids.

"Let's paddle up the eddy. Get as far as we can, then cut back in and do it again," I suggested. We would only catch the last hundred feet or so of the rapids, but that would be better than nothing, I thought, considering it might be the last excitement of the trip.

"Ram the bank!" Kathy yelled, as she dug her paddle deep into the calmer water and pulled hard.

We left the eddy at full speed and entered the rapids at a shallow angle heading upstream. It worked well. Our hard paddling carried us quite a ways before we lost our momentum to the flow of the river. Without much effort we brought the canoe around and were swept along in the rapids, but we had gone farther to the left than our first trip down and we were heading towards a large birch tree hanging off the outside bank of the turn. The only way around was to the right, but we were too late. The current was strong and we had no maneuvering speed. In a matter of seconds we were going to be entangled in its half-submerged limbs.

"Go left, go left!" Kathy yelled and pointed towards the bank. She was right. To the left there was a hole where the limbless trunk was suspended from the bank. It was only two or three feet high at the apex and got lower as the tree sloped into the water, but it looked like there was enough room for us to get through.

We dug our paddles into the river with renewed strength, heading for the opening. As Kathy ducked under the tree's trunk it looked like we were going to make it. Then I heard the distinct sound of leaves dragging along the bottom of the canoe, and we began to slow down. As we lost speed the current took us sideways, away from the bank and into the narrower part of the opening. Before I could do anything effective the gunnel of the canoe caught under the trunk and brought us to a sudden stop.

"The wine!" I heard Kathy yell from the other side of the tree.

As we struggled to regain our balance in the unstable canoe, it rocked back and forth, breaking loose from the tree. For a moment we were moving again, then a branch, just inches above the gunnels, hit me in the chest, pushed me back and pinned me in my seat. By the time we stopped moving it had slid up my chest and was stuck under my chin, choking me.

I got my hands under the limb and pushed up to get it off my throat; however, instead of the limb going up, the stern of the canoe went down. It wasn't until a wave of ice-cold water fell into my lap that I realized what was happening and stopped—but not for long, because there was no other way to get out from under the limb. I turned my head sideways to reduce my profile and pushed up again. While little waves lapped over the gunnels, the limb slid slowly up my cheek, scraping over my ear and up the side of my face. Just as it cleared my head, the stern slid beneath the surface of the river.

As the canoe filled with frigid water I rolled out of my seat and dove away from the tree, wanting to put as much distance as I could between its ensnaring limbs and myself. Between my fears and the current, by the time I surfaced I was at the end of the rapids. Kathy was about 10 feet upstream reaching out to get a paddle that was floating off to her left. A few feet past her I could see a portion of the canoe's bow above the water.

Treading water in blue jeans and wool shirt was getting more difficult by the second. I could feel my rubber boots getting heavier. It was taking everything I had just to stay afloat. I would have headed for shore, but we had to get the canoe.

"Grab the bow," I yelled to Kathy, who was still closer than I was. But she was distracted and couldn't hear me over the sound of the rapids, so I began swimming upstream as hard as I could.

By the time I got to Kathy I was exhausted. Being submerged in 40-degree water was taking its toll. My arms were getting sluggish, making shorter strokes. Even my thoughts were slowing down, but I could see that we were going downstream faster than the canoe.

Not wanting to swim any farther than I absolutely had to, and barely capable of anything more than impulsive thought, I put my hand on Kathy's shoulder and pushed off towards the canoe. That, plus a few soggy strokes, and I had it by the bow. When I glanced back at Kathy, all I saw was her cowboy hat rocking gently among the choppy waves. Then her head popped up.

"What the...," she sputtered, glaring at me as she swept wet hair from her eyes.

Before I could apologize she went after her hat, then everything in the canoe that could float was spread out around her.

While Kathy went after our things, I swam the submerged vessel towards the sandbar below the rapids. It was slow going. Even though it had only been two or three minutes since we swamped, both my extremities and my mind were numb. I could barely move or think. The cold water didn't seem to be affecting Kathy as much. In the time it took me to reach the rocky beach, she'd made three trips into the river and back, gathering up even things that had sunk. She also helped me pull the canoe out of the water and dump it.

"Why'd you push me under?" she asked as we sat down beside the overturned canoe.

"I was going for the canoe," I told her.

"Why didn't you just swim over to it?"

"Uh... I was tired and..." At that point I began to shudder. Slowly at first, but within seconds my body was shaking uncontrollably. "This is ridiculous," I said. "I c-can't stop sh-shaking."

Kathy took a closer look at me. "Hypothermia. That's the trouble with you skinny guys. No body fat," she said, her voice softening as she realized how cold I was.

"No-o-o shh-it," I agreed.

"Better get out of those wet clothes. I'll get a fire going."

Thanks to the dry wood left behind by high water, bark from a birch tree, and the Bic lighter she always carried in her pocket, Kathy had a fire going within minutes. We stripped off our wet clothes and hung them on the drying rack I'd put together with a few sticks. By that time my shaking had turned to violent tremors.

"Wh-at is it with you?" I asked. "I'm sha-aking my ass-s off and you lo-ook like you just got out of a s-steam bath." The analogy wasn't far off. Steam rose off her underwear as she stood with her back to the fire.

"Will you quit lookin' at my butt," she scolded.

"I ca-an't help it," I explained. "It's ste-eaming."

Kathy peered over her shoulder, one eyebrow noticeably higher than the other. "Well, I'll be darned. It is." And we both enjoyed our first good laugh since the canoe went under.

As our spirits improved, and my body absorbed the fire's heat, the shaking began to subside. I was feeling better, beginning to relax, when I saw something in the river. "What's that?" I asked, pointing.

"Looks like something in a black bag," Kathy observed. "Maybe a sleeping bag." We looked upstream and saw more debris floating towards us.

"Must be from one of the other canoes," I guessed. A pack of Marlboro's was bobbing in an eddy not far from us. "I think that's what Dave smokes."

We grabbed sticks and began snagging everything we could, but a lot of the stuff was out of reach so we had to go swimming again. Later, as we sat by the fire drying off, the alders at the upstream end of the sandbar began thrashing back and forth. Could be a bear, I thought, wondering if we'd have to get in the water again to get away from it. Then Dave came crashing through, almost falling as he broke from the woods.

"Did you guys see any of our stuff?" he asked as he walked towards us.

Kathy and I exchanged glances. Dave didn't look good. His shirt was torn, and he was limping slightly. "Yeah, we got a whole bunch of stuff." I nodded towards the things drying by the fire. "Where's everyone else?"

Dave sat down and stared at the fire, then at me. For the first time, I noticed his eyes were either very tired or incredibly sad. "Jesus, Tom. You wouldn't believe what happened."

He went on to tell us how he and the twins came around the corner in the river and saw the logjam. Instead of going around it the way we had, they got pushed up against it.

"We were having a hard time pushing off, so Liz got out on the log jam to drag us to the end." He paused, shaking his head. "Her foot slipped off the log, she came down on the canoe and it flipped. Liz didn't go in and I pulled myself out. But her sister... Becky just disappeared."

"What are you talking about?" I asked. My brain was still numb from the swim.

"We looked around and Becky was gone. Under the logjam." When Dave saw our looks of horror, he added. "She's not dead. But we thought she was. I mean, she was down there forever. Jesus, it really was forever."

"Becky went under the logjam?" I was astounded. The current runs through the tangled mess of trunks and limbs, following a labyrinth of small channels. Once you are pulled under it's nearly impossible to avoid being drawn into the logjam, trapped and drown.

"It was freaky as hell," Dave continued. "When Becky when under, Liz flipped out. Didn't move, just started sobbing and trembling all over. Turned white as a sheet." Dave picked up a stick and poked the fire. "Then she stopped, just stood there staring straight ahead, eyes wide open. Like in a trance."

"What happened to Becky?" Kathy asked.

"Unbelievable! It was easily a couple minutes after she went under. I really thought she was gone. But she just popped up on the other side."

"Is she okay?"

"Yeah," he said, visibly relaxing for the first time. He told us Becky had trouble breathing for some time, kept coughing up water. But, other than a few scratches, she seemed all right. He straightened himself up. "I've gotta get back. Neither of the twins will go near the canoe. Guess we'll hike out to the road and get them back to town. I don't know what the other guys are gonna do."

"We'll wait here for a while," I told him. "Maybe the

night," I added, getting a nod from Kathy.

Dave slung the trash bag full of their things over his shoulder. "Thanks. I'll let them know you're here," he said as he headed back upstream. At the edge of the woods he turned and waved. I don't think Dave ever noticed that Kathy and I were in our underwear.

Within an hour the other canoes came through the rapids and pulled out. Kathy and I were set to go, but by that time it was getting late so we decided to stay where we were for the night. After dinner Kathy and I sat on the edge of the river, talking and watching black swallows feed on the bugs that hung out just above the water. When the light began to fade we set up our tent.

"I'll finish up," she said, climbing inside to lay out our sleeping pads and bags.

"Great," I told her, and headed for the warmth of the fire.

A few minutes later Kathy sat down beside me. "You did that on purpose." Her voice was low and threatening. "Didn't you?"

"What?" I had no idea what she was talking about.

"Your sleeping bag. It's sopping wet." She was watching me closely. "You mean you didn't know your stuff bag leaked?"

"No, I..." Then it dawned on me. "You mean, too wet to sleep in?" And I began to laugh.

"You jerk," she exclaimed, pushing me over and pinning me on my back among the rough stones beside the fire. "You planned this. Didn't you!" She was laughing too. "Admit it."

"Look, we don't have to share your bag. I can sleep out here with the mosquitoes and bears. On the rocks, wrapped around the failing embers of the fire."

"Good," she replied.

But by the time we were ready to sleep the night had cooled quite a bit. Kathy, being a considerate person, was kind enough to share her sleeping bag with me, and our relationship took on a new dimension.

The ill-fated canoe trip ended the next day at the first pullout near the road. A few hours later Kathy and I were cruising down a back road outside Fairbanks. I was driving Spot, my first time at the wheel of a pickup, and enjoying it. As our speed climbed, the truck's light rear began to slide around on the loose surface of the gravel road. The little drifts didn't bother me. Spot was so big and heavy it seemed unlikely he'd go anywhere quickly. Kathy looked at me and I knew she felt it too.

"Punch it!" she said.

I pushed down on the accelerator and the beast rose off its front springs, lunging forward as eight big cylinders flooded with gas. The exhaust roared through the header manifolds and abbreviated muffler system. It was mesmerizing.

"See?" she yelled. Spot's rear end had settled down.

"Let me see if I've got this straight," I queried. "As long as I keep pushing on the gas, Spot stays on the road."

"Something like that," Kathy smiled.

In the short time I'd known Spot, he'd grown on me. He was solid and, in his own way, dependable. As Kathy put it, "Chevys run shitty forever." And there were little things to appreciate, like the hole in the seatbelt buckle that made a perfect beer bottle opener. I liked driving Spot and was happy to be with Kathy.

"You know, Kat...," I began. "About last night." I looked over at her. She was still smiling, waiting. "Look, I really like you. I mean, God, you're a hard-body..."

"What?"

"Sorry. What I mean is I really enjoyed last night. But if what we did is going to screw things up between us."

I didn't want to go back to the way things were, but there was Kathy's boyfriend in Montana, and she didn't know about Sara, which could affect how she felt about us. And we were working together. That also complicated things. So I thought I should offer her an out.

"What do you mean, a hard-body?" she asked.

"Jesus, Kat. That's all you've got to say? After me telling you your friendship is worth more than sex."

When she didn't reply right away, I thought, what the hell, and told her how I felt about women who were physically fit. How their muscle tone and conditioned strength showed in everything they did. Out of the corner of my eye I saw her smile.

"Well, I had a good time too," she confessed. "I don't know how you feel about this. But, you know, back at camp, I'm not sure that we should move into a tent together or anything like that, but…"

"I agree," I told her.

When we got to the hangar, Kathy stayed downstairs talking to Craig while I went up to my room. Sara had obviously been there while I was gone. There was a pair of jeans draped on the chair, a magazine on my desk, and a black notebook lying on the bed, open. I picked it up and read:

You direct me across country
you have never been before
what is more
each step is taken
for the love of it
you move me
beyond mountains
or pine trees gathering snow
and don't know
the tears my eyes shed
I am wed
to the world we share
you out there
somewhere facing flight

the air you breathe
the light you radiate
makes my way here
I live on this
the wind my kiss

Damn good poetry, I thought, knowing very little about the art but appreciating the message. Poetry was another thing Sara and I didn't have in common. A wave of guilt rolled over me. With the way I felt about Kathy, I really had to let Sara know it was over. That she had to stop using my room while I was gone because I had a girlfriend.

- 8 -

DAVE LOSES IT

Kathy and I spent the rest of our four-day break together, and kept our relationship low key when we got back to Alpine Creek. One evening, on the way to her tent, I ran into Dave. I was surprised to see him coming down the trail that led to my tent. He wasn't the type to be visiting. Also, there was something strangely familiar about the way he was moving. So I stopped and watched.

It was nearly dark. Dave and I were almost a hundred feet apart in low brush. He was hunched over, creeping along, looking off to the left toward Chris and Kathy's tent. He's spying on the girls, I thought, feeling embarrassed for the poor guy. But then he switched his attention to the right and I realized why the way he was moving looked familiar. Dave was "walking point."

In Vietnam the guy leading a column through the jungle was the point man. He walked alone, well ahead of the other soldiers, to trigger booby traps and ambushes set up for the advancing troops. Point men had notoriously short life spans so they moved cautiously, like Dave was doing.

He continued along the trail towards me in a crouch, looking from side to side while I stood watching, feeling a bit strange but too intrigued to do anything else. Anyway, at any moment I expected him to look up, see me, and the weirdness would end. But he just kept coming, apparently in another world.

When Dave was only 20 feet away it was almost frightening how distracted he appeared to be. I was certain that he was going to bump into me and decided it was time to say something. But just then he looked at me and froze. Although he was looking right at me, obviously surprised, he didn't say a thing. Neither did I. We just stood there staring at each other.

131

Then Dave spun on his heel, but just as quickly turned back and looked at me again. He had the strangest expression on his face, a comical frown.

"Nice evening for a walk," I said, mainly to add the reality of sound to the scene.

Dave spun around again. It looked as if he was going to take off running up the trail the way he'd come; however, after a moment, he turned again and walked right up to me, staring intently at something over my left shoulder. I was tempted to turn and look, but didn't want to take my eyes off of him.

"Yeah," he said, finally looking at me. "It's a nice evening." We stood there for a long uncomfortable moment before Dave turned once more and walked away.

Several days later Dave snatched Bill's revolver right out of the holster on his hip, pointed it into the trees and said, "Bang, bang, bang." Then he gave the gun back to the surprised cook, and wandered off into the woods. That evening Fred mentioned to the group assembled around the fire that Dave would be working in camp for a while. Fred was hoping that some time off would give Dave a chance to relax, but it didn't work.

The next day, moments after I took off for a plot, Dave walked up to Ken, Kathy and Will, the crew waiting for the next flight, and told them, "You've got to do something." His eyes were wild with fear. "There's a bomb in the helicopter!"

"What?" Ken asked, as calm as Dave was crazed.

"There's a bomb in the helicopter. Up on that ridge," Dave exclaimed, pointing at the Clearwater Mountains to the north. "It's going to blow up any second!"

Kathy and Will looked at Ken, who shrugged. "Tom just took off that-a-way. Just a couple of minutes ago," he told Dave, pointing south.

Dave stared at Ken for a few more seconds then took off running for the Clearwaters at full speed, heading for the ridge he'd pointed out.

"Look at him go!" Will exclaimed.

"Unbelievable," Ken agreed. "I'd have trouble crawling

through that stuff." Dave was running up a very steep slope through chest-high alders.

"Think he's gonna hurt himself?" Kathy asked.

"Hope not. We'll have to go get him," Ken said regretfully.

Five minutes later, about halfway up the ridge, Dave stopped in his tracks. They could see him staring uphill. A moment later he turned and came down the mountain at a normal pace. When he got back to the group, Dave walked by as if they weren't there.

"Well, Dave?" Ken called after him. "What happened?"

"What?" Dave asked, not even looking back.

"On the ridge. With the helicopter and the bomb, and..."

"Oh," Dave replied absentmindedly. "Yeah. The bomb was under the seat. There wasn't anything I could do."

When Dave didn't show up for dinner, Fred and Ken went to his tent to check on him. Dave was sitting in the lotus position on his sleeping bag, legs crossed, hands on knees, back straight, eyes level. When they asked him how he was doing, he didn't respond. The next day, the project supervisor in Anchorage drove up to take Dave back to the city. It took a while to coax him out of his tent. Apparently, Dave was reluctant to leave because he had found the center of the universe, which to his amazement was right where he was sitting.

Later that night at the campfire, Ken was sympathetic. "Who'd want to leave if they'd found the center of the universe?"

"I don't think Jim would have minded if Dave stayed here either," Chris added.

In an effort to protect Dave's privacy when he radioed Anchorage, Fred hadn't mentioned that Dave was a little crazy, just that he needed a ride to the hospital. The project supervisor who'd come to pick up Dave, thinking it was a routine matter, had brought his teenage daughter along for company.

"Good thing Bill had those handcuffs," Will said.

Seeing that Jim was worried about his daughter's

safety, the cook offered to let him borrow a set of handcuffs he just happened to have.

"Who the hell brings handcuffs to a field camp?" Tim asked.

Tim was right. Bill was weird. And using them on Dave was overkill. When they handcuffed him to the armrest in the backseat, he was smiling. There wasn't much doubt in my mind that Dave was pretty crazy, but he hadn't done anything wrong and they were treating him like a criminal. One of the guys could have ridden along if they were worried about him becoming violent. They didn't have to chain the poor guy to the seat of the van.

As the conversation around the fire moved on to another subject, I couldn't get Dave out of my thoughts. Consensus was that Vietnam had messed him up. I had to agree. For a long time I thought people shouldn't use war as an excuse for their problems. However, too many veterans were killing themselves, or worse, innocent people. And there were obvious similarities in the cases. It was hard to believe that their issues were all personal and not related to war. Like a lot of other vets Dave needed help, not to be handcuffed.

The crew's first plot the next morning was in the Clearwater Mountains. Our flight path took us up and over the ridge that Dave had climbed looking for the helicopter with the bomb under the seat. His uphill run had indeed been impressive. Cruising up the slope just above the vegetation, we got a good feeling for its steepness and the thickness of the alders covering it. They looked impenetrable. It amazed me what a crazed person could do.

At the top of the slope there was a small valley no more than a hundred yards across. In the center was a small lake, its blue-green surface rippling in a light wind. I was surprised. For a month I'd been flying all around these mountains and never knew the beautiful spot existed. I was also a bit shocked to see signs of fall among the low bushes along the side of the lake. I wasn't ready for it, not in August. But fall comes early in Alaska, especially in the mountains.

At the end of the lake, the valley turned left and dropped quickly. As we flew along a sheer rock wall on the west side, Alice's shadow raced across its gray face beside us. Around the distinct silhouette of the helicopter was a halo. Ahead of us a stark pinnacle of pale granite rose into the crystal-clear blue sky. All I could do was shake my head in amazement at the beauty of it all.

When Kathy and I got back to Fairbanks on our next four-day break, quite a few people were in town. One or two contracts were over, but most of the pilots and mechanics were between jobs. John Russell was back for a few days. It was the first time we'd been in town together since he'd told me about his affair with Darcie, and I had been looking forward to seeing him. What he had done was undeniably shitty, but it had been years, Darcie was gone, and holding a grudge would be more work than it could possibly be worth. John was visibly relieved when I told him I'd put his indiscretion behind us, and we agreed to get together for a beer later.

After a nice long shower, which always felt good after 10 days in a field camp without hot water, Kathy and I climbed into Spot and headed north. Outside of Fairbanks we followed Goldstream Creek for 15 minutes to the town of Fox. Amid endless piles of tailings from the gold dredges that worked the area for years, stood the Howling Dog Saloon, one of the three buildings in town. The Dog wasn't very attractive, a nondescript brown structure, and its floors were seldom swept, but that didn't bother the patrons. Most of them lived in the woods around town, where there were few flush toilets, much less hot showers.

Only Bear, the bouncer, was sitting at the bar when Kathy and I got to the Howling Dog. We ordered whiskey and talked to him until Baldini showed up and sat down. Then Rusty arrived. Not much later John Russell and Johnny Burns walked in, but they never got past the foosball table. Craig and Sheryl were next. And when Mike Parker joined us, it was officially a Tundra party.

In the meantime the place had filled up. Within a few

hours people were shoulder to shoulder. On one of my trips for refills at the bar I literally bumped into Dillon, a geologist with the state's Department of Land and Natural Resources. I'd been Dillon's pilot on several jobs, and we got along well enough until Craig hired Lurch, a friend who flew with him in Vietnam.

One of Lurch's first jobs was flying for Dillon. On learning that Lurch hadn't flown much since Vietnam, and that he didn't have any time flying in the mountains, several of the other geologists refused to fly with him. They were within their rights. Nevertheless, I got mad at Dillon because I thought he'd been instrumental in blackballing Lurch. I'd gone so far as to write him a nasty letter about my feelings.

"I'll be damned. It's Tom Smith," Dillon said when he recognized me. I could see a few of his teeth through the black mat of his beard, but I couldn't tell if he was smiling or snarling.

"Dillon! Are you going to apologize to me or not?" I asked, feigning indignation.

His eyes grew wide. "Didn't you get my letter?" he asked. In his rebuttal to my letter, Dillon had written, "You are out in left field. I do not owe you an apology." And ended it with, "Were you sober when you wrote?"

"I got your letter," I said, smiling. "You're right, you don't owe me an apology. But you're still an asshole."

"So are you," Dillon laughed.

While Dillon and I talked about where we were working and what kind of summer it had been, two guys and a girl set up on the small stage across from the bar. As they tuned their instruments the bar fell silent, then went wild when they began to play. The packed room heaved and swayed as almost everyone began to dance.

It was too loud to talk so I said goodbye to Dillon and went back to Kathy, who suggested we go outside. So far, dancing was the only thing Kathy and I didn't enjoy doing together. We stunk at it individually and together we were even worse. But we did play volleyball well, and behind the

Howling Dog was the best volleyball court north of Fairbanks.

Kathy and I made our way through the crowd to the back door. Outside it was darker than I'd expected. At eight-thirty the sun was already on its way down. In one month we'd lost three hours of daylight. It was as unsettling as the steady drop in temperature. Or seeing fall colors in the middle of the summer.

The game in progress involved a contingent of students from the university against several Tundroids and an aging hippie couple. Burns and Russell were starring. Russell for his audacity and skill, Burns for his dialogue. Kathy and I sat on the bench that ran along the wood fence that surrounded the court and waited for someone to leave the game so we could step in.

"What do you want to do after FSL?" I asked her. Our next 10-day stint at Alpine Creek was the last for the season.

"For one thing," she said, looking at me then back at the game. "I've got to pick up Jamie in Anchorage."

I had completely forgotten about her boyfriend from Montana. "Jesus, Kat," I said, feeling something like panic. "Can't you just tell the guy you're busy or something? I mean, I'm trying to be cool about this, but it's tough."

"I know," she said sympathetically. "But I made these plans before I even met you. And I specifically promised not to blow him off. He's a nice guy. I can't do it." Then she changed her tone. "But you and I have almost a week after FSL. Let's do another float trip. Remember the Delta? That looked pretty good."

On the south side of the Alaska Range not far from Alpine Creek the Delta River flows north from the Tangle Lakes. For about 40 miles it winds its way through the mountains before joining the Richardson Highway above Black Rapids. The one time we flew that stretch of the Delta it made quite an impression on us.

"It did," I agreed. "Except for those nasty waterfalls at the end of the lake."

The float trip was a good idea, but that didn't resolve

the issue of Kathy and her previous boyfriend. However, before I could come up with a rebuttal to her "I promised" rationale, Sheryl came out of the bar and sat down beside us

"Do you believe all the people in there?" she asked. A light wind stirred the leaves of a trembling aspen outside the fence. The warm breeze was relaxing. "Sure is nice out here, though."

"Hey, you guys. Get on over here," Burns called, inviting us to get into the game. Several of the college students were leaving for the bar.

"We're on our way," I told him, then to Kathy and Sheryl, "Let's go."

"Not me, Darlin'," Sheryl replied in her sweet southern drawl as Kathy and I joined what was left of the kids from the university.

"Play for shots, mon?" a guy in dreadlocks on our team asked, wanting to know if the newcomers would honor the Howling Dog tradition of buying shots of tequila for the winners.

"No problem," I told him.

The first two games were fun. The college students we'd joined were energetic and our friends from Tundra were doing a good job of not getting beaten. Everything was going well until the middle of the third game when Craig got hurt. He was playing at the net across from Kathy when the ball came down between them. Craig went up, Kathy went up, and they met in a perfect body slam. Kathy landed, staggered a few steps, but stayed on her feet. Craig, however, stumbled backwards and sat down in the sand, cradling his left hand.

"Goddamn it, Craig," Johnny Burns chided. "That was a girl you ran into. Get up and pretend nothin' happened, man. Come on now, you're embarrassing everyone here."

"I think she broke my thumb," Craig complained.

Kathy looked worried. "I'm sorry, Craig. Can you move it at all?"

The others were less sympathetic, harassing him until he got up and limped over to Sheryl. "You poor dear," we heard her say as he sat down beside his wife.

The game broke up not long after that. Kathy and I went into the bar where we found what was left of the Tundra crew sitting at a table in front of an enormous speaker near the stage. Craig was holding his thumb against the side of a cold bottle of beer while he watched the band. Sheryl, a bit bored, was watching the strange assortment of people on the dance floor. But I couldn't tell about Otter. He was either listening to the music with his eyes closed or asleep.

"Let's dance," I suggested to Kathy.

"What?" she asked, not sure she'd heard me correctly.

"Come on. We'll never get any better if we don't try."

One dance later we were back at the table. "Where's Craig?" I asked Sheryl.

"He wasn't feeling so good. Went outside for some fresh air, I believe," she told me.

Kathy sat down with Sheryl and I found Craig out back in the volleyball court. He was standing on the wooden bench, apparently looking at something on the other side of the tall fence that surround the court, his chin just clearing the top of the boards. Then, while I watched, he rose up on his toes and barfed.

"Gross," I protested.

Craig turned and grinned. "Yeah," he agreed. "I'm tryin' to see if I sober up quicker if I get rid of all the beer."

Made sense, but in my experience throwing up was painful. "Doesn't it hurt?" I had to ask.

"Sure does," he replied. "I keep hittin' my chin on the fence." And we both laughed.

When Craig was finished we went back into the bar and sat down with Kathy and Sheryl, the only ones left of our group.

"Wanna come back to our place?" Craig asked during a break in the music.

Kathy and I followed Craig and Sheryl to their home on a hill outside of Fox. After a raid on the icebox, Craig suggested we go for a walk, something we did now and then.

Behind their house there were miles of woods where we often saw grouse, ptarmigan, owls, moose, and occasionally a fox or a bear. Sheryl had to be at work by eight so she went to bed, but the rest of us took off up the hill. It was around three o'clock, barely enough light in the eastern sky to see where we were going.

Not far into the woods we crossed the Davidson Ditch, an aqueduct built to supply water to the mining claims around Fox. The six-foot-wide, three-foot-deep canal began northeast of Fox near the headwaters of the Chatanika River. It wound around ridges, went under streams and crossed valleys to circumnavigate a small mountain range to deliver 56,000 gallons of water a minute to the dredges on Goldstream Creek.

The Ditch carried water nearly a hundred miles with an average drop of only two feet in elevation each mile. Considering that it was constructed in 1925 using rudimentary surveying equipment and hand tools, the degree of accuracy achieved was phenomenal.

We walked and talked until the woods were full of light, then we turned around. On the way back to Fairbanks, Kathy brought up the Delta River again. It definitely was going to be a good trip, lots of white water. She thought we ought to see if Chris wanted to come along. As we pulled into the hangar parking lot, Kathy thought of something else.

"You know, I've got to get into grad school in the next couple of months. I was thinking about Vancouver, but Fairbanks has a pretty good wildlife program. Maybe I'll go up there tomorrow and check it out."

"That would be absolutely perfect," I told her as she got out of the truck.

When I got up the next morning Kathy had already left for the university, so I wandered downstairs. The helicopters sat side by side in the cavernous hangar, so peaceful and still, taking a break from their extraordinary life in the air. No one else was around, so I climbed into Alice, closed the door and relaxed.

I always felt comfortable in the cockpit. Whether it was

sitting quietly in the hangar or getting the shit kicked out of me in the mountains, there was always a connection. To me the helicopter was an avatar of sorts. Without each other our lives were nowhere near as interesting.

On my way to the pilots' room I saw Craig in his office. "What are you doing here so early?" I asked, pulling his dog out of the chair in front of the desk.

"Had to get this done today," he said, pointing to several files and piles of paper.

"How's your thumb?" If it was too badly sprained he might not be able to fly.

"Felt like I hit a damn wall," he told me, holding it up. The digit was a little swollen but didn't look that bad. "Kathy's one tough girl," he added respectfully.

"Or you're a wimp," I suggested. We tried to laugh but were too hungover.

"Did you see Burns and Russell?" Craig asked. "They were just gettin' in when I got here an hour ago."

"Nope. But speaking of Russell. I forgot to ask him about Denali." I'd heard that he didn't get to the top of the mountain.

"Ya mean you didn't hear about the dead people?" Craig winced as his voice rose, but went on to tell a strange story about John and his climbing party. How they were almost to the summit, maybe a day away, when they walked right up to a German couple sitting in the snow, their arms around each other for protection, frozen solid.

"That's the reason they didn't summit?" I was surprised. "The dead people freaked them out?"

"That probably had somethin' to do with it," Craig said. "But there was a bad storm movin' in. So they came back down."

"What a drag," I said. "Go all that way and see that... okay, enough of this shit. Let's talk about something that goes better with a hangover."

"Did I tell you about the preacher who called up and sounded just like Vinny?" Craig asked.

I'd known Vinny since we were kids. He'd been living in Anchorage for the last few years but spent most of his time as far away from the city as he could. When he wasn't working somewhere in the bush, he was hiking, backcountry skiing, or on his sailboat in Prince William Sound. He was also a practical joker.

"I'm sittin' here tryin' to figure out this Forest Service contract," Craig went on, "when I pick up the phone and this guy says he's the Reverend Devork." It obviously hurt, but he was laughing. "The reverend tells me he wants to put up a radio tower out towards Kotzebue to broadcast the word of God to the heathens."

"He actually used the word heathens?" I asked.

"Yep."

"I can see why you thought it was Vinny."

"It sounded just like him," Craig confirmed. "Anyway, I start playin' along, telling him that he should start right here in Fairbanks with the heathens at Tundra. He's agreeing with me, an' we're cursin' the heathens together, when I start figuring out that maybe this guy isn't Vinny."

By then I was laughing too, and it did hurt. "What did you do?"

"The only thing I could. Told him I had another call and hung up."

"Not bad," I told him. We sat in silence for a moment. "It sure would be nice if I could get out of this thing with Sara that easy." Craig didn't say anything but he was watching me closely. "Looks like Kathy might stick around. She's up at the university right now checking out their graduate school. But it's not like she's completely sold on the idea either, and Sara might be enough to change her mind."

"Sara can make a scene all right," Craig agreed.

"Recently?" I asked warily.

"Just a few days ago. At Jan's house," he told me. "It was a real fancy party, hors d'oeuvres and everything. Sara's sitting there in the sun and just takes off her shirt. No bra or nothin'."

"Nice tits," I pointed out.

"Bout perfect," Craig agreed. "Little bulge at the bottom, pointin' straight out... anyway, this old lady got all upset. Kept tellin' her to put her shirt back on. It was pretty funny."

That's it, I said to myself, Sara was out of control, and I had a bad feeling about how far it might go---for good reason. Shortly after we got together, in bed late one night, a girl I'd been seeing off and on for quite a while became the topic of our conversation. Although I'd always been open about the relationship, and Sara treated it casually enough, I felt uncomfortable, like when I'm flying along in smooth air but know there's severe turbulence in the area. "Are you mad at me or something?" I asked. "You know, because of her, I mean."

"Too much!" she'd exclaimed, sitting straight up in bed and staring at me. "Just a minute ago I was thinking about cutting your balls off. That is so far out!" The Zen of it completely overshadowed the violence of her thoughts, at least for Sara.

After the incident at Jan's party I decided that it was time to get Sara out of my life once and for all, and that there was only one way to do it. As long as she was in Fairbanks I'd have to deal with her. We had the same friends.

I knew that Sara wanted to go to Colorado to see a guru that lived outside of Boulder. There had also been an advertisement on the radio recently for one-way bus tickets to anywhere in the country. It caught my attention because they were so inexpensive. I didn't know if Sara would go for it, but it seemed worth a try.

I told Craig I had something to do and asked if I could borrow his car to go downtown. When I got back to the hangar with the bus ticket, Kathy was back from the university.

"Well, I did it," she told me. "I've applied to the graduate school. Too late for this semester, but I think I'll get in after Christmas break."

We were both very pleased and went outside to relax in the midday sun. Although the thunderstorm season was over there were a few late bloomers marching down the Tanana River towards Nenana. Magnificent works of nature standing tall against a perfect sky. I leaned back against the wall of the hangar and watched.

"Look at them build," Kathy said. "Must be five or six thousand feet."

"More like seven or eight," I told her.

"You should know," she admitted. "But they don't look that tall."

"I think Alice needs a test flight," I said.

Kathy was close, but I was closer. The one we climbed was around 6,847 feet. Near the top I turned into the cloud's gossamer folds, skimmed the surface of a snowy ridge and flew down its convoluted side. At the bottom of the ridge the valley was tight and we were going too fast, so we punched into the wispy wall on the other side. Inside the cloud it was grey, getting darker by the second, then lighter as we blew out the other side and back into bright sunlight.

It never ceased to amaze me how different the monstrous clouds could be. The one we were playing with was young, just beginning to grow, and out in the wide Tanana Valley. But add a couple thousand feet of growth and catch the same cloud a hundred miles upstream, where the valley narrows from 20 miles to two, and it's a different story.

The one that got me was obviously a mature storm cell. The trees below me were moving around in relatively strong gusts of wind, but my passengers were waiting for me in a small clearing about two miles from the base of the cloud.

I was making my approach to the clearing, about 200 feet above the tops of the trees, when it got me. With hardly any warning the winds picked up the tail, rolled the helicopter on its side and drove it towards the ground. My movements on the controls had no effect. They were completely overpowered by the force of the wind. Fortunately, with less than 50 feet to go, the turbulence let up. The second I got the helicopter under control, it hit again. I pulled in so much power to stay out of the trees the low rotor rpm horn came on.

For a few long minutes I battled the winds, never having control of the helicopter for more than a few seconds at a time, and ended up not far from the road to Tok. By that time all I wanted to do was get on the ground. There was no escaping the turbulent air, so I headed for the highway.

I didn't know if I was going to be able to land in those winds but figured a controlled crash was a better option than letting the wind put me in the trees. More than once I didn't think I was going to make it to the road; however, when I got below the trees along the side of the road, the winds dropped considerably and I made a decent landing. As I sat there, safe on the ground, my legs began to shake uncontrollably.

The flight with Kathy was different. Where we were, the cloud was no more threatening than a mountain of whipped cream. I flew slowly, making my turns, climbs and descents as smooth as possible without leaving the cloud's translucent surface. After exploring its rising spires and cavernous valleys for five or 10 minutes, we dropped back down to the Tanana flats, where we cruised the open fields inches above the tall rushes and grass that swayed gently in a strong wind.

At one point we flew over the wreckage of a B-25 bomber. It was in surprisingly good shape, considering the airplane was 35 years old and had landed in a stand of black spruce trees. There were a number of the World War II–era aircraft scattered along the Tanana River southwest of Eielson Air Force Base. It was the route the planes flew from California to Fairbanks. Most likely it had been on its way to Russia, part of a loan package to help the Soviets fight the Germans.

The problem was that the B-25 was a medium-range bomber. It could carry enough fuel to get to Alaska, but any error in navigation, even a strong headwind, could run them out of gas. Sometimes, like the one below us, their engines quit within sight of the airfield.

Back at the hangar Kathy and I got a couple of beers. In the pilots' room we found a topographical map of the part of the Delta River we were planning to float. There were numerous hash marks indicating rapids, and lots of sharp dropping turns.

"Are you sure you want to invite Chris along on this?" I asked. "It looks like it could get a little scary in some parts."

"I see what you mean," Kathy agreed. "But I already asked her and she said she'd love to go."

"Is she going to ride along with us, or is it going to be two canoes?"

"Hadn't really thought about that yet," Kathy admitted. "I don't think she knows anyone around here. But it sure would be nice to have our own canoe. Who do you think we could get to go with her?" I asked.

"Craig might have to work," I began, and that was it. I really couldn't think of anyone, at Tundra or in town, who might have the time and the experience for a trip like that. Then I thought of Vinny. It helped that Craig and I had just been talking about him.

"Vinny," I said.

"What?" she asked.

"A friend of mine from back east," I told her. "Lives in Anchorage but might be up for it. He's a really funny guy and knows how to handle a canoe."

A few minutes later I had him on the phone. Vinny was hesitant at first, but not after I told him what a good-looking woman Chris was. As I hung up Craig walked in. He was in his softball uniform and looked like a 30-year-old kid. That must be it, I thought. He's reliving his childhood. Nothing wrong with that, I conceded.

"Y'all goin' to the game tonight?" he asked.

Kathy and I looked at each other and shrugged. "See you there," I replied.

The game was well under way by the time we got to the ballpark. We'd stayed longer than planned at the Blue Marlin, a small dark hole of a place in the basement of a rundown building where they served the best pizza in town… possibly the whole world. It was the meatiest, cheesiest, greasiest pizza anywhere. Before the second bite the juice began to drip off your elbow. The place got closed down at least once a year by the state health department, but their pizza was so good people kept coming back.

As we joined the group of Sand King fans in the bleachers, a foul ball popped over the fence and landed on the hood of a pickup truck with a loud bang. The fans went wild. People always seemed to have a good time at the night games in Fairbanks. It was a good excuse to get outside and enjoy the long evenings. It was also part of the community feeling.

Even though there were 70,000 people living in and around Fairbanks, for many reasons, the collective mentality was that of a much smaller town. The geographic isolation, where even independent people become dependent on each other, and the economic boom and bust character of a society on the edge of civilization, where lateral employment is essential, create loose but very deep bonds.

Around nine o'clock I took Spot for a beer run, and on the way stopped by the bar where Sara worked. She was in the middle of a dance when I walked in. Her slim body moved slowly, innocent and seductive, like a child unaware of what she was doing. When she saw me the detached look on her face turned into a smile.

After her dance she came over to the bar. "You looked good," I told her.

"Thanks," she replied.

I tried to think of something else to say, but everything that came to mind was so lame in light of what I was there to do. So, I handed her the bus ticket.

"What's this?" she asked.

"Look, Sara. You know about Kathy, the girl I've been working with the last few months." She started to say something, but I didn't stop. "I think we're going to spend the winter together. You told me once that you came back this summer because of me. I figure I owe you a trip back."

She looked at the piece of paper in her hand. "You're giving me a goddamn bus ticket and telling me to get out of town. Is that it?" Sara said calmly. I just stood there, looking at her, waiting for it to be over. "Whatever," she said finally, and walked away.

When I got back to the ballpark, the game was over. The Sand Kings were standing around rationalizing the game they'd almost won and Kathy was talking to "Pine Tree" Pete. Pete was on the team and also worked for Alaska State Forestry as a Helitack crew chief. They were a gung-ho lot of forest fire fighters who went to fires in helicopters. Rumor had it Pete was leaving the ranks to join management.

"Hey, Smith," he greeted me. "Whazz happenen?"

As his nickname implied, Pine Tree Pete was tall, almost six and a half feet. He had a beak of a nose and his head was long and came to a point of sorts. Or maybe it just looked that way from my perspective.

Pete was very tall and a little obnoxious, but I thought he was a decent guy until we were on the Wood River fire together.

9

THE WOLF AND THE MOOSE

The Wood River fire didn't start at the Wood River. It flared up on the Blair Lakes range in the beginning of summer. Bombing on the range that time of year often set things ablaze. The military helicopters from Fort Wainwright always got right on it, but this one kept getting away from them.

After a few days the fire left the bombing range and began burning trees on state land. By that time it had grown to 5,000 acres; however, even though it was fairly large and burning out of control, no one was worried. There were so few firefighters in the state, and so much land, only forest fires that threatened private property were fought aggressively.

But if the fire changed directions and headed back onto the bombing range it would look bad for State Forestry, so they decided to send a Helitack crew to keep track of the blaze. They gave the job to Pine Tree Pete, who in turn called Craig for a helicopter to take them to the fire.

The Helitack crews carried chainsaws, digging tools and backpack water bags. Their job wasn't to put the fire out. They couldn't. Instead the crews tried to control the fire. They cut firebreaks to direct the way it spread, turned it when they could and tried to keep it away from good sources of fuel. By slowing it down they kept the fire from growing as quickly, and gave the weather a chance to change to rain. When they limited its fuel the possibility that it would burn itself out increased.

By the time I got to the head of the fire with Pete, it was working its way through a stand of large timber, 50-foot spruce, and it had doubled in size. It was the middle of the day and the sky above us was blood red. A light wind pushed the fire to the west, but it was also drawing air in from the advancing side. The combination of good vertical fuel and gentle winds from both sides made the smoke and flames go straight up, giving us an unobstructed view of the death of a forest.

While Pete assessed the fire, I watched it consume the tall dark figures set in a wall of flames. One by one, orange fingers found them, writhing around, up and down their trunks. In seconds, bright red torches and black streamers of smoke burst from their bark, growing quickly until they joined and consumed the tree.

Not only was the fire spectacular, it was behaving well, moving slowly among the tall trees. Consequently, the Helitack crew had it easy until the third day. Around noon the wind picked up from the east. Within minutes the fire took off, jumping the fire line on the west side and picking up speed. A few days later the fire had grown to 30,000 acres, churning along in a hundred foot wall of fire and smoke several miles long, heading for the Wood River less than 10 miles away.

The firefighters would have been happy to let the fire run to the river and burn itself out, but there were several cabins along the Wood. Once it was apparent the fire was going for them, it had to be stopped. Forestry sent out another helicopter and several more crews. Normally one of Pete's bosses would have stepped in at that point; however, because Pine Tree was being considered for promotion, they let him keep the fire.

For the next week Pete did everything he could to stop it. He brought in more crews and had me shuttling them back and forth from sunup to sunset. But the fire kept rolling along towards the cabins. Finally Pine Tree realized he wasn't going to stop it by himself and radioed his boss in Fairbanks for help in the form of retardant drops. Fire retardant is a mixture of water and chemicals that's dropped out of airplanes to suffocate the fire. The planes would have helped a lot, but Pete was told there weren't any available.

The next day, the wind picked up to 20 mph and the fire really took off, surging ahead with less than a mile to where we were camped around the cabins on the side of the Wood River.

Day turned to night in the thick smoke. Hot ash and embers rained down, searing skin and burning holes in everything. While the Helitack crews packed their gear to move, Pete and I jumped in Alice and flew around to the back of the fire. From there we'd be able to get a good idea of what was happening because there would be a lot less smoke. What we saw was impressive.

A solid wall of fire, 200 feet high in spots, was stretched out along a north-south line for five miles. Twisting in the intense heat, giant columns of smoke rose above the flames. It was an enormous fire, completely out of control, but to our amazement and delight the wind had shifted slightly to the south. There was still a chance the fire might miss the cabins.

"Let's get those guys back on the lines," Pete said.

In order to save time I cut across the south end of the fire. The wind was really blowing there, pushing the smoke and flames over. I could look right down into the heart of the blaze. Incredibly, in the middle, where it should have been the hottest, there was a patch of black spruce trees apparently untouched by the fire raging around it.

"Look at that," I told Pete. "Why aren't..." At that moment the little stand of spruce exploded. A bright orange ball rose rapidly toward us, then just as quickly disappeared, leaving behind little fingers of flame, all that remained of the trees.

When Pete told the crews the fire might miss the cabins, they went back to work as hard as their exhausted bodies would let them, cutting firebreaks and soaking down the cabins. But in the end the flames were just too close. The temperature was well over a hundred degrees. Some of the firefighters were having trouble breathing, and none could keep themselves hydrated enough to work. When a guy finally passed out, Pete told me to start moving them away from the fire.

There was only one more thing we could do to save the cabins, light a backfire. Backfires work on the scorched earth principle. Big fires need so much air, even a fast-moving fire will draw it in from all sides, including the front. A line of fires set in front of a big fire will be drawn into it, effectively burning the fuel the larger fire is about to consume. Pete didn't want to set the backfires because he had other things to do, so I picked an older firefighter who looked calm and collected. It was going to be hot and smoky.

Moving slowly, almost at a hover in the dense smoke, the firefighter and I crept along the tops of the parched trees until we could see the wall of flame at the front of the fire. Then we landed. When we got out of the helicopter, it was like stepping into an oven, but the air was surprisingly clear. Apparently the back draft was so strong it was drawing clean air in under the smoke.

With such a hot environment, and plenty of air, the half dozen small fires we lit spread quickly through the grass and into the bushes and trees. It was strange watching the hungry flames envelop the vegetation. After spending all that time trying to contain the fire, I was setting it free. It would have been interesting to watch it grow, but the blast furnace temperatures stung our skin and burned our eyes.

The backfires saved two of the cabins but the rest were lost. A few days later they sent Pine Tree Pete home. And that's when I found out I didn't like him. Among the firefighters Pete worked with it was a tradition to have a nice meal on the last night of a fire. On the Wood River fire the dinner was going to be a great big Virginia ham. Everyone was looking forward to it because the fire had been long and hot, with nothing but surplus military food to eat. When Pete was let go, he took the ham with him.

Traditions, customs, and rituals are very important among people like pilots and firefighters. They are part of the mentality that keeps us alive. When a situation is critical and what to do next isn't exactly clear, you have to rely on established procedures and each other. That was Pete's problem. He didn't care about anyone but himself.

When they turned the lights off at the ballpark, Kathy

and I said goodbye to Pine Tree and the rest of the team, then headed home to get some sleep. Unfortunately, we stopped by the hangar and walked into the middle of another party. Tom and Cookie had just come back from their summer in the bush and a dozen Tundroids were helping them celebrate the end of their first field season in Alaska.

Tom Lynch and I met in a hangar at the Long Beach Airport where a management company was interviewing helicopter pilots for job openings on the other side of the world, Indonesia. Along with two dozen other ex-military pilots we were flown to Jakarta and put up in the Hotel Indonesia, one of the finest on the island of Java, and told to charge everything.

For several months we were treated to a life of luxury while waiting for the central government to issue our commercial pilot licenses. The process was incredibly slow due to a virulent system of graft. During those days of leisure I spent a lot of time around the hotel pool enjoying Tom's indelicate wit.

Once we had our licenses we were sent to work. I went to Borneo where I was working with a seismic crew from New Zealand, slinging dynamite, gasoline and food to the native crews chopping seismic lines through the jungle. Tom went to one of the other islands, but we managed to get together now and then on our breaks. When I left Indonesia he stayed but we kept in touch with the occasional letter. The last one came from Abu Dhabi and read:

Greetings from a secret port nestled in the bowels of the Middle East. Here is where they would administer the enema. How about furnishing some details about Alaska. Some guys here have made enquiries concerning work and I've carefully screened out the reliable, conservative types to leave a nucleus of

known felons. If interested, advise me.

Two months later he showed up in Fairbanks with his girlfriend, the irrepressible Cookie. It had been a good summer for them. They had spent it working out of an upscale lodge on a pristine lake in the wilderness; however, there was one more thing they wanted to do before heading back to California.

"So, Smith. What about that hot springs trip?" Tom asked, reminding me of a date we had made earlier in the summer. After I told him about one of my favorite spots, Kilo Hot Springs, he made me promise to take them there before they left Alaska.

"Let's go," I said. Kathy and I had two days left on our break.

The next morning the four of us climbed into Alice and flew northwest. About 70 miles later we passed Rampart, a small and isolated native village, then crossed the Yukon River and flew up Canyon Creek into the Ray Mountains. At a fork near the headwaters of Canyon Creek we turned north through a small pass and crossed the Tozitna River to Twilight Creek.

We followed Twilight along the south slope of Mount Tozi, turning northwest again as we entered the headwaters of Gishna Creek. On the far side we climbed a long and gentle grass-covered slope to a broad notch between two barren peaks, the entrance to Spooky Valley. In the notch several tors, large freestanding columns of rock left behind by the process of erosion, stood like sentinels.

As we flew between the 40-foot monoliths, tendrils of clouds rose vertically from near ground level to materialize around us like ghostly greeters. Ahead, scattered around the basin of Spooky Valley, were smaller versions of the tors we'd just passed. The misshapen columns of rock were in disarray, but there was something purposeful about them, as if they'd been caught midstride in their advance up the valley and were patiently waiting for us to move on.

Ten minutes later we landed beside the hot spring and spent a long day bathing, drinking wine and enjoying life. The next day Kathy and I left on our last trip to Alpine Creek, where work had become secondary. The summer was coming to an end. We'd accomplished everything Fred and Ken had hoped to get done. With only a few plots left to survey it was time to relax and enjoy the land we would soon be leaving.

Most of the crew spent their free time reading and lying in the sun. Fred tinkered with his truck and Ken fished, using only dry flies so he could watch the trout rise to the surface to take the lure. He was slow and deliberate in his movements; the eight-foot rod seemed to be an extension of his willowy body. I envied the contentment he found in his pastime.

Not much about my life changed. I still flew the same amount of time; however, with the summer coming to an end my attitude changed. Instead of sitting in the helicopter reading or napping, I spent more time appreciating where I was, taking walks or just sitting and watching what went on around me, which was mostly animals eating each other.

Whether it was a great big brown bear going after a little ground squirrel, or a small spider cautiously working its way among the rocky debris of a windswept ridge to capture an insect many times its size, almost all the wildlife I watched was simply looking for a meal. What makes it interesting is how they go about it.

The year before, while I was working on the north side of the Alaska Range, someone in the back said he'd seen a wolf stalking a moose in the river we'd just crossed. By the time I turned around the wolf was gone, which didn't surprise me. Where I'd worked in Southeast Alaska the woods were full of the clever animals. I was always finding fresh tracks and scat, but the most I saw of them was the flash of a head or a tail disappearing into the undergrowth.

When we got back to the river the wolf was gone but there was a large moose standing on a sandbar in the middle of the wide river. Not wanting to harass the big guy I continued on my way, but couldn't help but think that the moose was lucky I came by when I did. The wolf was probably after him. During the course of the day I made three more trips over the same spot in the river. Each time the moose was there, hanging out on the sandbar or wading in the water. When I came back by myself at the end of the day, the moose was on the same sandbar, but he was lying on his side, dead. The wolf, or more likely, wolves, hadn't gone far, I realized. That's why the moose was in the same area all day long. The wolves had kept him there, out on the sandbar in the hot sun with no food or shelter, wearing him down until he couldn't defend himself, and then they attacked.

Wanting to find out if it really had been wolves that killed the moose, I lowered the collective and made a low approach over the tree line on the edge of the river, then came in to a hover beside the carcass. Judging by the paw prints and the way he was being eaten—tunnels had been gnawed into his abdomen—it appeared to be wolves. My curiosity satisfied, I was about to take off when something caught my eye. I looked up and there on the sandbar right in front of me, about 20 feet away, was a wolf.

When I'd come in over the trees on my approach to check out the carcass I must have cut him off from the woods, and he was doing what anyone should do in a similar situation. The wolf was standing absolutely still, the only way to remain unseen when you are caught in the open.

His head was down with body aligned to present a small profile. I could see his feet were braced to run in any direction, but not a muscle moved. And he was staring at me. Not at the loud threatening helicopter, but right into my eyes.

At that moment the wolf knew he'd been seen. His head and shoulders moved left then right, checking both ways around the helicopter. As he moved I could see more of his body. The animal was big, probably 30 inches at the shoulder. He was thin. A domestic animal his size would weigh 120 pounds or more, but he was lucky to be 100. In fact, the wolf looked more like a mangy dog than a skilled predator. Then he bolted and that impression changed.

In one smooth motion his long body extended to the right, going at least 10 feet before his front paws hit the ground. With all four paws planted firmly he banked hard left. The gravel flew as he dug into the sandbar and sprinted past me. His courage, stealth, strength and speed were truly remarkable.

Wild animals are always looking for food and spend most of their time in that pursuit, but they also find time to relax.

When one of the drillers at the Bornite mine scalded a major portion of his body, I had to fly him to the hospital in Kotzebue. I did everything I could to get him there quickly during the hour and a half flight. The poor guy was in terrible pain. On the return flight by myself, however, I relaxed and did what I like to do... fly close to the ground and follow the contours where they lead.

The sun was going down behind me and the grass-covered hills glowed amber and gold in its dwindling light. A strong wind blowing off the Chukchi Sea swept the tall grass into great rolling waves. My airspeed indicator said the helicopter was going 130 mph, but with the tailwind my ground speed was more likely 160.

I was so close to the ground, traveling so fast, the big bruin never heard me coming. I caught the old brown bear sitting on her butt, propped up by her forelegs, watching the setting sun. It was obvious the sow was enjoying the sunset because she was facing due west, sitting right on the crown of the hill, where the experience would last the longest. And she was so obviously relaxed, like anyone watching the sun go should be.

Animals look for food, and relax now and then. A few even take time out to entertainment themselves, even the serious-minded ones.

Sitting in the sun one warm spring day, about to doze off, I heard the sound of gravel rolling down the side of the ridge not far from where I'd parked Alice. My passengers had left, heading the opposite direction well over an hour before, so I knew it wasn't them. Probably frozen gravel thawing and gravity taking over, I thought and closed my eyes again. When

I heard the same sound a second time, I knew it was more likely an animal and got up to see what it was. A hundred yards down the steep slope a large brown bear was crossing the stone-strewn hillside.

While I watched, the bruin made his way to the edge of a snowfield in a streambed relatively protected from the sun. When he got to the hundred-foot-wide swath of snow, he paused. It looked as if he was considering whether or not to get his feet wet. But that was probably the furthest thing from his mind as he threw himself on his belly and began sliding.

As he slid down and across the snowfield, the big bear rolled onto his back and, with paws up in the air, began a slow 360-degree turn. A few feet from the far side he came to a stop, stood up, shook the snow out of his fur, and continued on his somber journey.

Watching large animals like wolves and bears was entertaining. They embody so much of what we love and fear about the woods. But they were few and far between, and leery of people; so, more often than not I settled for smaller creatures, which I found are capable of extraordinary feats.

Not long after shutting Alice down, I regretted not returning to camp while my passengers went about what they had to do that day. As soon as the door opened the bugs attacked in such numbers and with such zeal, at least a dozen made it in before I could close it. After capturing or killing the intruders, I got my book and began to read. Then the temperature began to climb.

Within minutes the cramped cockpit was stifling, forcing me to take my chances outside. Immediately a horde of mosquitoes descended. The onslaught was so intense it literally drove me up the side of the aircraft to sit on the small cowling in front of the rotor mast. To my surprise, most of the mosquitoes didn't follow.

Approximately seven feet in the air there were almost no bugs at all. They seemed to prefer the airspace closer to the bog. But before long the horseflies found me and continued their harassment, concentrating on the patch of thinning hair on the top of my head. Fortunately there weren't too many of them, and I was able to get some reading done.

A few pages later a swarm of dragonflies showed up and began darting around the helicopter with the horseflies. I put my book down to watch. Their bulbous, multifaceted eyes seemed so efficient in guiding their high-speed maneuvers, and I loved the fluttering sound their transparent wings made when they stopped in midflight. For brief periods of time they were like hummingbirds and helicopters, capable of three-dimensional flight.

Not long after returning to my book I became aware of a sound. It was light, intermittent and without a consistent direction, but coming from somewhere nearby. A strange little crunching noise so faint I wasn't sure I was hearing it, until finally I happened to look up just as a dragonfly ran into a horsefly. The crunching sound ensued and seconds later an inert horsefly fell to the ground.

The dragonflies were catching the horseflies in midair, latching onto them and biting through their brittle exoskeletons. With faultless flying and blinding speed, the kill and feast was over in a heartbeat. If not for the partially eaten remains I found around the helicopter as proof, I might not have believed what I'd seen.

Because there were so many of them, birds got my attention too. Eagles weren't as interesting as I thought they'd be, not much more than a large lazy scavenger with a taste for fish. And their high-pitched chirp of a call is embarrassing. But the sharp-eyed hawks hunting the fields and the deft falcons soaring the mountain slopes are true sovereigns of the sky and know more about flying than any of us.

Although I've always had an affinity for birds, most of the time I use them for wind indicators. They always take off and land into the wind, so I watched them when it was time for me to do the same. One day, however, I found there was more to learn from a bird than that.

Normally I would not have been in that part of the Brooks Range on top of a sharp ridge with it blowing as hard as it was, but the wind came up unexpectedly and my passengers were out of radio range. However, I wasn't too upset, because being on the ground was better than having to come in and land in those conditions.

A standard approach into the wind wouldn't work because of the turbulence on the leeward side. Even a crosswind landing might be impossible. The wind was going over the ridge at 30 mph or better. But because of cavitation the air was barely moving where I sat. To go from that much airspeed to none in a landing would be extremely difficult, and potentially disastrous.

As I sat there waiting for my passengers I noticed a hawk on the windward side of the ridge. He was only feet from the ground and his wings were motionless as he rode the strong and gusting wind. As he approached the ridge I had to wonder what the raptor was going to do. If he tried to go over the ridge he'd get hammered. If he tried to land with a tailwind, like a helicopter, he'd crash. But he just kept coming, riding the updraft without a beat of his wings. When he crested the ridge, instead of going over or landing downwind, he executed a steeply banked turn and came around into the wind for a perfect two-point landing.

A few days later, on another windy day, I mimicked his technique. I caught an updraft on the windward side of a ridge and, the closer I got to the slope, the smoother the air was. At the top of the ridge I did a steep turn to the left and let the wind push my tail around. Other than a little awkwardness on the pedals as the aircraft's nose came into the wind, the landing was flawless.

Every so often I learned something from a raptor, but most of the birds I watched were just going about their life. Many of them were migratory waterfowl swarming to the northernmost part of the continent to feed on the rich seasonal growth and have their young in an environment of abundance. Their lives weren't as dramatic as the raptors hunting the mountains' slopes, but they were every bit as much a part of life, and death.

A flock of ducks had gathered in a bend of a river on the north side of the Alaska Range. It was a common sight, ducks resting in calm water for a day or two before continuing their migration south. However, a week later they were still there. It was fall, and the weather was deteriorating, but the flock stayed right where they were. Curiosity got the better of me and I flew by to see what the attraction was. The flock took off at the sound of the approaching helicopter... all but two. One couldn't fly and the other was her mate. I checked on them every day, hoping they'd be gone. But they were always there, together. When the river iced over, I avoided the area.

I took it easy the last few days at Alpine Creek, enjoying myself like everyone else, but it was also a little depressing. Working for FSL had been the best flying job of my career. The right people in the right place at the right time, and it was coming to an end. But when it actually came time to say goodbye, it wasn't that bad.

Everyone had something planned. Fred and Ken were going back to Anchorage to compile the summer's data. Linda had plans to visit friends in Fairbanks for a while. Paul was going to get a degree from a college in Seattle. Rocky was talking about checking on a girl he knew in Texas. Will was going to play music in Anchorage. Tim was thinking about hanging around, or maybe heading down the Kenai Peninsula, and Chris was going on a canoe trip down the Delta River with us.

After the hugs and goodbyes, Chris, Kathy and I climbed into Alice and headed to Fairbanks. On the way, we made a detour to take a closer look at the route we'd be following to Black Rapids, beginning with Long Tangle Lake.

The water was clear and peaceful as we flew down the narrow lake. Its shores were the slopes of opposing mountains that rose quickly to rocky peaks. Several ducks flushed, and near the end of the lake a moose pulled pondweeds in the shallows with her calf.

It looked good, we agreed, as we left the lake and flew down the moderate rapids at its wide outlet. A mile later we were at the waterfall. The river dropped off the edge of a ragged cliff and fell 20 feet onto jagged rocks. At first glance there wasn't a way around or down the cliff. Then, concealed in a narrow ravine, we found a well-worn portage.

After the waterfall the river deepened, ran faster, and was full of rocks and turns. We spent the next half-hour flying low and slow, sometimes hovering to check out the worst parts. Although it was an intimidating stretch of water for canoes, from the vantage point of the helicopter we always found a way through the rough parts, until we came to a sweeping turn about halfway to Black Rapids.

It didn't look that bad from a distance. The river was deep with very little white water or other signs of trouble. We would have flown right by if Chris hadn't noticed something shiny below the water's surface. When I rolled Alice around for a closer look we all saw it, but had no idea what it was.

"It's a canoe," Chris said in a subdued voice.

We could barely make out its aluminum body deep below the surface. It was flattened against the upstream side of an enormous boulder, twisted beyond recognition, with nothing but the pressure of the fast-moving water to keep it in place.

"There's another one," Kathy added, pointing to a green blur a little farther downstream.

"Let's walk our canoes around this part of the river," I suggested.

The next morning we got up early, packed up everything we'd need for the float trip, and waited for Vinny to show up from Anchorage. Around ten o'clock the phone rang.

"Hey, Tommy. Come pick me up, will ya?"

"Vinny? Where the hell are you?"

"I'm over at the airport," he said. "I had to fly up."

"Where's your truck?" The plan had been to leave Spot at the Tangle Lakes and his truck at Black Rapids. That way we wouldn't have to hitchhike back to Spot.

"In Anchorage. Damn thing wouldn't start this morning. I borrowed this guy's jumper cables, but Norma killed his battery too, so I got out of there pronto."

By noon we were on the road, canoes and gear piled in the back of Spot with the four of us packed in front. The air was crisp and clear, the sky bright blue and we were in good spirits. High in the mountains we were heading towards, it was already winter. The snow line was down to 7,000 feet, a thousand feet lower than the week before. But where we were it was 65 degrees and fall was just beginning to show in the birch and aspen trees.

We followed the Tanana River for an hour until the road forked, then followed the Delta River into the north side of the Alaska Range. On our left Donnelly Dome, a round hill several hundred feet high, had a dozen Dall sheep grazing unabashed on its grassy slopes. Moments later we were in the mountains. Grass-covered ridges became steep rock-strewn slopes that rose thousands of feet above us.

The valley closed in so tight that, as we passed the Black Rapids Roadhouse around two in the afternoon, the sun had already left the valley floor. Ten or fifteen miles later the Delta River turned southeast into the mountains while we followed the road through Isabel Pass back out of the mountains. On the south side of the Alaska Range we took a right turn onto the Denali Highway, a well-maintained dirt road. By four o'clock the canoes were unloaded and we were paddling up Long Tangle Lake.

The weather stayed clear and warm; there was even a gentle tailwind helping us on our way. Long Tangle Lake wasn't much wider than some rivers, but unlike a river its shores were shallow and thick with alders, willows, cotton grass, sedges and rushes, making prime wetland habitat. Pintails, scaups, mallards and goldeneyes, taking a break on their way south, kept a wary eye on us as we paddled by.

Vinny and Chris seemed to be getting along well. Sound travels well over still water. Vinny was telling Chris about a power line he'd recently put up for the residents of Kobuk, a native village in the foothills of the Brooks Range.

"Yeah," he said at one point. "The big boys wanted to dig holes in the permafrost, sink enormous anchor plates. It would've made a mess. But I ran into this guy in a bar…"

"What?" Chris asked surprised.

"In a bar in Anchorage," Vinny said, not noticing her disbelief. "He knew a lot about this stuff."

"So, you held the poles up with… how'd you do it?" Chris was on the verge of laughter, but the technique Vinny used to anchor the poles was actually based on sound, albeit unconventional, logic. Plus, it was working.

"Rebar! Ten-foot lengths of three-quarter-inch rebar, pointed on one end and screwed together. Drove 'em thirty, forty feet into the permafrost with a gas-powered jackhammer. Then we anchored the poles to the rebar. They're not going anywhere. We did it in the middle of the winter, on snow machines, so we didn't leave a mark on the tundra."

Vinny deserved credit for not using heavy equipment. It leaves a mess forever in the ground that's almost always frozen. Once the permafrost is disturbed it stays that way. There were tracks on the North Slope made by the first motorized vehicles to reach that area, some more than 50 years old. And they look like they could have been made yesterday. Another thing Vinny did was hire locally. He'd bring in a few skilled people from Anchorage or Fairbanks, but the rest of the crew came from the village. That way the natives got back a portion of the money they put into project, while learning marketable job skills.

Kathy was listening to Chris and Vinny, too. "Two peas in a pod," she commented.

"Two bimbos in a boat," I added, as we broke into laughter.

We kept going until it was almost dark and then, having consumed a fair amount of beer, went to sleep almost immediately. The next day we heard the waterfall half a mile away and had no trouble finding the portage around it. By noon we were making our way down the first stretch of white water below the falls. The rapids were easily twice the size of the ones we'd encountered on the Chena, but the crests were farther apart, not as choppy. It was wild but very smooth. The ride was exactly what Kathy and I liked, fast but not scary.

Another thing we liked about the river was there weren't any sweepers. It moved too fast and the trees were too small. When the banks eroded, the trees that fell in were swept away. But there were a lot of submerged rocks. They're not as dangerous as sweepers. They won't trap you underwater; however, they're hard to avoid and can hang you up, fill the canoe with water and even flip a canoe over.

A few hours later we came to the stretch of water where we saw the sunken canoes, and played it safe by getting out and walking down the bank, holding our canoes by their bowlines as they drifted along the shore. Several miles and a lot of white water later we came to a spot where the river widened and slowed down. On the east bank, where the evening sun would stay the longest, there was a level area large enough to camp.

Even though it was fairly early to be stopping, we decided to enjoy our evening more than we had the day before, and pulled out. After our tents were up we stretched out in the sun. A perfect day, I thought, cool, clean mountain air, blue skies, fall colors, white water, exercise, excitement, good friends and wine. Before long we all dozed off.

When I awoke the sun was not far from the towering peaks to the west, and it was chilly. Vinny and Chris were making a fire and Kathy was rummaging around inside her pack not far from where I lay. While I watched she pulled out her fishing gear.

"Brought all this stuff along. Might as well use it," Kathy said when she noticed I was awake. Then she turned and walked down to the water.

I got up and joined Chris and Vinny. The fire was going well. "Anything I can do?" I asked.

"How about a sauna?" Vinny suggested.

"Great idea," I agreed. "It has been a strenuous day."

While they began dinner, I took the nylon fly off my tent and found a limb not too far from the fire that was around four feet above the ground. After tying the apex of the tent fly to the limb I took a few good-sized rocks and staked out the bottom, like a tepee.

Meanwhile, Kathy had put our canoe in the water. The bow cut a straight line as she paddled, which is not an easy thing to do with just one person paddling. Once she was in deep water she laid down the paddle, picked up her fishing rod, drew the tip back and whipped it forward.

As her lure sailed neatly out over the water, Kathy yelled, "Shit!" and lunged forward, almost tipping the canoe over as she grabbed at something in the air. Just as abruptly, Kathy stopped what she was doing, picked up her paddle and headed back to camp. "The sucker just flew right off," she said, when she was close.

Evidently, she'd forgotten to tighten the little nut that holds the reel on. We didn't have fresh trout for dinner, but we did have thick New York steaks, red potatoes roasted in butter, and a fresh spinach salad. For dessert we took a sauna.

First, using sticks, we rolled red-hot rocks from the fire into a pit I'd dug under the tent fly. Then, with a bottle of water to make a little steam, we crawled into the small tepee. As Vinny came in, I noticed that he'd put on a little weight.

"You look a little like Tube Dog," I remarked.

Tube Dog lived next door to Vinny in Anchorage. She was a nondescript, shorthaired dog that looked like a furry brown keg of beer with legs.

"It's Kobuk, Tommy," he explained. "They feed me what I like."

"Lots of dead animals?" I guessed.

"Exactly," Vinny confided. While I poured water on the hot rocks, filling the sauna with steam, he went on to tell us a story about one of the more unusual meals he'd shared with his native friends. "We were hunting and found this caribou head. All that was left from someone else's kill. But it wasn't that old. So the guys I'm with, they're funnier than shit. They pick up this frozen head, put it on the back of their snow machine and take off for the hot spring near Cosmos Mountain."

"I know the place," I encouraged him.

"You should've seen it, Tommy. They threw the head in the hot spring and cooked it."

"Gross!" Chris said, feigning horror. "You're not going to tell us you ate it.""Isn't that like cooking road kill?" Kathy asked.

"More like a 'fresh frozen' entree," Vinny laughed.

"Oh, my God! Cut it out," Chris implored. "We just ate."

Not wishing to offend Chris, Vinny let the story rest. But later he told me that his Kobuk friends had stuffed the head with cloves of garlic and rice. When it had cooked for a couple of hours in the hundred-degree water, they ate the "soup."

Cringing at the thought, I had to ask, "Did you have some?"

"Of course I did," he said. "You know I love rice."

The third day of the trip went as well as the first two. Late in the afternoon we pulled out at the Black Rapids Roadhouse, wet, tired and with no worries in the world other than how to get back to Spot. Knowing that there was little to no traffic on that road, we began hitchhiking right away.

Three hours later we were standing in the same spot. Only two cars had gone by, and neither of them had even slowed down. With so few opportunities for a ride, Vinny and I did the logical thing, went into the roadhouse for a beer after convincing Kathy and Chris that a car would be more likely to stop for two good-looking girls than four people.

Not long after it got dark they joined us in the bar. "No luck?" I asked.

"One guy stopped, but he was only going a couple more miles," Kathy told us.

"I guess the theory about girls getting rides easier without guys isn't true," I surmised.

"Nope," Chris said. "You were right. That was the only car that came by. And it did stop."

There wasn't any point in going back outside. No one would stop for us after dark. Besides, even if we did get a ride down the main road, it was another 25 miles of dirt road to

Spot. We'd be walking all night. Then I looked at the bartender, a big man slouched in a chair behind the bar reading a magazine. We'd been there for hours and he'd barely acknowledged our existence, much less talked to us. But parked by the backdoor was a dusty Chevy Malibu. It had to be his.

"Excuse me," I said. "Bartender."

He looked up from his magazine. "Yeah."

"When you go home tonight, which way are you going?"

"Delta Junction." Spot was in the opposite direction.

"Nice try, Tommy," Vinny said respectfully.

I was about to suggest we start walking, when the bartender closed his magazine and I saw the cover. He'd been totally engrossed in the latest issue of Field and Stream.

"He's a hunter," I whispered to Vinny. "For Christ's sake, tell him some of your hunting stories. He'll love you. Then maybe he'll give us a ride."

"No problem," Vinny smiled. Turning to the bartender, he said, "Hey, buddy! Did you read that article in the March issue about huntin' in Russia?"

Vinny charmed him right up to the caribou-head soup. Even Martin, the macho bartender, couldn't handle the thought of dining on brains and minute rice. But a bond had been created, and the situation had gone from horrible to good. However, I didn't think we could ask him for a favor yet.

"You guys sure like hunting," I told the group. "But you don't know what it's all about until you've been on the ultimate hunt."

"What's that?" Martin asked.

"Another man with a gun." I paused. "Like I did in Vietnam."

Martin bit, but a little harder than I expected. He reached under the bar and pulled out a great big, long-barreled .44 revolver and laid it between us on the bar.

"I've had this thing under there since I began workin' here," he told me. "Just waiting for an excuse to use it." In a voice full of emotion, Martin continued. "I didn't get to go to Vietnam. But I wouldn't mind killin' a man if I had to."

Okay, I thought. Where do we go from here? But the situation developed nicely, with Martin doing most of the talking about combat books he'd read and articles from Soldier of Fortune magazine. It wasn't long before I felt comfortable enough to ask for a ride to Spot.

"Sure," Martin said. "I can run you up there. But I got to stick around till two." Then, to my surprise, he reached in his pocket, pulled out his car keys and tossed them to me. "Don't wreck it."

Kathy and I spent the next week hanging out in Fairbanks, sleeping late and taking it easy. Other than her taking off with her boyfriend from Montana, who was flying into Anchorage that weekend, everything would have been just about perfect.

I'd given up trying to talk Kathy out of seeing him because she had her reasons and wasn't going to change her mind. I thought about giving her an ultimatum or something, but knew how I'd have dealt with that kind of thing when I was her age... "See you later!" But it was still driving me nuts. I'd seen a picture of the guy in her photo album. He was younger, taller, had a nice smile, and was a whole lot better looking.

The evening before Kathy was going to leave, we were at The Office, a downtown bar where we ended up with some friends. I'd had enough Jim Beam to realize just how much I was going to miss my friend and was ready to tell her how much I loved her, that I could handle this and would be waiting for her.

"Kat. I gotta tell you something," I began.

"Okay," she said. "But let me go the bathroom first."

When she got back, she was laughing. "You wouldn't believe what I just saw in there. This girl... she had on a leather flight helmet. Like the ones you see in World War I movies. And these fake glasses with screwy eyes in them."

A sinking feeling came over me. "My height? Wavy brown hair to here?" I asked.

"Yeah," Kathy said, confirming my fear. "You saw her, too?"

"No."

Goddamn it, I thought. That girl was Sara, no doubt about it. I'd seen the flight helmet before, along with her authentic Symbionese Liberation Army beret. What a time for her to show up. If Kathy found out about Sara now, she couldn't help but have second thoughts about coming back to me.

"She was standing there," Kathy continued. "Right in front of me. And the eyes popped out of her glasses on these long springs. I…"

"She what? She was right in front of you?"

The sinking feeling changed to shock. Sara knew who Kathy was and had come right up to her without saying anything. That was not good. I wasn't exactly sure why. I didn't think she was a threat to Kathy; however, Sara was crazy and she was getting too close.

"Yeah, she…" Kathy paused, seeing how uncomfortable I was.

"That was Sara," I told her, feeling responsible for whatever was going on, and that Kathy should know about this crazy woman. "A girl I used to know."

"You mean the topless dancer you were sleeping with?" She laughed. "The one who keeps leaving her stuff around your room. Boy, what a wacko."

"How the hell do you know about her?" I asked, completely surprised, and more than a little relieved.

Kathy told me that several of the women at Tundra had let her know about Sara a long time ago. It didn't seem to bother her that much, which gave me even more reason to tell her how much I appreciated her, which I did for the rest of the night.

The next day I found a note:

Hello Love,
    Well, guess I'm off. Will be in touch as

soon as I know my plans—max two weeks.
Probably call Tuesday or Wednesday. Hell,
you already know all this, but I do want to
thank you for not keeping me chained in
your yard. Have a feeling everything will
work out fine.
Chow,
Kat

That night I found Sara and handed her a one-way plane
ticket to Colorado and her High Lama. "Thanks," she said.
While I was out flying the next day, Sara came by the hangar
and picked up the rest her things from my room. She also left a
note:

Hello Tom
As today there is no time like the present.
Still I appreciate your direct way.
I believe with
a little
blue sky sunshine food drink
the future will
care for itself
open
and
well

Sara

10

THE HIGH ONE

Two days later I was in the White Mountains, 40 miles northeast of Fairbanks, working for Mapco, a resource exploration company. Their geologists had been in the area for years, studying and mapping what they could see of the earth's crust so they could speculate about what lay below, and what minerals those geological formations might contain. Now it was time to bring in the core drills and see exactly what was under the ground.

Core drills look a lot like the drills used to extract oil, a tower of latticed steel, only smaller. And the bits on the core drills are hollow so that they can bring up sections of rock from hundreds of feet below the surface. My job was to take the crews to the two drills operating on Cache Mountain, about 20 minutes from camp, and every so often move the drills from one site to another. If I wanted a distraction from the loneliness I felt without Kathy, moving core drills in the mountains was a good one.

Flying in the mountains, navigating the maze of ridges and valleys, knowing where the wind is and using it, working my way through a difficult landing, is mostly right-brain work, sensing things and being creative. Moving drills is completely left-brain, calculation and execution, total concentration. Of the two I prefer right-brain thinking, but life without precision would not be as rewarding.

When you move core drills you get to see just how precise you can be with a helicopter. Like a three-ton erector set, they come apart in pieces: the base, draw works, engine and boom. Each section is carried underneath the helicopter at the end of a cable anywhere from 20 to 100 feet long. The cable clips into a cargo hook in the center of the aircraft's belly. We used the Hughes 500Ds almost exclusively on drill moves because they are stronger and more stable than the Jet Rangers.

The first step in a drill move is breaking it down. A guy on the ground hooks the cable to the boom, the 30-foot tower that holds the lengths of drill pipe in place above the hole. Once the helicopter is attached to the boom, I take the slack out of the line so it doesn't fall over when it's detached. When the drillers pull out the last bolts holding it in place, I lift the boom straight up then take it to the new drill site. Next I go back for the draw works. That is the winch, cable and gears that lift, lower and turn the pipe. After that I pick up the big diesel engine that runs everything. Lastly, I take the base, which is the steel undercarriage of the drill. When I have all the parts at the new site, I put them back together.

Taking a drill apart is demanding, but putting it back together is stressful. When you pick the pieces up, all you have to do is keep the right amount of tension in the right direction on the cable until it's loose, then fly away. You have to watch out that something doesn't get hung up, or that you don't pull too hard in the wrong direction before the part is free. Both of those can bring the helicopter down. Also, the parts are always about the maximum amount the helicopter can lift, so you can run out of power if you're not careful. But all of that is compounded when you reassemble the drill.

When you come in with a piece of the drill there are a few more critical factors: groundspeed, wind direction, rate of descent, how much power you pull and when. All of that is important because of the weight of the part and the fact that it is in a descent. It's going to take more power to stop the load than it did to pick it up. Power management is everything, and it all has to come together precisely at a chosen point right above the drill. You simply don't have the power to move around on the steep side of a mountain once you've come to a hover.

If you do run out of power at that point, the main rotor system loses lift or the helicopter begins to rotate, usually the latter. In a revolution or two, no more than a couple of seconds, the aircraft is out of control. The only thing you can do on the side of a mountain is jettison the load and get flying again. Once you are moving forward at 20 mph the helicopter will stop spinning.

Once the drill part has stopped in exactly the right spot, you have to set it in place as quickly as possible. The longer you wait, the harder it is to keep it where you want, because the helicopter is operating at maximum performance in disturbed air on uneven terrain. Of course you can't rush, because the bolt-holes on the part have to line up with the bolt-holes on the drill.

To make the job a little more difficult, the only way to tell exactly what the load below you is doing, is to lean out the door and watch. It's a lot like riding a bicycle while looking at the road beneath the pedals. Precision and control are not only important in taking the drill apart and putting it back together, there's also a safety issue. If anything goes wrong, you will probably maim or kill the three or four drillers waiting to bolt the part in place.

The guys on the ground are a lot of help when it comes to putting the drill together. I can get the piece within an inch or so of being in place, but it's the drillers who manhandle the part into exact alignment. If I screw up and run out of power, or my engine quits, the first thing I'm going to do is jettison the part of the drill I'm carrying. If I'm right above the drill, there's a very good chance someone is going to get hurt.

You really don't have any other choice than to get rid of the load the instant you know you're in trouble. Otherwise, the drillers will have both the load and the helicopter coming down on them. There isn't enough inertia in the rotor system to hold the helicopter and a heavy load at a hover for more than a second. If you let the load go right away, there should be enough energy left in the rotor system to move the aircraft away from the drillers; however, the chance of making a successful landing at that point is not very good, especially on the side of a mountain.

Along with the drills and their crews, I move everything

else involved in the process: water pumps, heaters, tools, thousands of feet of water line, water reservoirs, materials to build huts, and the dreaded drill pipe. The trouble with flying drill pipe is, unlike most loads, it doesn't streamline. Most loads are held in place by the drag of forward airspeed. Some rotate, or swing around a little, but the 20-foot lengths of drill pipe slung below the helicopter respond differently.

At a hover the pipe gets caught in the rotor wash and begins to spin. If you aren't moving in a few seconds the load gets going so fast it begins to oscillate and then gets out of control. In flight the bundles of pipe ride smoothly enough, pulled off to one side or the other by the flow of air against them, until you get going more than 30 mph. Above that speed it can slip off its cushion of air at any time. When that happens the pipe whips to the opposite side of the helicopter, yanking violently on the cargo hook and rolling the machine from side to side. The only way to stop the pendulum-like action is to slow down or pull in more power. Then around 45 mph it does the same thing all over again, except it's more violent.

Almost everything to do with moving drills is difficult. I found myself breaking rules all the time to get the job done. From little things we tried to avoid, like hovering with a heavy load and a tailwind. To bigger things we were never supposed to do, like fly to the top of a mountain that's inside a cloud.

One night, 13 hours into a 12-hour day, I was sitting near the waterline at the foot of a ridge waiting for the clouds to move. The waterline was an orange hose two inches wide that ran up the mountain to the drill. A thousand feet above me three tired and very cold drillers were waiting to be picked up. While I sat there I noticed that I could see 20 or 30 feet of the waterline inside the cloud, and I began to wonder.

I knew the side of the mountain. There wasn't anything to run into. Twenty feet of orange hose was enough to stay oriented to the slope, and it would take me right to the drillers. However, flying into a cloud would be breaking one of my cardinal rules. But I wouldn't actually be flying into the cloud, I reasoned, I'd be hovering over vertical ground. About the only thing I had to worry about was losing sight of the hose. But it would be right outside my door, I assured myself, only a few feet away, and it was really bright. I could follow it in the dark.

Hungry, and not feeling like hanging around all night waiting for a cloud to move, I picked the helicopter up and moved over for a closer look. Then I followed the waterline into the cloud. A few minutes later I was sitting beside the drill. It helped that we were north of the Arctic Circle and nothing grew over a few feet tall in that part of the Brooks Range, and that there was plenty of light at eight p.m. But I was really impressed with how easy it had been, flying inside a treacherous cloud, and quite pleased with myself until the drillers were loaded and we started back down.

Hovering up the mountain I could see the waterline well because it was right outside my door, rising in a straight line to the drill. Coming down the mountain, although the hose was still out my door, I could only see a few feet before it disappeared under the aircraft's belly. Not nearly enough to stay oriented to the mountain. I ended up having to turn the helicopter around so that my door faced away from the mountain. That way I could look straight down at the waterline and see more of it. Unfortunately, from that perspective, the pipe was so far away it often disappeared in the mesmerizing mist of the cloud.

Of course, once you start doing things like following waterlines into the clouds, it's not long before you find yourself in trouble. Only a week or two after I went up the side of the mountain, we were in the Ambler River Valley waiting on clouds again. We'd been trying to get to the side of a steep ridge near the headwaters, but the clouds were keeping us out, hanging several hundred feet below the spot the geologists had picked for us to set up the drill. Finally they thinned and lifted enough for us to get in.

Everything went well for most of the day. A few clouds drifted around the ridge to the south, sometimes keeping me away from the site, but it wasn't until the last part of the drill move, the boom, that I had a real problem. Most of the parts of the drill go together in a couple of minutes, but the boom is long and gets caught in the rotor wash. Most of the time it takes several tries just to get it in the right spot. Then the drillers climb up on the drill to set the attaching bolts. The slightest movement and I have to begin again. It's difficult and dangerous, so they move slowly.

About halfway through the process of setting the boom, a larger-than-usual cloud rolled over the ridge and headed straight for us. I didn't like the looks of it, but the drillers were busy fitting the bolts in place. The only communication we had was hand signals, and before anyone took the time to look up at me, the cloud had enveloped us.

When the drillers were done bolting the boom to the drill, it was time to make a decision. I couldn't get to the landing spot for the site. The mountain was so steep we had to put the landing pad several hundred feet below the drill. The waterline wasn't in yet, so I couldn't follow that down, and the mountain was too rugged to work my way down without something to follow. Of course I could take off and fly out of the cloud, but I really didn't want to do that. Not only would I have to go from a hover to instrument flight, a dangerous transition with no ground reference, I'd also have to climb up into the cloud or risk flying into another mountain. By then I'd be completely lost. The best plan at the time seemed to be to stay where I was.

About 20 feet in front of the drill a narrow ledge protruded from the slope. It was barely visible, but it looked level and was wide enough to support the landing gear. If I moved over there I could wait for the cloud to blow over. Then I checked the fuel gauge. There were less than 10 gallons left, about 23 minutes in flight, maybe 30 or more at a lower power setting. Not a lot of time, but enough to make it worth a try, I figured, and moved over to perch on the ledge.

While I sat there balancing on the little rock protrusion, waiting for the cloud to move on, I began messing around with the cyclic trim. In the Hughes 500 there's a little cap on top of the cyclic that I control with my thumb. It activates electric motors that move the cyclic short distances in any direction, helping me counteract forces in the rotor system. Before long the cyclic was trimmed up so well, I could take my hand off of it for up to half a minute before the helicopter began to roll off the ledge in one direction or the other.

Originally, I was going to sit on the ledge and give the cloud time to move. If that didn't happen, having no other option, I'd planned to fly out of the cloud; however, when I got the helicopter balanced, I realized that I could probably undo my seatbelt, climb out onto the ledge, jump off and scramble to the side before the helicopter came down on top of me. It seemed like a good idea until I weighed the risks, including an uncoordinated exit from the aircraft, premature rotation off the ledge and flying parts when the aircraft hit the ground, all of which might kill me.

Meanwhile, the needle of the fuel gauge moved lower. When it touched the top of the empty mark, I began to worry. I really didn't want to jump out of the helicopter. Unknowns aside, I didn't want to ruin a perfectly good helicopter; however, I might have waited too long to fly out of the cloud. With so little fuel left, I might lose the engine at any moment. In desperation I looked down the mountain, towards the spot where my fuel was stored only a couple thousand feet away. It took a second to sink in, but it looked as if the cloud had lifted off the side of the mountain a bit, 10 or 15 feet at least.

I couldn't make out the valley floor yet, but I could see at least a hundred feet down the mountain. Even farther, there was a rock outcrop visible in the haze. I knew I could easily lose sight of the mountain, but then I'd just get on my flight instruments, which I would have had to do anyhow, and it would be a lot safer in flight than from a hover. So, I picked the helicopter up and nosed it over. Within a minute I was parked beside the fuel drums in the sunny valley below the drill.

There is also a paradox in drill moves. Although you can't relax for a second, you can't be tense. The control movements necessary for that kind of flying are small and precise. Tense muscles can't do that. They hold on then let go, way too erratic. Over time I learned to relax my body without losing concentration; nevertheless, every night after a drill move, when I lay down to go to sleep, my head would shake uncontrollably as the tension in my neck muscles released.

The technical flying was the rewarding part of moving drills, but it was gratifying to know that, in using my helicopter as an airborne crane, bringing the drills in and out with minimal impact on the environment, I was helping keep one of my favorite spots as safe as possible.

Until the Mapco job, almost all the drill moves I'd done were in the western part of the Brooks Range. A place so unspoiled, you could fly for more than a hundred miles without seeing a straight line, the universal sign of man. No towns, roads, telephone lines or even remote radio towers. It is the Middle Earth of Alaska, lying between the uninhabitable reaches of the North Slope and the more populated regions to the south. The kind of place where wolves didn't feel the need to hide, and mythical creatures became real.

One calm afternoon I was doing some nap-of-the-earth flying along the slope of a gentle mountain. Low-level flight is a scenic way to get from one place to another. Generally you fly in a fairly straight line, somewhere around cruise speed, at a consistently low altitude. Nap of the earth is slower, 30 or 40 mph, and lower, as low as three or four feet above the ground. Unlike other types of flying, instead of heading in one direction, you follow the terrain. Not just up and down drainages, but along the subtle features of the land, up a little rise, around a small knoll, down the fall line of a steep slope, along the foot of a small cliff. Nap-of-the-earth flying is slow and rhythmic.

The wood nymph I saw couldn't have heard me coming. The skids were almost in the grass as I came over the treeless ridge several hundred yards downwind from where she was crouched by the side of a stream. I could tell she was small, maybe three or four feet tall, and her lithe body appeared to be draped in white gossamer.

Even though I was staring right at her, I didn't see the nymph until she moved. A shimmer of soft light taking form as quickly as it melted into the willows. In the next instant I wasn't sure I'd seen anything at all. However, because I'd been looking right at her, with nothing on my mind, the picture was there.

Unfortunately, the job with Mapco wasn't in the Brooks Range. Our camp was in low hills covered in stands of densely packed black spruce trees, crisscrossed with four-wheel-drive roads and littered with trash.

A lot of the stuff left around the backwoods of Alaska was interesting. An old wooden-wheeled hay wagon with trees growing through it on the side of the field was a work of art. And the rusting hulk of an ancient bulldozer at the end of an overgrown road in the middle of nowhere raised the question… where was it going? Then there was the large boiler way up a mountain valley with no sign of anything else made by man within 50 miles. What did it power? And what about the one-room house that sits in the middle of the dirt road about a mile northwest of the Farwell Lake airstrip.

Things like the gold dredges left around Fairbanks were state treasures as far as I was concerned. They were living museums, places where you can see an artifact in its own environment, climb around on it, explore, and try to figure out what it did and how it had worked. But the stuff left around the foothills of the White Mountains, where we were working, was different.

Beer cans, toilet paper and plastic bags full of garbage littered the sides of the roads and the few pullouts. Along the rutted roads punched into the woods by four-wheel-drive vehicles were the dumps left behind by hunters, would-be homesteaders, and squatters. People who had dragged everything they could into the woods, made it through a miserable winter or two in tents or a plywood shack, and then left it all to rot. Deeper in the woods, at the end of the ATV trails, were the tattered tarpaulins of hunting camps, their dumps dug up and scattered by bears.

The Mapco camp fit well with its surroundings. Like most seasonal operations at the end of the season, the small exploration company was trying to squeeze in one last job on dwindling resources. Rather than set up a decent camp, they rented an old cabin and its dilapidated outbuildings on the side of the road between Central and Fairbanks. The little cabin served as cookhouse and office, while its sheds were set up as bunkrooms for the drill crews and the pilot. Each night, as I struggled to get to sleep amid the snores of the drillers, I was acutely aware of how dramatically life had changed since Kathy had left.

The quality of my life sucked, which made her absence even more difficult to deal with. I wasn't really jealous. She'd been going out with Jamie before we met, and made a promise. I had to respect that. If she didn't honor her promise to him, why would she honor one to me later? That's if there was going to be a later. What really bothered me was the loneliness, feeling like I'd lost my best friend and she might not be coming back.

One morning, while I was going through the preflight for my Hughes 500, I heard the distant sound of a flight of geese. Minutes later they were crossing high overhead, at least a hundred of them, their calls to each other reverberating in the cold clear air, and I realized how much I wanted to join them, head south, go anywhere to escape the snoring at night and feeling bad all day.

That evening I caught a ride with the cook who was on her way to Fairbanks, where I rented a well-used Ford Fairlane from Rent-A-Wreck. A few minutes later I was at the hangar and there was a party going on. Almost everyone who worked for Tundra was in town, pockets full of money and celebrating the end of the season. From then on I drove back and forth to Mapco each day.

With flying and the nightlife at the hangar, life was good again. I rarely had time to think about Kathy. Unfortunately, one by one my friends left town. Ernie was the first to go. I think he went to a job in the Gulf of Mexico. Then

Baldini and Russell took off for different parts of Africa. When Johnny Burns left for Kansas, life around the hangar began to drag. Then one of Mapco's drills broke down and they decided not to fix it. With only one drill operating there was very little to do, and I had a lot of time to miss Kathy.

When she had been gone more than a week, I began to think I might not see her again. She said it might be two weeks, but she could have come back earlier if she wanted to. She hadn't even called. The more I thought about it the worse it got, then Vinny called.

"Tommy! Scotty, Porgy, Brodie and me are heading into Denali right now. We'll wait for you at Wonder Lake. I don't think you want to miss this one," he said, and hung up. Scotty and Porgy were Vinny's younger brothers, and Brodie was a friend from home.

Not many things could have cheered me up more. I needed a distraction and Vinny was perfect. We always had a good time together, and with his brothers and Brodie along, it would only be that much better. After a call to Craig, to get him to cover for me on the Mapco job, I filled up the Fairlane and took off for Denali National Park.

Two hours later I was in the park and heading towards Wonder Lake. Although I was on my way to see my friends, the 95-mile drive from the entrance to the lake, alone, would have made the trip worth it. The hard-packed dirt road that winds its way through the foothills of the Alaska Range is smooth and wide. And with the tour buses finished for the day, I had it all to myself.

It took me a while to get used to how the Fairlane handled on dirt. She was heavy and didn't like to come out of the corners because the shocks were soft. But the tires were worn so it drifted easily and that helped me get through the corners. The car had a powerful engine, so I drove it like Spot. Whenever it wanted to get out of a sideways slide I stepped on the gas. Before long I was up to 70 in the straight stretches, great clouds of dust boiling up behind me, feeling better than I had in a long time.

About halfway to Wonder Lake it got dark. I couldn't see as far through the corners and began to slow down, which was a good thing. When I came around a long sweeping turn to the right, parked on the outside of the turn, facing the wrong direction and taking up a good part of the road, was a pickup truck. If I'd been going any faster I might have slid into it. I was all set to give the driver a dirty look as I rolled by, but realized it was Norma, Vinny's truck. I locked up the brakes and slid to a stop.

"Hey, Tommy," Vinny greeted me. The four of them were standing around a lantern on the tailgate, eating. "We were wondering what kind of wacko was coming down the road. We've been watching your headlights blink on and off as you came around the corners." He laughed. "You were haulin' ass."

"Didn't want to be late for dinner," I told him, picking up a paper plate and helping myself to the stew simmering on the Coleman stove. It was good.

After dinner we drank rum, told stories and laughed until, one by one, everyone crawled off to sleep. As frigid air flowed down the mountains, I snuggled deep in my sleeping bag, glad the Fairlane was there to keep the wind off me. The next morning, while we stood around the tailgate waiting for the little gas stove to boil water, I noticed light-colored bird feathers scattered around the bed of the truck.

"What've you been doing, Vinny? Smuggling chickens to the natives again?" I asked.

"Ptarmigan, Tom. They're Ptarmigan," he whispered. "And you ate them?"

"No way, Vinny." I was really surprised. The feathers were everywhere. "You didn't shoot them here, did you? Right in the middle of a goddamned national park?" That was a major crime. Vinny just grinned at me.

"Don't let him bullshit you, Tom," his brother Scotty said. "We shot them outside the park."

"Yeah," Porgy added. "On the other side of Peter's Hills." He paused. "When we were in Petersville yesterday."

He began to chuckle. "You know, after we went for a swim in Peter's Creek."

Our laughter was interrupted by the sound of an engine revving up and gears grinding as a green school bus came around the corner, slowing down to give us room as he went by. It was the first of the park busses to come along that morning, loaded with tourists on their way to see Denali. Then the brakes squealed and the bus came to a stop in its own cloud of dust. A middle-aged hippy wearing headphones leaned out the driver's window.

"What are you doin', McClelland?" he asked Vinny. "Killin' the critters?" I saw a few of the tourists draw back in shock. It was an older group. Even I cringed, and moved to block their view of the Ptarmigan feathers.

"Just the tasty ones," Vinny laughed. The bus driver laughed too, ground the gears, and drove off. "His name's Bob," he told us. "Nice guy. We've done some skiing together." Vinny had told me about the skiing he and his friends did around these mountains. Their mantra was "Ski to Die!"

A couple hours later, when we left for Wonder Lake, I noticed a sign I hadn't seen the night before because Vinny had parked in front of it. In big yellow letters the park service sign stated: "NO STOPPING OR STANDING—GRIZZLY CROSSING AREA."

We pulled over several times on our way to the lake. The mountains were that beautiful, fall colors right up to the snow that was only a few thousand feet above us. At a stop at the highest point in the park road, I noticed that fall was already past its prime. The purples and reds were still intense, but the lighter colors were almost gone. Winter was not far away.

Early that afternoon we reached our destination, Wonder Lake. Dark and calm, it sits alone at the foot of Denali, minuscule compared to the mountain above. However, in the best tradition of irony, the little lake takes the mountain, shrinks it down and captures the behemoth in the flawless reflection of its still water.

Later that evening when the moon rose, it was full. Standing around a blazing fire, glasses of rum in hand, we watched as it bathed the mountain in its pale white light. Then, high above the darkened plain around us, the enormous mountain began to float. It was an optical illusion. The bottom half of Denali was as dark as the night, which left the snow-covered top of the mountain free to drift in space. It was surreal and a phenomenal sight.

We drank too much while we watched the moon rise and set on Denali, and ended up crawling off to sleep not long before sunrise. So it was the middle of the morning when Vinny opened the Fairlane's door. "Get up, Tommy. You've gotta see this," he told me, laughing. The world around my car was white. It had snowed a good two inches during the night and covered everything in sight. I didn't see what was so funny until I realized that the large lump in the snow not far away was Scotty in his sleeping bag.

After a large breakfast of bacon and eggs, I left for Fairbanks. Craig was only going to fly the morning crew change at Mapco, so I had to get back for the afternoon shift, and I had to be sober. Neither of which would happen if I hung around with those guys any longer.

When I pulled into the hangar parking lot, Craig's car was still there. "Kathy called," he said as I sat down in the chair in front of his desk. I didn't move, waiting for more, but Craig was enjoying the look of anticipation on my face. When that expression changed to anger, he quickly added, "She'll be in town day after tomorrow."

"That's it? Anything else?" My chest was tight.

"Oh, yeah. She said she missed ya," he added. And I breathed a sigh of relief.

Kathy got back to Fairbanks the day she said she would, and it was as if she'd never left. We were good friends who had missed each other a lot. But I had to ask, "It's over, right? I mean, between you and him."

"Yep," she said.

"I mean. You didn't make any more dates or anything like that?"

Kathy looked at me for a moment. "You're joking. Right?" she asked.

I was and wasn't. Life had changed when she left, and changed just as quickly when she got back. A little more assurance wouldn't have hurt.

The sun was still up 12 hours a day, and it was unseasonably warm for the end of September, but fall was peaking around Fairbanks. Every evening, when I got back from the White Mountains, Kathy and I went for a walk or rode our bikes. It was hard to believe, but snow and freezing temperatures were only a hundred miles away, creeping over the Brooks Range on their way down from the North Slope. Then, in the first week of October, I went out for the morning crew change and found the drill buried under a half foot of snow. The water lines were frozen, and Mapco finally called it quits.

A few days later, while I was bringing in the last parts of the drill, the camp boss came out and signaled me to land.

"There's a plane overdue," he told me. "Troopers came by and said it was on its way from Fort Yukon to Fairbanks. Their flight plan had them coming right by where you were workin'. You didn't see them, did you?"

"Nothing all day," I told him. "Want me to go look for them?"

"Might be a good idea," he said.

"What kind of aircraft is it? How many on board?" I asked.

"Troopers said it was a single-engine, red and white, with a family in it. Two grownups and two kids."

Back in the White Mountains the weather was the same as it had been all day, overcast but not particularly bad. A few peaks were in the clouds, but everywhere else it was clear. I followed Beaver Creek towards Fort Yukon, the route everyone takes to Fairbanks when the weather's low. My focus was any place the little plane might have put down in an emergency landing, but I also watched for broken limbs or other signs of a crash in the trees.

I was pretty sure that's what had happened to them, an engine failure or something. There were a lot of places to put a plane down, including Beaver Creek itself, so there was a 50-50 chance they'd be okay. However, something the troopers told the camp boss bothered me. No one had received a distress call from the airplane.

Sudden impact is what usually keeps pilots from getting off distress calls. But that didn't mean it wasn't an engine failure, I told myself. It was a family in the plane, probably a weekend pilot doing the flying, and he might not have had it together enough to get out a radio call for help, especially if the weather had him close to the ground to begin with. Nevertheless, as I flew by Rocky Mountain, the only peak in the area that was in the clouds, I looked up its barren slopes and got a bad feeling.

About 50 miles from Fort Yukon I radioed flight service, got the last known location of the plane, and flew directly to that spot. After circling that area I headed for Rocky Mountain. The feeling that the missing airplane was there had only gotten stronger.

Twenty minutes later I was over the North Fork of Preacher Creek. It was just south of Beaver Creek and paralleled it straight into Rocky Mountain. About halfway up the cloud-covered valley it became too narrow for a plane to turn around, so I began scanning the ridges on either side. That's where airplanes end up when they enter a valley they can't get out of.

When I got to where the clouds met the mountain without seeing any wreckage, I relaxed. They aren't here, I thought, and began a turn to leave. Then, just above the cloud line, among some large boulders, I saw something red. With a sick feeling in my stomach I circled back and clearly saw the wings and fuselage of a single-engine airplane.

They'd hit hard, almost straight in, and there were no signs of survivors. It didn't take long to figure out what had happened. The pilot had simply flown up the wrong valley. Instead of taking Beaver Creek along the north side of the White Mountains on his way back to Fairbanks, he followed the North Fork of Preacher Creek right into the side of the mountain.

It was an easy mistake to make. Beaver Creek and Preacher Creek are only 15 miles apart, about the same size, flow in the same direction, and their approaches are similar. Unless you know what the area looks like in bad weather, it's almost impossible to tell the two valleys apart.

Flying up the wrong drainage was the first mistake he made, but it probably wasn't what got them killed. More likely it was being too close to the clouds. When weather forces a pilot to fly lower than he's used to, his natural reaction is to keep as much distance as he can between himself and the ground. Unfortunately, up against the uneven surface of the clouds, visibility is limited. It's like trying to see out from under a blanket, you can't see the walls of the room. Judging by the way the airplane hit, nose high and going fast, he didn't see the mountain until the very last moment.

As I envisioned what had happened to the little plane and the family inside, a wave of sadness overwhelmed me, mostly for the kids. I felt so sorry for them, the lives they no longer had, and the terror they must have felt. My parents had died in a similar fashion. An error in judgment and things went terribly wrong.

A strong wind was blowing across the little dirt airstrip on Virgin Gorda, an island in the Caribbean. It caught the single-engine plane carrying my parents and another couple and drifted it into a flagpole just off the runway. When the wingtip hit the pole the opposite wing rose, caught the wind and flipped the plane over. It was fast. My father died instantly, mom never regained consciousness.

Like the family in the airplane on the side of the mountain in front of me, the last thing my parents saw was the ground coming up at them. I could feel their panic, knew what it was like to see the end coming. My door gunner and I were in a free fall for more than a hundred feet when we got shot down and crashed in the jungle. The last thing I saw was the limb of a tree coming up through the chin bubble. Hopefully, like me, they didn't think they were going to die.

I doubted anyone in the small red and white airplane survived the crash, but thought I'd better make sure. If people were alive I could have them in the hospital in less than an hour. While I flew along the side of the mountain, looking for a spot to land, I was surprised to hear another pilot calling my aircraft number. He was on the Flight Service Station frequency I'd been monitoring. Evidently he was in radio contact with a rescue team somewhere on the side of the mountain below me. The message he relayed was that they had a fix on the wreckage and everything was under control, so I headed back to camp.

With the Mapco job over, and not much work scheduled, Kathy and I had some time to enjoy fall and life in Fairbanks. We got up late, went out for long breakfasts, and spent the rest of the day outside. If it was cool we ran around the back roads of the airport or along the Chena River. When it was warm we took long bike rides or went canoeing. And if it was sunny and hot we just found someplace comfortable and enjoyed it.

We relished those days because each one was noticeably cooler than the last. The air got crisp and clear, the nights cold, and the woods grew quiet. Then the beaver pond beside the dirt road we ran on froze, as did the road itself a few days later.

On one of the last comfortable afternoons in October we were floating the Chena River through Fairbanks. When a blast of very cold air swept down the river, I made some comment about getting ready for winter.

"That reminds me," Kathy said unenthusiastically. "I've got to make reservations for Colorado pretty soon."

"What?" I asked, not liking the sound of that at all.

"I talked to my mom the other day. I guess the family's getting together for Christmas in Colorado again," she told me.

"What the...," I exclaimed. "Leave! Goddamn it, Kathy, you just got back from a trip."

"I'm sorry, Tom. But it's my family. We've been doing this almost every Christmas since I was a kid." There wasn't much I could say. Family vacations are a priority; nevertheless, the thought of her leaving again hurt.

"Yeah, but..."

Kathy gave me a sympathetic look and said, "But first, how about we do something fun. Float a river, or a road trip to Homer."

It was getting too cold to camp, but Homer, a picturesque fishing village 400 miles south of us on the tip of the Kenai Peninsula, was a place I liked to visit, and fall would be further away. But then I got an idea.

"Okay," I said. "But instead of Homer, how about we go to New Zealand?"

11

THE OTHER SIDE OF THE WORLD

I had been thinking about taking a trip to New Zealand for years, probably since I visited Australia on a one-week rest and relaxation break near the end of my tour in Vietnam. Kathy was all for it too, so we began making plans. We decided to do the trip on bicycles and camp to keep expenses down.

Next I checked with Craig. There was hardly any work scheduled, so he didn't have a problem with me taking off for a few months. And when I looked into tickets, I found a two-for-one deal on Pan American. A few weeks later we put our 12-speed bikes in boxes and got on a plane to Auckland.

The first few miles on our bikes were a little scary. The shoulder of the road leaving the airport was narrow and the traffic heavy. Most of the drivers, trucks in particular, made little effort to give us any leeway, often coming within inches of our handlebars. Making matters worse was the weight. Our bikes were loaded with food, water, cooking gear, a tent, sleeping bags, clothes, spare bike parts, and backpacks. All of it strapped onto front and rear racks, or stuffed into panniers, nylon bags that attached to the bike racks like saddlebags. The weight made steering extremely sensitive. Turning the handlebars more than a few degrees was cause for the front wheel to veer sharply and dump me on the ground.

Around the time we got used to the way our bikes handled, we found out it was safer, and more pleasant, to stick to the side streets. Auckland was relatively modern and hectic, but the residential areas hadn't kept pace. The little motel we stayed in was from a different era, sometime around the 1950s in the United States. From the bedspread to the lampshade, everything in our room was handmade, and tastefully homey. It was like we were staying in someone's guest room.

In the morning there was a knock on the door and we

found the local paper and a pint of milk on the stoop. The milk was in a glass bottle with an inch of cream at the top.

That day we left the city behind. Traffic all but disappeared. Instead of concrete buildings and diesel fumes, there were little farms, fertile fields, and forests. The first town we came to was Albany. It was late in the afternoon so we looked around for a hotel room, but the town was full of vacationers. There wasn't even a place to camp. Albany was by the sea. It was the beginning of New Zealand's summer, and the Kiwis apparently loved to go to the beach.

The next town we came to was tiny. Nothing but a road intersection with a few red-roofed homes on one side and the grocery store and post office, also with red roofs, on the other, but no campground.

"Let's get some stuff for dinner and camp along the road somewhere," Kathy suggested.

In the store we found everything we'd need, including a decent bottle of wine to go with the steaks for dinner, and fresh berries for breakfast. Not far from town we found a pasture with a fine view of the mountains. It was getting late so we rode up to the house above the field and asked the lady who answered the door if we could camp in her field for the night.

"Oh, no," she said. "You've got to stay with us. We've lots of room."

We gratefully declined and spent a pleasant evening grilling our dinner over an open fire at the edge of their pasture. The next morning we began pedaling into the mountains that had looked so inviting from our tent. A few hours later we were dying, down to our lowest gear and barely moving up the steep grade of our third or fourth pass.

It was impossible to keep the sweat out of my eyes and my thighs were killing me. Even the tops of my feet were sore. To get my heavy bike up the steeper pitches, I had to pull up against the toe-clip on one pedal as I pushed down on the other. The only thing that kept me going was having Kathy in front of me, steadily pulling away.

Our plan was to keep heading north, towards Cape

Reinga on the end of North Island. It was one of the more remote and rugged parts of the island with sand dunes, beaches and small sheltered coves. Also, because we were in the southern hemisphere, we thought temperatures would rise the farther we went in that direction. After Fairbanks we wanted to be warm. But once we crossed the mountains, the wind picked up and the temperature dropped into the 50s. The beach at the town we reached that night was windswept and cold. The next morning we headed back over the mountains to warmer weather.

Two days later we were well south of Auckland, pedaling up a gentle grade towards Tongariro National Park to see the volcanoes. It was sunny and warm, the winds were calm, and there was almost no traffic.

"This is just great!" I exclaimed, having decided that traveling by bike was the only way to get around.

You sit up higher than a car, so the visibility is better. And the speed of the bike is perfect; slow enough to take in everything along the way but fast enough to get somewhere. More important, you are out in the open, can feel the sun on your skin, smell a patch of flowers as you ride by, enjoy every aspect of the day. Compared to traveling in a car, a bike is the equivalent of flying low level with the doors off.

"What?" Kathy asked.

"I haven't enjoyed anything so much for a long time. I just love this. Being outside, cruising and seeing the sights. Sharing it with you."

"What?" Kathy said again. "Turn around. I can't hear you."

It's hard to understand what someone is saying while they are riding in front of you. Unfortunately, it's hazardous to face backwards for long. So I turned, looked at her, and said, "I love you."

"Why, thank you very much," she replied.

The route we picked to Tongariro and the park's volcanoes took us to Rotorua, a picturesque town on a perfectly round lake. There was a classic old hotel with world-class lawn bowling greens and a natural hot spring.

The next morning we decided to ride around the lake with a stop at the hot spring. There was a good breeze blowing when we got on our bikes, so we figured it would be best to ride into a headwind the first half and have it at our backs when we had less energy. But the wind followed us right around the lake, blowing 180 degrees from where it had been in the morning. We were beginning to dislike wind.

From Rotorua there was a lot of uphill to the high plateau of the volcanoes. It was slow going, two miles an hour at best, but the scenery was diverse and changed constantly as we climbed. In a matter of hours we went from fields and forests to sand and sage. On the second day, we arrived on the shores of Lake Taupo, more of an inland sea, sans salt, than a lake. As we pedaled around the north side of Taupo, it began to blow, coming straight at us so strong we ended up lying flat on our bikes, chins to the handlebars. While dirt and sand peppered out faces, the wind howled in our ears to the point of distraction. That night it was so loud in our tent we drank a bottle of wine just to get to sleep.

We awoke to a strange sound. Silence. The wind had died; however, before long it would have been nice if there were at least a breeze. We had pedaled up and onto the slopes of the volcanoes where there was very little soil. The ground consisted of cinders, dry and very hot when the sun shone on the dark surface.

Later that day, as we pedaled along in a stupor, I thought it was a hallucination when I looked up and saw the snowcapped peak of Mount Nagauruhoe, dazzlingly white in a bright blue sky. Just as surprising, and even more comforting than the sight of snow, was the large brick hotel at the base of the mountain, with tall chimneys, slate roof and grand portico.

"What do you think?" I asked Kathy when we stopped to stare at the sight.

"I think the reservations are for Smith, party of two," she replied.

Fortunately, we had packed a set of decent-looking

clothes for just such an occasion, but we needed a bath to get rid of the layer of windblown grit that had built up on our perspiring bodies. Not far from the long drive leading up to the hotel we crossed a nice clear stream and stopped for a bath. An hour later we checked into the Chateau Tongariro.

It was an old hotel, somewhere between grand and institutional in design, but unique in its solitary setting among the volcano's peaks. True to its era the rooms were spacious and the dining exceptional, with elegant settings of linen and crystal.

As we relaxed after our meal, sipping brandy while the sun went down outside the tall window beside our table, I noticed an older gentleman making his way across the large dining room. He caught my attention because he was moving so slowly, but deliberately, in our direction. Every so often, he'd pause as he shuffled along, look up, orient himself to the room, and then continue. Finally he was beside our table, looking back and forth between the two of us.

"Are you the young couple I saw today from the window of our tour bus?" he asked in a soft and metered voice. Then he raised his hand to his bald pate and made a brushing motion, and I remembered that after our bath in the stream I'd brushed Kathy's hair for her. "You were brushing..."

"That's right," I told him. "That was us."

"I can't tell you how much it meant to us," he turned and gestured in the direction of his table, "seeing you two young people. Enjoying life so much in such a wonderful place." There was a comfortable pause. "Thank you," he said with a nod of his head, first to Kathy, then to me. Without another word he turned and began the long trek back to his table.

"That was cool," Kathy said as she watched him go.

"To the little things in life," I added, raising my glass. "And the perspective of age."

The next morning, instead of getting back on our bikes, we put on our packs and hiked into the volcanoes above the hotel. We wandered among cinder cones hundreds of feet high, feeling like we'd gone back millions of years in the near-lifeless environment. The only water we saw above tree line was boiling hot and trickled from clefts in the barren slopes of the volcanoes. Steam hissed from fissures amid brilliant shades of red, yellow and brown growths of slimy algae. The smell of rotten eggs, hydrogen sulfide gas, was too strong for breathing in some spots. It was a fascinating, although hostile, environment.

From the park we rode our bikes to a train station 10 miles away and caught the express to Wellington, a small city on a picturesque bay. We'd planned to spend most of our vacation on South Island hiking in the mountains around Queenstown, but it was the middle of November, more than a week into our trip, and we weren't even halfway there, so we got on the train to make up a little time. After a night in the relatively busy city of Wellington we took the ferry to South Island and began pedaling again.

In Nelson, on the north end of South Island, we checked into a motel and lounged around the pool for a few days. But we were falling even further behind schedule. After consulting our map we decided it would take at least another week to get to Queenstown on our bikes. The first 50 miles were nice, but then we had to go up several passes through the Hope and Matiri ranges. Actually, it looked like 75 miles or more of torturous pedaling up and down mountains. Then the road followed a beautiful coastline for 300 miles before going back into even taller mountains. After very little debate, we decided to do a one-way car rental.

With our bikes packed in the trunk we headed south. It was a treat to travel without regard for the weather, and effortlessly climb one hill after another. Along the coast between Greymouth and Haast we spent a lot of time looking around, saying, "We could live here." At every turn in the road there was a valley in the mountains or a cove on the coast that would have been a perfect place to build a home.

At Haast we turned inland. In a lush rainforest we hiked among tall tree ferns while green parrots flew overhead. From there we drove way into the mountains to Lake Wanaka. Along its shore, grassy slopes rose thousands of feet to the rocky peaks of the Southern Alps. They were nearly as impressive as the mountains in Alaska, but a lot more accessible.

Fifty miles later the main road turned east as it wound out of the mountains towards Christchurch. Not wanting to leave the alpine pastures behind, we checked the map and found a road to Queenstown that stayed in the mountains. We enjoyed every mile of it, but the car didn't. At first the road was surfaced, then hard-packed dirt, but the last 40 miles were a one-lane washed-out track, which was another nice thing about driving a rental car, the original sport utility vehicle.

Queenstown was all that we'd heard it would be, scenic and unpretentious. The town lay against the mountains on the sunny north shore of Lake Wakatipu, and looked across miles of placid water to the aptly named Remarkable Mountains. It was such a pleasant place we decided to stay for a while before beginning the hike we had planned. Not too far from our favorite pub we found a house for rent by the week. To get there we had to walk through a park landscaped with botanical gardens and lawn bowling greens. And we had to remember to bring something for the ducks.

A week slipped by while Kathy and I took long rides around the lake, had picnics in the park, drank beer in the pub, and went over the plans for our hike in the Southern Alps. We decided to walk up the Rees River to the north end of the Forbes Mountain Range. There we'd cross a low pass to the headwaters of the Dart River and follow it to the beginning of Routeburn Track. That would take about six days, we figured.

The next part of the hike would be a trail that crossed the Humboldt Mountains to Milford Sound. It looked like the entire thing would be around 70 or 80 miles. At 10 miles a day, plus a few weather days, we figured a week and a half would be enough time for the trip. With two weeks to go before Kathy had to be in Colorado, the hike fit perfectly.

Our packs weighed close to 40 pounds apiece by the time we were ready to go, and that was without our tent or sleeping pads. The clerk at the mountaineering store that sold us our maps told us there were huts along the trails, and that they were maintained for hikers, complete with woodstoves and bunks with mattresses. He even showed us where they were on our map.

In the last week in November, the beginning of summer in the southern hemisphere, we caught a bus out of Queenstown to Glenorchy, an intersection in the road at the north end of Lake Wakatipu. After the bus pulled away, and the dust cleared, we looked around.

"What do you think about this?" I asked.

"The valley everyone's wanted to walk," Kathy confirmed.

Fluffy sheep grazed in lush pastures on both sides of the one-lane dirt road meandering up the valley towards our destination. Every so often one pulled its head from deep in the grass to check on us, but never stopped chewing. The few who weren't eating lay in the shade of large mushroom-shaped trees, ruminating. On the right side of the valley a waterfall dropped hundreds of feet into a small pool. On the left, Mount Earnslaw rose 8,000 feet. Its snowcapped peak the centerpiece of the Forbes Mountains.

We shouldered our packs and began walking. Every few miles there was a waterfall. Fed by snowmelt on the upper slopes, they cascaded off cliffs in long white plumes on both sides of the valley. After six or seven miles, the dirt road we were on came to an abrupt end. A large tributary of the Rees River, Invincible Creek, had washed out the bridge. All that was left was a few wooden piles fighting the torrent of spring runoff.

The creek was 50 feet across and looked fairly deep, but we had no choice. To our right was a cliff, and to the left was the wider and deeper Rees River. With shoes, clothes and packs held overhead, we waded into the creek. The water was frigid and the bottom rocky. The first thing I did was stub a toe, then another, each one hurting more than the last until they began to go numb.

The current was strong, pulling on our legs. As the water rose to my waist the fluctuating current made my footing even less stable. Turning sideways helped a lot, as did leaning into the flow, but before long we were moving our feet only inches at a time to keep our balance. We considered turning back, but decided that would necessitate getting broadside to the flow, which would increase our chances of being swept away. Besides, we were almost halfway across.

As we lay on the stony bank letting the sun warm our abused feet, Kathy pulled out the map to see if there were any more tributaries ahead of us like the one we'd barely made it across. Seeing there weren't, we continued towards the first hut on the map, agreeing we shouldn't try to get any farther that day.

Two hours later the trail crossed Arthur Creek and there was a nice hut just as the shop clerk had described, but it had a padlock on the door. There were three other little buildings, also locked up tight. With sheep parts piled here and there, it didn't take long to figure out that the buildings were temporary dwellings for shepherds, not huts for hikers to spend the night as the store clerk in Queenstown had stated. But it was only midafternoon, the sun was warm and we weren't worried. Besides, the map showed another hut just up the trail.

A couple miles later we could see the second hut depicted on our map. It appeared to be a small cabin perched on a knoll in the middle of the valley, a perfect place to spend the night.

"Hope this one's open," I mentioned as we got closer, feeling the weight of our packs and 12 miles of hiking.

"Well, it's unlocked anyway," Kathy pointed out when we were at the doorway.

The hut wasn't locked because it didn't have a door. There wasn't a floor either, and part of the roof was falling in. Most likely it was another sheepherders' hut, but abandoned. The only thing left behind was a rotting table and two bed frames with sections of chain-link fence stretched between the frame members for mattresses.

At that point I was glad we packed as heavily as we had. In our packs were steaks, fresh red potatoes, salad makings, and a bottle of Cabernet Sauvignon. We slugged down the wine, devoured the meal, and felt great until we could barely keep our eyes open a few minutes later. I groaned at the thought of our soft sleeping pads back in Queenstown but was too tired to care. Within minutes of lying down on the cruel ridges of bent wire, both of us were sound asleep.

The next morning, not far from where we'd spent the night, there was a fork in the trail. Most of the foot traffic went to the left, following a sign to Lennox Falls. Our trail led up a tight valley to the right and showed little sign of use.

Not long after lunch we lost what was left of the trail. We weren't worried, though. Our maps were good, plenty of detail. We'd find it again before too long. And we still had the Rees River to follow if we needed to. It wasn't much more than a stream at that point, but still big enough to follow.

Anyway, it wasn't the kind of place Kathy or I minded being lost. The day was pleasant, and the little forest we were in was enchanted. Ancient trees no more than 20 feet high formed an emerald canopy above our heads. Moss hung like mist from their twisted limbs. Breezes, fragrant and gentle, stirred the leaves overhead. Even the occasional bird's song was soft, adding to the tranquility we felt.

We took our time wandering through the forest. It wasn't far to the Shelter Rock, the next hut on our map. We weren't going any farther that day and had decided we'd break in if we had to. It was the last hut before the pass between the Rees and Dart Rivers. We really wanted a decent night's sleep before heading over the pass.

Unfortunately, we didn't have to break in. The hut was in even worse condition than the last one. Three walls of loose stones, the tallest not more than four feet high, surrounded a fire ring. The roof, corrugated tin held up with sticks, was big enough to cover two bed frames that had, once again, chain-link fence for mattresses. On either side of the hut, there was an active avalanche chute.

"You know, there might still be a few avalanches this time of year," Kathy mentioned as we crawled into our sleeping bags. The Rees River Valley was very tight at Shelter Rock.

"I'm not worried," I told her. "If the avalanches didn't stay in their chutes, there wouldn't be anything here."

Moments before I heard the sound of tons of rock and ice thundering towards us, the tin roof a few feet above our heads began to rattle. The ground was shaking. Kathy sat up and yelled, "Avalanche!" About the same time there was a low but powerful sound of rushing air. The metal roof shook violently and rose a few inches on the strong blast. Then everything, even thought, was lost in the roar of the maelstrom descending the slope above us.

When the avalanche came thundering down the mountain, I was certain we were going to die. But in the morning, upon inspection, we were surprised to find that it had stopped about 500 feet from where we slept.

Cold, tired, and sore, we began hiking toward the Rees Saddle, the pass we had to cross to get to the Dart River. With nothing else in sight we picked an animal trail and followed it along the side of the mountain. As we began to climb, hip-high plants resembling miniature yuccas sprung up along the trial. Now and then we came too close to their spines and were rewarded with an aching stab. As we progressed up the mountainside the trail narrowed. Before long we were cursing, having been stabbed numerous times. Finally the trail disappeared altogether. In full retreat, we had to endure getting stabbed all the way back to Shelter Rock.

"It's was like a trap," Kathy said, rinsing blood off her legs in the stream.

We ate an early lunch, took a swim, and stretched out on a large flat rock to soak up its warmth. On our second attempt at the pass we followed the streambed then turned straight uphill. It was a lot steeper than the side-hill approach of our first try, but it was more direct. Several hundred feet up the slope we stepped out onto a snowfield that took us all the way to the top of the ridge.

The pass, surrounded by majestic peaks under a brilliant blue sky, felt like the top of the world. Once again we were in great spirits as we began our descent into the Dart River drainage. However, not far from the pass the map showed the trail going to the left, along an incredibly steep slope on the side of Mount Cunningham for at least two miles, but there was no sign of a trail.

Between huts and trails that weren't there, we had to wonder about other things on the map, like the little footbridge we had to cross after the long side-hill hike ahead of us. If we got to the bridge and it wasn't there we were going to have trouble crossing the Dart. From what we could see, the river was a deep canyon at that point.

With the sun on its way to the horizon and no place to go back to, we kept going. Not more than five minutes later Kathy slipped on a rock ledge and put several nasty gashes in the side of her thigh. The wounds weren't deep but bled quite a bit. After that things slowly got worse.

The slope we had to cross was covered with a long-bladed grass that had been flattened and left wet and slippery by the recently melted snowpack. As we progressed, the angle of the slope got even steeper, and we began to worry about being able to stop ourselves if we slipped. Not far away was the gorge cut by the Dart. If we couldn't stop, that's where we would go, plunging off the cliff into the snowmelt-swollen river.

Hands raw from grasping blades of grass, toes cramping in their effort to keep traction, we kept going, painfully aware of the situation we had worked ourselves into. And that there was not a lot of hope of returning the way we had come, even if we had to. Fortunately, the bridge across the Dart River was where the map showed it, and we couldn't have been much happier. The sun had set, it was almost dark, and there was no place to sit, much less sleep, anywhere on the Mount Cunningham side of the river; whereas, on the other side of the bridge the ground was flat.

We debated crawling in our sleeping bags right where we were, but there was an obvious trail at that point, good enough to follow by flashlight if we had to, and the map showed a hut only a mile or two away. Just as the trail began to blend into the night we found it, open, with a fireplace, stove, and bunk beds that had beautiful thick mattresses. It was so comfortable we spent the entire next day there, mostly asleep.

The rest of the hike and our last week in New Zealand went well. However, during takeoff on our flight home we lost an engine. As the nose of the airplane came off the runway we heard a distinct change in the tone of the engines. Then the nose came back down with a thud. The plane swerved from side to side as the pilot slammed on the brakes to avoid going off the end of the runway, but it was over so quickly we didn't really have time to worry.

From Los Angeles Kathy went on to Colorado for Christmas with her family, and I went back to Alaska. When my plane touched down in Fairbanks it was pitch black outside. The stewardess said it was 36 below zero. As I walked from the plane to the terminal the snow was so cold it squealed shrilly underfoot. My skin bristled against the bitter cold that cut through my thin jacket, and I cursed.

12

THE LIFELESS HEART OF WINTER

When I climbed into Spot the next morning the seat was frozen solid. The engine block heater and battery blanket were plugged in so the truck started easily enough, but I could hear the valves clicking away without the benefit of lubrication. It was 28 below. For the first mile I had to go slowly because there was a pronounced dip every time the wheels rotated. The tires had frozen solid, leaving a flat spot where they'd been in contact with the ground.

By the time I got back to the hangar it was eleven o'clock in the morning. Sixty miles south the sun was just coming up over the Alaska Range. When I got out of the truck and stopped to look at the pale orb low in the southern sky, I realized that the sun wasn't giving off heat. I turned my back to it, then faced the sun again, and my skin could not detect any discernible change in temperature. It was weird, and a little disconcerting, like being a zombie.

After summer in New Zealand, winter in Fairbanks was depressing. Not only was it bone-numbing cold, there was nothing to do. I was the only person living at the hangar. Within days, I was sleeping 12 hours at a time. When the conditions were right, boredom and lack of sunlight, the body goes to sleep, or at least mine does.

Although sleeping all night and day seemed like a viable option, I had things to do. The hangar had been my home for several years. It had been perfect, a place full of friends and good times. However, Kathy and I enjoyed our time together, especially peaceful nights, and we were getting tired of communal living. In several months the seasonal pilots and mechanics would be coming back. They'd need the space in the hangar and we'd need some privacy, so before we left on our bike trip I'd begun looking at houses.

Other than the fact that I hadn't told Kathy what I was doing, because I wanted it to be a surprise, looking for a house was something I would normally be doing around that time. Wherever I moved, I paid attention to the real estate market. It's the only type of shopping I really enjoy. When I felt comfortably knowledgeable in the local market, and if I planned to stay in the area for a few more years, I would buy a house or apartment. It makes sense. Why pay rent when you can be paying down a mortgage on an appreciating piece of property? You can also make improvements that don't cost a lot but will raise the resale price.

My brother, Peter, and I bought a house in Denver while we were going to college at the same time. He was getting his master's degree in nuclear engineering while I was struggling to get any undergraduate degree. We paid 14,000 dollars for a three-bedroom house two blocks from school. After we each came up with 1,500 dollars for the down payment, our monthly payments were less than our friends were paying for a one-bedroom apartment. Each time I sold a house I kept enough for the down payment on the next one.

It didn't take long to find what I was looking for. Just across the runway, in a small, relatively nice subdivision between the airport and the Chena River, was an inexpensive house for sale. It was only 390 square feet and cost about the same amount as a new 4x4 pickup truck. By the time I got back from New Zealand the paperwork was done and, after a quick closing, the house was mine. Ten days later Kathy was coming back from Colorado.

The little place was cute but cold. They'd used sawdust as insulation that, over 40 or 50 years, had settled to the bottom foot or two of the walls. But once I put in a woodstove, it was hard to keep the house from being uncomfortably hot. Just to make sure we weren't cold, though, I also bought a king–sized heated waterbed. The only drawback to the bed was it took up so much of the bedroom, the door to the bathroom couldn't be opened. So I got rid of the door. By the time Kathy got back from Colorado the house was livable, and she loved it.

Although the house was comfortable, it was undeniably small. Not long after I got out of bed in the morning, typically a few hours after Kathy had gone to school, I'd end up going to the hangar to see what Craig was doing. He came to work around 10 and we'd bullshit while he took care of paperwork. Around noon we'd go to lunch. After a few hours of lunch, we'd go back to the hangar and watch a video or play foosball.

I wouldn't have been able to make it through the part of the day Kathy was at school if not for Craig. In the middle of the winter your world shrinks. As the cold and darkness close in, cutting you off from the rest of life, your existence is the building you are in, then the room. Conversation becomes one of the few live stimulants left for the mind. That's where a friend like Craig is invaluable. We could talk about anything and everything, and his perspective was invariably unique and entertaining. While returning a rented chainsaw one afternoon, we drove past the store three times because we were so engrossed in our conversation.

Around five I'd go home and wait for Kathy to get back from school. Most of the time she'd cook dinner; however, in the depth of winter we went out more often. Because we were going to the restaurants for stimulation as much as the food, our favorite place was Tiki Cove. It was downtown in the Polaris Hotel, which was, at 11 stories, the tallest building in town.

Although the elevator always smelled a little of urine, and the food was below average, we kept going back.

"It's the view," I maintained, as the reason for our patronage.

"Nope," Kathy insisted. "It's the chairs."

In the northwest corner of the bar there was a table with two large wicker chairs facing the window. Their tall backs screened us from the rest of the restaurant and, in effect, reality. Looking out the window we couldn't see that much, a short stretch of the Chena River meandering off into the night, but it was enough to create the illusion that there was a world out there. So we'd drink Mai Tai's with pretty little umbrellas in them and talk about places thousands of miles away.

Another spot we frequented, especially if we were out late, was the Sunset Strip. It had a good bar and they served dinner all night. Their steak-n-eggs plate, complete with home fries or grits, toast and a sprig of parsley, was my favorite.

As the winter wore on, our sedentary lifestyle began to take its toll. We were putting on weight, 10 pounds in two months for me. We were also tired all the time, lethargic in body and mind, and getting more and more unhappy about it.

"Let's go skiing," Kathy suggested on one of her days off near the end of February.

We had cross-country skis but hadn't used them because it was so cold. But on that day it was sunny and almost zero, the warmest day in quite a while. Encouraged by the relatively warm weather, we clipped into our skis and headed out behind the hangar. By the time we were past the frozen beaver pond we were stripping off layer after layer of winter clothes to keep from sweating.

"What a good idea this was," I complimented Kathy.

The sun was low on the horizon. Its rays lit just the tops of the birch trees around us. Their limbs were encased in a thin coat of frost that sparkled like leaded glass. Being in the woods was such a pleasant change, and the feel of my skis gliding over the snow was mesmerizing.

We had a great time and vowed to go skiing whenever we got the chance; however, the temperature took a dive again. After a few days of sitting around we decided to give it a try even though it was 10 below. A few days later we went out when it was almost 20 below.

At that temperature, when we exerted ourselves, the frigid air seared our throats. Quite quickly we discovered that, by using our scarves to make a baffle several inches from our mouths, we could effectively preheat the air enough to make breathing comfortable. The only problem was that the moisture in our breath accumulated in the wool as ice, which burned our cheeks. Nevertheless, we gladly put up with it. Going out at colder temperatures allowed us to ski whenever we could, including at night.

One full moon night it was near 30 below zero and we stayed out for hours, entranced by the world around us. At that temperature the trillions of tiny crystals that made up the snow on the ground were frozen to perfection. They caught the cold light of the moon and turned it into brilliant pinpoints of red, yellow, blue, even an emerald green. Sixty miles away the sheer rock faces of Mount Deborah, Hess and Hayes, stood out in perfect relief, more clearly than any summer day.

That was one of the last cold snaps we had. It was March. Every day was noticeably longer and the temperature was climbing. With the change in weather I got to fly again for the first time in months. Two electricians had to get out and repair a radio repeater. As the starter whined and the turbine engine spooled up, I felt myself change, wake up, and pay attention in a way I hadn't in recent memory. Minutes later we were climbing into the early morning sky above Fairbanks. Sunlight poured into the cockpit and the world opened up in front of us bright and beautiful. What a way to start the day, I thought to myself.

We flew to Fort Yukon, refueled, then took off northwest to Big Rock Mountain. On its snow-covered summit we found the repeater. Far below us the Chandalar River wound its way through the mountains in a series of smooth bends and frozen rapids. While they went to work I relaxed. Alice's cockpit, like a greenhouse in the sun, was close to 60 degrees. Warm and content, I soon fell asleep.

A couple of hours later one of the electricians opened a back door to get something from his toolbox. The blast of cold air he let in was a rude awakening from a pleasant nap. The temperature had dropped more than 20 degrees, near zero. More disconcerting, the sun was almost on the horizon, a dull glow in an overcast sky.

"Ready to go?" I asked the guy rummaging around in the back.

"Couple more minutes," he replied as he trudged off through the snow.

By the time they'd finished, the sun was setting and it was below zero. I was angry as I flipped on the battery switch and engaged the starter. Twice I'd gone out to tell them we had to leave, that we wouldn't have enough light to get back to Fairbanks. But they knew I wouldn't leave them there and ignored me.

When the turbine speed peaked at 13 percent, I cracked the throttle. Nothing happened. I could hear the igniter clicking away behind me in the engine compartment, so that wasn't the problem. I opened the throttle further, dumping more fuel into the engine, but still no "whoosh" from the exhaust cones as it ignited.

Knowing there would soon be a dangerous amount of fuel in the engine, I rolled the throttle closed. The first thing to check was the fuel boosts. I pulled the circuit breakers, resetting them one at a time. They both showed a rise on the fuel pressure gauge, so I knew the boosts were working.

I tried to start the engine again but the same thing happened. No ignition. I was down to one, possibly two attempts before the battery would be dead. At that point my outlook on life changed. I was no longer upset with my passengers. I was worried. It might drop to 40 below on the barren top of that mountain at night. There was survival gear, including sleeping bags, in the baggage compartment, but it would be a miserable 10 or 12 hours before anyone came looking for us.

The igniter in the engine seemed to be working, and there was the distinct smell of jet fuel coming from the exhaust cones, so there was fuel flow. The only thing that I could think of that would keep Alice from starting was the fuel itself. Even though I had refueled in Fort Yukon, most of it was four or five months old. There could easily be moisture in fuel that had been sitting around that long. At five below zero, and dropping, it might be enough to inhibit ignition.

I got out of the helicopter and drained the fuel sumps, looking for contamination. There wasn't any, no ice or dirt, but the fuel had been stirred up and a critical amount of moisture

209

could be in suspension. Regardless, the only thing left to do was give it another try. When I pushed the starter button for the third time, the voltmeter dropped from 24 to 13 volts.

This is my last try, I said to myself, and to the helicopter, "Come on, girl. This isn't funny."

The turbine barely made it to 10 percent before the battery peaked, well below the lower limit for starting, but that was all it was going to do, so I opened the throttle. Immediately the fuel ignited, resonating in the exhaust cones and releasing my fears.

I would have sat back and relaxed at that point, but the exhaust temperature was on its way to the red line. The turbine wasn't turning fast enough to exhaust the burning gases and the temperature was heading towards 900 degrees. Immediately reducing the fuel flow solved the heat problem, but the throttle was extremely sensitive. Shutting the engine down completely was a genuine concern.

There were a few nerve-racking minutes, but they were well behind me as we lifted off and dropped into the Chandalar Valley. Unfortunately, our problems weren't over. We still had to get back to Fairbanks. By the time we were on our way up Beaver Creek on the north side of the White Mountains the light was almost gone. If not for the trees along the river, I wouldn't have known where the ground was. Everything else was covered with snow.

Fortunately, I knew the area well from the job with Mapco. As we passed a valley where one of the drills had been, I glanced up it to confirm our position and saw something I'd never seen before. Right before my eyes the drainage became a mountain.

I actually flinched. It was that surprising. The slopes on either side of the valley, no more than half of a mile long and not very wide, had reversed their angle. In the blink of an eye the valley had become a ridge. It was so bizarre I did a circle to try to recreate the optical illusion, but couldn't. It had to be some sort of whiteout effect, I figured. The conditions were right, complete snow cover, overcast skies and low light. The weather in Alaska never ceased to amaze me. It was like no place I'd ever flown.

The day after I got back from repairing that radio repeater, where we might have frozen to death if the helicopter hadn't started, we got a taste of spring. The temperature shot up to 52 by noon. While Kathy and I were skiing around the airport, we heard a new birdsong. Life was returning to Fairbanks. For the first time in months, I was glad to be there. Then Craig called me into his office.

"Got a job with Fish and Game on Kodiak for you," he told me.

Kodiak is a large island in the Pacific Ocean south of Homer. I'd never been there but had heard it was beautiful, rugged and wild. The island was also hundreds of miles to the south, where it had to be warmer. Also, it sounded like interesting work.

The job was to fly support for the state's Department of Fish and Game in their annual salmon pre-emersion count. We would be going all over the island.

"You're gonna be down there almost a month," he added.

The idea of leaving Kathy for that long bothered me, but Rusty was the only other pilot. He couldn't leave for that long because he had the last race of the dogsled season coming up in a few weeks.

"Well, it would be pretty rude of you to hang around on the payroll all winter and then not take a job when it comes up," Kathy pointed out when I told her about my reluctance to go to Kodiak.

"They're putting me up in a hotel," I added lamely. "Think you can take some time off? Come down with me for a while. I think Alaska Airline flies in there."

She couldn't. Kathy was actually going to be in Anchorage at the time for a briefing on what FSL was going to be doing for their summer field season.

On the third of March, Alice and I left for Kodiak. On the way we stopped in Anchorage, where Kathy had been for the last few days.

I found her in Ken's office going over some aerial photography. Later, as we walked down the hall I felt compelled to comment on the inspirational poster taped to the wall above Ken's desk. Generally, their colorful scenes and corny messages didn't do a lot for me. But the poster on Ken's wall was oddly appropriate, considering that Kathy and I were going to be apart for a month.

It showed a bird, a sparrow or something, taking flight from a hand. In the background was a gilded birdcage with the door ajar. The verse on the poster read:

> *If you love something, set it free*
> *If it comes back to you, it's yours forever*
> *If not, it never was*

"You know that poster on Ken's wall?" I asked Kathy.

"The one with the bird?"

"Yeah," I said. "I think I'd write it a little different. Like… if you love something, put it in a cage. If it beats itself to death on the bars, so what. It would've left anyhow."

She laughed.

KODIAK

The skies were clear when Alice and I left Anchorage the next morning. Within minutes we were over the broad mudflats of Turnagain Arm. There were several stories of people sinking into the silty glacial runoff and being drown by the incoming tide. After a half-hour flight down the scenic Kenai Peninsula, past Homer, we flew straight out into the Pacific Ocean. To the right a plume of smoke rose from Augustine, a perfectly symmetrical volcano on the far side of Cook Inlet rising 4,000 feet out of the water. Minutes later I couldn't see land in any direction.

The wind had been from the northwest, but gradually shifted 180 degrees and increased in strength. The quartering headwind would certainly slow me down and increase my fuel consumption. There really wasn't anything to worry about. Even at the reduced forward speed, I had plenty of fuel, but the wind was also pushing the sea into large swells.

For this contract Alice was equipped with fixed floats, large rubber pontoons attached to the landing gear above the skids, so I could land in the ocean if I had to. However, it was difficult to feel entirely comfortable. There was a good chance the helicopter would roll over in the large swells. In the 40-degree water, my life expectancy would drop to a couple of minutes.

By the time I got to the Barren Islands, about halfway to Kodiak, the wind was blowing over 35 mph. Plumes of spray trailed off the crests of breaking waves. As I flew over the little islands the water below me went wild. Giant, breaking waves were coming in from every direction, smashing into each other in explosive collisions, which didn't make sense. Waves don't change course in the middle of the ocean. Finally

I realized it must be the islands. They rose more than a thousand feet from the ocean floor. Like boulders in a river, they were interrupting, it seemed, an extremely strong flow of water.

When Afognack, the large island north of Kodiak, appeared on the horizon it was a welcome sight. As I crossed the shore and flew down a wide valley that bisected the island, I was relieved to be back over land, but stunned by what I saw below me. So much for the wild and unspoiled, I said to myself. The entire valley, a mile wide and at least 10 long, had been clear cut. Slash and debris covered the ground. The streams were choked with it. Massive erosion was at work on the sides of the valley, cutting deep gullies in the steeper slopes. Unbelievably, there was no sign of reforestation. It was one of the worst jobs of logging I'd seen.

Crossing the channel between Afognack and Kodiak, I flew over a rusty freighter heading out to sea. Newly felled trees were chained to her decks, stacked nearly as high as the bridge. Behind the smokestack the rising sun of Japan's flag flapped in the wind. The wood was probably on its way across the Pacific Ocean to be made into plywood. From there it would just as likely be shipped back to us for sale. Minutes later, crossing the north shore of Kodiak Island, I had to laugh. The rugged coast was lined with concrete bunkers built during the last World War to protect the island from a Japanese invasion.

When I landed at the airport I checked the outside air temperature gauge. It was almost 50 degrees, 30 degrees warmer than Fairbanks. The light wind blowing across the runway smelled of sweet grass. Across the bay the small town of Kodiak sat on the sunny side of a long harbor where small rocky islands protected it from the open ocean. Tall, treeless mountains, the kind I loved to fly in, rose up behind the town and followed the coastline to the south.

It was perfect, but I already missed Kathy and called her after checking into my hotel, and every day after that. She missed me too, but admitted she was getting a lot of work done with me out of town. After we hung up, I went for a walk, heading towards the harbor where the tall outriggers of the long-line boats swayed back and forth in the evening sky.

Every type of boat that worked the waters of Alaska was tied up in the marina, from the big, steel-hulled crab boats to the gillnetters small enough to fit on a crabber's deck. Each boat was different, had its own character, but they all had one thing in common. They were working boats. Their solid hulls were dented and scraped, paint-chipped and rust-streaked, their rigging patched and worn. The smell of fish guts was second only to diesel fuel. They were beautiful, hard-working machines.

My favorites were the older wooden boats. As I walked by, I read their names: the Alaskan Star, Northern Queen, Carolyn Mae. The wear and tear on their old hulls was distinction, not damage, and their age something to be proud of, proof they had survived life in some of the worst water in the world.

The fishing vessels creaked and swayed against their moorings, taking a well-deserved break from life at sea. A good day for these boats was plowing along in three or four foot swells, dragging miles of lines or tons of nets. A bad day was fighting winds blowing 50 knots while struggling through seas 40 feet high. Even worse than the wind and sea is ice. Wind-blown seawater freezes and coats everything when it's cold enough. Covered in ice, the boats don't respond well in the heavy seas. Eventually they get so top-heavy they turn turtle. Roll upside down.

Loving the rugged coast of Alaska as much as I did, it was impossible not to think about owning my own boat, something around 30 or 40 feet in length, small enough for one person to handle if they had to, but big enough to be comfortable. There was a lot of money to be made fishing. In a good season, sometimes in just a few days, a boat could bring in hundreds of thousands of dollars. But when it came down to it, that's all I did, look at boats and daydream. Fishing commercially is a cold, hard, dangerous way to make a living.

As the sky darkened I left the docks and walked into town. Along the hillside above the harbor were the old houses of the early Russian fur traders, intricately worked wooden homes built more than a century ago. The rest of the old town was flattened in 1964 when a 9.2 magnitude earthquake sent an enormous wave rolling into the harbor. Fifty people were killed and most of the fishing fleet lost. Only the homes built on the hillside or farther inland survived the tsunami.

It was a quaint little fishing village before the earthquake. But when they rebuilt, practically everything was made out of concrete. It was understandable. Cement is inexpensive and much stronger than wood. But it looked terrible.

The contract with Alaska State Fish and Game began the next morning at the airport. My passengers were nice enough, three young men who were looking forward to the work ahead of them. The annual emersion count was designed to give commercial fishermen an idea of how many salmon would be returning to Kodiak's waters in the years ahead.

Every fall salmon spawn in streambeds all around the island. In the spring their fry head out to sea for three years before returning to lay their own eggs. By sampling spawning streams, Fish and Game can estimate how many salmon should be returning in the years to come. It was important work and the guys were glad to be outside after a long winter doing paperwork in the office.

After introductions and a safety briefing, the senior guy, Larry, took out his map and showed me the streams he wanted to visit that day. After clearing the airport traffic area, we headed south along the coast, looking for a pass through the mountains to Saltery Cove, the first stream we wanted to sample.

Fir trees, stunted by the harsh environment of wind and salt, looked like sculpted bonsais among the rock outcrops of the rugged shoreline. Above them the grassy slopes of the mountains rose quickly, golden in the morning sun. At the end of Middle Bay we picked up the American River and followed it into the mountains. Five minutes later we were nearing the pass at its headwaters. There was a strong wind coming down the valley, so I knew it was going to be bumpy. If there's one place turbulence is predictable, it's the downwind side of a mountain pass.

Even though I knew it was coming, with the first jolt of rough air, my grip on the controls tightened. The grass and shrubs were flattened on the right slope of the pass. The air was really moving over there, but it looked like it was steady, so I pulled in some power and moved over to that side of the valley. A few healthy bumps later we were up against the mountain and the air was relatively smooth.

On the other side of the pass I lowered the collective to begin our descent into Saltery Cove. We should have been going down as much as 500 feet a minute; however, we were going up, riding a very smooth, fast-moving updraft. I could have pulled away from the slope and left the updraft behind, but it felt too good. I really missed flying in the mountains.

Near the top of the ridge I'd all but forgotten about my passengers and what we were there to do. Pulling back on the cyclic I put the helicopter in a nose-high attitude, then rolled it to the left. With the strong updraft underneath us, and zero airspeed, we came to a high hover facing away from the mountain. I held Alice there for a second, then nosed her over 40 degrees and plunged down the side of the mountain.

With a big grin on my face I looked over at Larry, expecting him to be enjoying it too, but he was holding onto the frame of his seat, staring straight ahead with his eyes wide open. Goddamn it, I thought. This is the first time they've flown with me. They probably think I'm crazy, or even worse, showing off. I brought Alice's nose back up to straight and level flight.

"Hey, I'm sorry, you guys," I said over the intercom. "It's just that for the last four months I've been trapped up in Fairbanks with no decent flying like this." I looked at the guy in the copilot seat. "You understand? Right?"

"Nope," he said as flat and cold as he could.

I felt bad. Most people don't feel what the pilot does in that sort of a maneuver, the smooth interface between machine and air. How could they, without having the controls in their hands? In fact, I didn't think anyone did, until I was flying some geologists around Medfra, a small community on the banks of the Kuskokwim River in central Alaska.

Alice and I was there on a show-and-tell, flying both state and federal geologists around some low grass-covered ridges that were once sand dunes, stopping frequently to examine their formation. Because the ridges were treeless and close together, I never got more than 50 feet above the ground as we went from one spot to the next.

Like most sand dunes, one side of the ridge was short and steep while the other was long and gentle. We were flying from the southwest to the northeast, so the approaches were up the steep slope with landings at the apex of the ridge. The wind was also from the southeast at 10 to 20 mph, giving us a gentle updraft. I'd ride up the steep slope, helped along by the tailwind, then make a 180-degree turn and land into the wind.

By the third or fourth landing I had it down. I'd hold a constant speed and altitude as we rode the updraft to the top of the ridge. As we crested, and the updraft dropped off, I gently pushed the nose down while rolling the rotor blades slowly to the left into a wide, perfectly trimmed turn. Halfway through the turn I slowly opened it up, rolling the rotor blades level and bringing the nose up to settle into a seamless landing.

I shot the approaches at a mean altitude of 20 feet, using minimal control movements and only one power change. It was so coordinated, in concert with air and terrain. I doubted I would ever feel more like a bird. Later that day I found out one of my passengers had gotten the same feeling.

Bill's attractive field assistant and I were sitting on a bank above the Kuskokwim River drinking beer. Bill was a nice old guy and the senior geologist on the trip. He was also a pioneer in Alaska's geological community, including being one of the first guys to go out looking for minerals in a helicopter.

"Bill says you're a natural pilot," Lisa said during a lull

in whatever we'd been talking about.

"What?" My mind had been on something else.

"He says you fly by feel and instinct more than anyone he's been in the air with."

Bill must have been referring to my landing on the ridges earlier in the day, which meant he felt the wind work with the helicopter. Seeing that his compliment was the nicest I'd ever had, I didn't bother to tell her that it was the wind on the dunes and Alice, not me. I just put the controls in the right place.

After apologizing again to my new passengers for scaring them, I made a beeline for Saltery Cove. A few minutes later Larry, the guy in the copilot seat, pointed to a good-sized stream flowing into the head of the bay and asked, "Can you land in those little rapids above the wide turn to the left?"

"No problem," I told him.

I made my approach upstream and came to a hover between some tall trees. The water was clear, running quickly over a gravel bottom, but only a few inches deep. When I put Alice down, we drifted a few feet before the pontoons grounded solidly enough to hold us in place.

When the blades stopped turning, my passengers put on their waders and stepped into the water. One of them cranked up the gas-driven air pump they'd strapped to the cargo rack. Then he stuck the tip of a hose into the streambed, forcing air into the gravel. Soon salmon fry were floating to the surface. The other two guys were downstream a few yards with large nets, catching the fry and doing a quick count before putting them back in the stream.

While they worked, I waded to the bank and went for a walk in an ancient grove of cottonwoods. The open-canopied trees formed a small forest along the west side of the stream, the kind of place that would be perfect for a picnic on a nice summer day. About 20 feet inside the tree line, I stumbled and almost fell when I stepped into a depression. It was a rut, worn deep in the soft soil. Then I saw that there were two of them, parallel tracks about two feet apart. About the time it dawned on me that I was looking at a brown bear trail, a strong musky smell filled my nostrils.

A well-worn trail with the smell of recent use was enough to make me wish I wasn't there, but the sound of something in the grass behind me almost stopped my heart. I whipped around so fast I nearly fell over again. Still in its winter coat, a black tip on the tail of its pure white body, a startled little weasel disappeared into some taller grass.

From then on my 12-gauge shotgun accompanied me on my walks. The average size of a male Kodiak brown bear is eight feet standing upright. A large one can be five feet at the shoulder when it's on all fours, which is a terrifying thought.

The next day on the job was just as nice. We followed the coast farther south into a picturesque bay and landed in a stream in the middle of a large field of tall dry grass waving gently in an onshore breeze. In the sun it was almost 60 degrees, and that morning I saw a red and silver fox, the first I'd ever seen. At our next stop I found a beaver slide, a well-worn chute down the side of the muddy bank on the stream we were sampling. I back tracked it to a thicket where the beavers had been harvesting willow.

For a week we had one sunny day after another, then it started to rain, and the wind began to blow. The morning it began I was the only one to show up at the helicopter. When I called Larry at his office, he was surprised I'd gone to the airport. He told me the weather that was moving in was so bad even the fishermen were staying home. In Kodiak they dealt with storms the way we handled the cold in Fairbanks. They stayed out of it if they could.

"I'll give you a call at the hotel when it looks like it's good enough to fly," he said. "Could be a couple of days."

I went back to the hotel, watched television, called Kathy, read, and occasionally looked out the window. Everything was gray, the clouds tearing across the sky, the heaving swells in the ocean, the concrete town, it was almost overpowering. By the third day I was bored stiff. Even going out to the bars wasn't much fun. Invariably I'd end up talking about Kathy and how much I missed her.

On the afternoon of the fourth and worst day of the storm I went for a walk, just to break the monotony, and ended up at the marina. The wind was howling through the rigging of the fishing fleet. Halyards and running gear slapped against metal and wood as the boats heaved and tugged against their moorings. Leaning into the force of the wind, tasting salt in the rain that stung my face, I made my way to the end of the pier. Being out in the elements felt good, but it was cold. As I turned to leave, I heard the whine of a turbine engine across the water.

As the familiar sound rose and fell on the wind, I searched the surging sea until I caught a glimpse of the bright orange markings of a Coast Guard helicopter. The big Sikorsky was right down on the dark water, fading in and out of the torrential downpour as it beat its way out to open ocean. It never ceased to amaze me, the conditions they flew in. When it came to bravery in the cockpit, in my esteem, the Coast Guard pilots were second only to the medevac pilots in Vietnam. As they faded into the storm I wished them well.

The weather improved the following day. In fact, it got unseasonably warm as we worked our way south, counting fry and enjoying the beauty of Kodiak. Towards the end of the island, we stopped in to see Ron and Don, two big game guides who spent the summer in an abandoned cannery on Otter Bay. Larry had known them for years and always stopped by to get the local news. On the way back to town I mentioned that the two men looked pretty old to be big game guides.

"Yeah," Larry agreed. "These days they're just two horny old men trying to have a good time."

"What?" I exclaimed.

Seeing my shock, he laughed. "They spend more time stalking the young guys they hire than any big game."

Evidently the old farts, both in their 80s, ran ads in hunting magazines looking for "healthy, young men to work as guides' assistants." As bad as it sounded, Larry said they were harmless, more voyeurs than molesters.

Other than Ron and Don there weren't a lot of people

living on the south end of Kodiak. It was windblown, desolate and relatively flat. Unlike the rest of the island, though, there were some great beaches. On a walk one sunny afternoon I stopped to watch a flock of seagulls work over a seal carcass in the sand. The large rock I'd made myself comfortable on was warm, so I lay back to absorb its heat. Through half-closed eyes, on the verge of dozing off, I noticed something moving to my right, coming towards me. It was furry and brown.

My eyes popped open and in one smooth motion I turned, rose on my right knee, brought my shotgun up and barked, "WOOF, WOOF." Twenty feet away from me a little brown fox disappeared in one bound. Kneeling there, trembling slightly, the gun halfway to my shoulder, no round in the chamber and the safety still on, I had to ask myself, "'Woof? Where the hell did that come from?" But I knew the answer. Any dog will tell you that it's an expression of fear in the guise of a warning.

After we finished the salmon pre-emersion count on Kodiak, we went to work on Afognack, the island I'd flown over on my way down from Anchorage three weeks earlier. The clear-cuts looked worse on the ground than they had from the air. It was a wasteland, nothing but weeds grew amid the carnage left by the loggers. Animal trails were abandoned in the woody debris, and uncontrolled runoff had left the streams silted and lifeless.

When we moved to a part of the island that hadn't been logged, the reality of the destruction was even more painful. We could see what had been taken, an old growth forest of ancient Sitka spruce. In 1912 the Katmai eruption, largest in the 20th century, deposited ash along the long horizontal limbs of the giant trees. Over time, sphagnum moss took root in the volcanic soil and hung in long gray veils. As I sat in the sunlight on a pillow of moss, in a sanctuary of immense beauty, there was no outlet for the sadness I felt, knowing that in a matter of months the long life of the trees around me would be over too.

The last part of the job for Fish and Game involved a

half-hour flight across Shelikof Strait to the rugged shores of the Alaska Peninsula and Mount Katmai. The wind was howling and an outgoing tide was running headlong into the large swells rolling in from the pacific. The collisions stood the water up in colossal waves while the wind tore their tops off, sending large sheets of seawater flying. I knew there was no way we could go down in that water and live.

Alice seemed to sense my discomfort. As I gazed out the side window at the malevolent seas below, out of the corner of my eye I thought I saw a red flash.

"Did you see that?" I asked Larry.

It would have been one of the master caution lights on the instrument console. Red usually meant "Land Immediately." But I had no idea which one of the lights had flashed.

"See what?" he asked.

I didn't answer because I was staring at the engine oil temperature gauge. I thought I saw it go up a good needle's width. Once again I couldn't be sure. You're screwin' with me, aren't you, I said to the helicopter.

It was a syndrome, inexplicable things happening in the cockpit at inopportune times that ended up being nothing at all. It happened to Craig now and then too. Even though I was relatively certain nothing was going on, I climbed up to 1,500 feet, which would give me more time for an emergency call if something did go wrong.

Our first stop was the mouth of a large river near the deserted town of Kanatak, one of the few settlements on the isolated peninsula. The town looked like a Western movie set. A dozen flat-roofed, two-story clapboard houses sat facing each other on a wide dirt street. Everything was weathered a timeless gray. The inhabitants hadn't taken much with them when they'd left. An old pickup in the street, tattered curtains in the windows; there were even plates in the cupboards.

It was good exploring, but towards the south end of town I began to feel uneasy, like someone was watching me. On my way to a log cabin off the main street, I got so nervous I turned around and went back to the helicopter. That evening, when I mentioned the creepy feeling to Larry, he told me about "Killer" Bill, a notorious trapper who still lived in the area. Story was he'd killed several of his partners in cold blood. Even bragged about it, but never said enough to get himself convicted.

For three days it never stopped blowing 30. So, as wild and beautiful as it was, I didn't mind when it came time to leave Katmai. We got back to Kodiak before noon, and I was in Fairbanks for dinner. That evening I told Kathy about a concern of mine.

"A couple times I almost forgot what you looked like," I told her.

She laughed. "I know what you mean. It takes more like two months for me, but it definitely happens."

"And that's not good," I added. "I mean, you forget what someone looks like. You forget about a lot of other things."

"Is there something you want to tell me?" she asked, only half-joking.

"Yeah, I love you. And I think we should have a one-month rule. No splitting up for more than a month because it's not good for a relationship."

Kathy stopped and looked at me in a way I'd grown not to like. "I guess this is as good a time as any," she began hesitantly. "About that rule. I've got some good news and bad news."

Preferring to temper the bad news with the good, I asked, "What's the bad news?"

"I don't think you're going to like this part at all," she said. "The university got funding for a research project on deer habitat this summer." She paused, really not happy. "I'm going to be on Hinchinbrook Island for two months. In Prince William Sound, it's…"

"You're not going to be working for FSL this year?"

"No," she told me. "They're having to really cut back the field season this year. The crew will be working out of field camps along the road. I'm not sure they're even going to be using a helicopter more than a couple of days."

"So you're going to Hinchinbrook by yourself?"

"Chris is coming with me."

Kathy had actually told me about this part of her Master's program, the independent study part. I knew she had to do it. And my going to Kodiak a few months earlier hadn't been much different, just not quite as long. Anyway, she wouldn't be leaving until June, which was still a long way off. Regardless, I felt like someone was taking something from me.

"This sucks," I said, dejected. Then I got an idea. "Know what?"

"What?" Kathy replied.

"I'll come see you."

"Sounds good to me," she laughed.

By the middle of April the sun was up more than 12 hours a day. Spring was in the air. Where winter drew the life out of me, summer brought it back. One night, on our way back to Fairbanks from the Howling Dog, I felt like cutting loose. It was the first time we'd been out of town since the snow had left the roads, and I was trying to get Spot over a hundred, just to see if he could still do it. We got close, a little over 90, but there were so many cracks and heaves in the asphalt from the recent thaw, that was about all I could get Spot to do.

The next morning I took Kathy to school because I wanted to use the truck. As we rounded a long right-hand turn into the school parking lot, Spot began to wobble. Before I could come to a stop, the left front wheel fell off.

"Goddamn," I said, looking at Kathy. "Can you believe that didn't happen last night? It's only been a mile or two."

"Thanks, Spot," she said, reaching forward and patting the truck's dashboard.

In what was becoming a tradition, just as the weather in Fairbanks began to get nice, Craig called me into his office.

"You're gonna love this," he told me, and I knew that I would be going to the North Slope.

Some wildlife biologists from the University of Alaska

wanted to study the peregrine falcons living in the steep cut banks along the rivers running north from the Phillip Smith Mountains to the Beaufort Sea.

As we worked our way through the Brooks Range on our way to Atigun Pass, I was impressed once more by the variety in the last chain of mountains in Alaska. To the west, where the mountains ended at the sea, the Brooks Range was a series of grass-covered rolling hills. But where we were, not far from the formidable mountains of the Gates of the Arctic National Park and Arctic National Wildlife Refuge, the mountains were tall, their narrow ridges and jagged peaks seemingly unassailable.

The temperature dropped the higher we climbed, and the snow got deeper. Even though Barrow's Flight Service Station was reporting unseasonably warm weather, until we reached Atigun Pass it looked like we were flying back into the dead of winter. Luckily, a valley opened on the other side of the pass. Large patches of the ground were snowless, and water appeared to be moving in the streambed. Miles away I could see a tractor trailer rolling towards us on the haul road, dust billowing behind it.

Half an hour later we landed on an abandoned pipeline construction site beside the haul road, a little gravel island in the middle of an endless expanse of mottled snow and tundra. The biologists wanted to camp in the study area rather than stay at the Happy Horse Hotel in Deadhorse, a half-hour flight from where we were. While we pitched our tents the wind was light and it actually felt warm.

The next day we began looking for falcon nests. We began on the Canning River where it entered the Franklin Mountains on the north side of the Brooks Range and worked north across the flat slope to the sea. The river was covered with ice but often welled up in spots to form bright blue pools. All the cut banks and rock outcrops along the Canning's banks were free of snow. We had no trouble locating several nesting sites. We also saw several small herds of muskox.

Every time we went out, the biologists found peregrines

on the rivers we visited. After a few days of clear blue skies and mild temperatures, it looked as if we might finish our work well before the 10 days planned. In fact the weather was so nice that, when it began to snow around noon on the sixth day, the little white flakes were a pleasant distraction.

The snow shower drifted in off Beaufort Sea and caught up to us as we were returning to camp for fuel. By the time we landed the sun was disappearing in an overcast sky. Before I had finished pumping the fuel, the horizon had disappeared. Ground and sky were the same dull shade of white. Even the falling snow had been absorbed in the one color.

It was obvious we weren't going to be flying for a while, so I slipped nylon covers over the upper fuselage, main and tail rotor blades, then crawled into my tent. After a few hours of reading by candlelight, I dozed off. When I awoke there was just enough light for me to see that the sides of my tent were caved in. I reached up and pushed. Ice-cold condensation ran down my arm as a mass of wet snow slid off the sides and the tent regained some of its shape. Still in my sleeping bag, I unzipped the tent fly and looked outside. There was nothing. The other tents, even the helicopter, had disappeared. So I read some more before falling asleep again.

The next time I opened my eyes my watch read six o'clock. Nothing had changed outside but it was time for dinner, so I pulled my clothes on inside my sleeping bag, unzipped the tent fly, and stuck my head outside just in time to catch an avalanche on the back of my neck. Before I could shake it off, cold water was trickling under my collar.

It didn't seem to be snowing anymore and, as my eyes adjusted to the anemic light, I could make out the shape of a tent about 30 feet away, then another. They were underneath two feet of new snow, nothing more than lumps on an otherwise level landscape. In the other direction I could make out the shape of my helicopter. Motivated by hunger, I trudged through layers of ice and snow to the nearest tent.

"Hey," I said to the mound of snow. "Anyone alive in there?" No response, not a sound, so I called a little louder,

"What's for dinner?"

"What?" came a muffled voice from beneath the mound of snow.

"It's me. The pilot. What are we having for dinner?"

"Dinner?" he asked, sounding puzzled.

Then a second voice, more distinct, joined the conversation. "What's he talking about?"

The other person answered, his voice also more distinct, like he'd pulled his head out of a sleeping bag. "He wants to know what we're having for dinner?"

"It's six in the morning, for God's sake," the other man declared.

"No shit?" I replied, momentarily put off. "Well, how about breakfast then?"

"The food's in Don's tent," one of them curtly replied.

Not expecting Don, wherever he was, to be any more receptive to the idea of food, I made my way to the helicopter. After chipping a thick layer of ice off the door I got inside and found a Milky Way candy bar, which I thawed in the fold of my armpit for several minutes and ate. Then I went back to my tent and sleep.

Two days later the storm passed and we left, apparently having seen all the nesting sites we had to.

In Fairbanks the weather was nice enough outside to do something Kathy and I'd been planning since she told me she was going to Hinchinbrook. We had to check her out with some weapons. There were going to be a lot of big brown bears on the island.

Kathy had taken a marksman course at school, shot a .22 caliber rifle and pistol at an indoor range. She said she did pretty well, but we knew she would need something a little heavier on Hinchinbrook. I borrowed a .44 caliber revolver and a 9-millimeter automatic. Plus I had my 12-gauge, not very pretty but functional, pump shotgun. It was company policy to carry a weapon capable of dropping a bear in a survival situation, and the single slugs in its magazine weighed almost an ounce apiece.

She picked up the automatic and looked at it. "A little light," she said, putting it down and reaching for the .44.

To make the experience as realistic as possible, we'd taken a large piece of cardboard and sketched a reasonable likeness of a large bear on it, head down in full charge. Her first shot hit the mock bruin in the left shoulder. We'd decided that was the high percentage shot. A large caliber weapon like the 12-gauge or the .44 would easily break the bear's collarbone, which, allegedly, would drop him on the spot. And if the bullet missed the collarbone, potentially, it could hit his heart. Kathy's second and third shots hit him in the head, the last one right between the eyes. She was just as good with the 12-gauge.

Around the same time the seasonal pilots and mechanics began returning. Burns, Russell, Ernie and Ken came back, as did most of the mechanics from the year before. Over the next few weeks, among the other rituals of life returning to Fairbanks, we took care of recurrent training, an annual requirement of the Federal Aviation Administration for most commercial pilots. The intention, to reacquaint us with our aircraft, mountain flying and pertinent federal regulations, was a good idea. Most of us had barely flown at all in half a year.

We also had our Part 135 check rides. It was a perfunctory flight with a designated FAA check airman who was there to make sure we knew how to fly, but a requirement of our commercial pilot's certificate nevertheless. Only the newest pilots failed the check ride, but they always made me nervous. As pilots in command we get used to being the final authority in our aircraft. Having someone in the copilot's seat, with the authority to ground you, is disconcerting. Especially when it's an employee of the federal government.

I also had to get checked out in the helicopter I'd be flying for the first part of the summer, the Bell 206L, or Long Ranger, as it was called. It only carried two more passengers than the Bell and Hughes helicopters I'd been flying for the last few years, but it was quite a bit longer and almost twice as heavy when fully loaded. I enjoyed the change. Heavier helicopters require a different control touch, more detailed plans and smoother moves.

In May the Long Ranger and I went to work for Alaska State Forestry. Instead of fighting fires, though, our job was to support the headquarters staff in Fairbanks. Occasionally I got to rush a Helitack crew to a new fire, but mostly I flew the senior staff around on show-and-tells and training missions.

Not very exciting work, but time literally flew by and the next thing I knew Kathy was on her way to Hinchinbrook Island in Prince William Sound, 300 miles to the south. Once again she left a note:

> Tommy
> This past year I've spent with you has been one of the best in my life—because of you. You've been kind, warm and pretty damn silly, and I sure do have a whole lot of love for you.
> Take care of yourself, just as I'll look after me.
> I feel terrible—hope you do too...
> See you in Prince William Sound

The next week the fire season came to an end and I went out on another contract. This time with the Alaska Geological Survey, flying Alice in the Alaska Range about 75 miles west of Denali. Before leaving I stopped by Craig's office to say so long. I also wanted to talk about how I was going to get to Hinchinbrook Island in the middle of a contract.

"Come on," he said after thinking about it for a minute. On the wall in the maintenance office there was a board with all the aircraft listed, along with the maintenance scheduled for them over the course of the summer. "We were planning on doin' Alice's twelve-hundred-hour when you got back from the contract with AGS," he rubbed the blond stubble of his beard.

"But there's nothin' says we can't get to it a little early. Maybe four or five weeks from now. That would be easier on the mechanics anyhow."

Every 1200 hours of flight time, helicopters have to go through a major inspection. The mechanics strip it down and check everything: wiring, flight controls, even the rivets holding the aluminum skin to the aircraft's frame. It usually takes a couple of days. I would have at least that long to get to Hinchinbrook Island and see Kathy.

"You're a great guy, Craig," I said, giving him a big hug.

"Get off of me," was his response.

I'd been in the Alaska Range for a week or so when Craig shipped me a letter along with some helicopter supplies. It was from Kathy:

Yep, miss you all but can't say I wish I were there. Right here, right now is fine by me. Shelter Bay is Eden. Mountains, the sea and all kinds of nice living, growing green things and critters of all kinds. Got sea lions, harbor seals, sea otters, eagles, brown bears, Sitka black-tailed deer, and all kinds of waterfowl and small furbearers here in the bay and surrounding waters— and around the camp. They are pretty much unafraid of us, so it's a paradise for a wildlife watcher. Only difficulty is with the bears, area is loaded with the large browns. Have run into two in the field. Both close: 100 and 50 feet. One ran off with yelling and arm waving. The closer one I stumbled upon while moving

231

from the forest onto the muskeg. He was coming toward me when I noticed him. I yelled "Yaah!" and waved my hat, because often they can't see well enough to know what you are. The bear stopped in his tracks but made no signs of splitting. So, I moved slowly out into the open and yelled some more—he moved into the woods but didn't leave. Finally decided to fire a shot into the air to get rid of him. Fired the forty-four, the brown moved off slowly and we went back to work. I was glad not to have to use the shotgun.

Kathy had a unique way of dealing with bears. Instead of trying to hide, or even stand still, she made herself look as large as possible. That's what the other animals do, like that fox being harassed by the golden eagle. The little guy wanted the enormous raptor to think he was a lot bigger than he really was. That it wouldn't be worth the risk of injury to make him a meal.

If her apparent size wasn't enough to dissuade the bear, Kathy got more assertive. "I figure sometime in their lives, someone, probably their mom, has yelled at them… and meant it. I do the same thing. Try to make them think they're doing something wrong." So she yelled at them, things like "bad bear" and "go home." And if her bluff didn't work, and he got too close? Fortunately, that never happened.

I was glad that Kathy was enjoying Hinchinbrook Island, but couldn't help but be jealous, even the part about the bears. She was experiencing all kinds of new things without me. Also, I missed her terribly.

Nevertheless, other than some mental anguish now and then, life was good. I was flying from the Terra Cotta

Mountains to the Revelations, a large part of the west end of the Alaska Range. Some of the ridges were so steep, grass couldn't grow on their slopes. My passengers, the geologists, loved the place. Bands of minerals, red and orange, yellow and green, were exposed from one valley to the next, giving them easy access to detailed information on the content and disposition of the geological formations. At the headwaters of the Swift River was the biggest isocline I'd ever seen. A perfect fold of exposed rock strata that was more than 1,000 feet tall. There were also waterfalls, and meandering streams that fed crystal clear lakes in deep green valleys set high in the mountains.

It was as nice as it gets, but a gnarly place to fly. There was a lot of wind coming directly over the mountains. Most of the time the turbulence was mild, but to keep me honest, every so often it would hit hard. Fortunately, there were lots of easy landing sites. Flying in turbulence is uncomfortable, but landing in difficult spots all day in it is nerve-racking. Once you get below 30 or 40 miles an hour the wind can do what it wants with you, including smack the helicopter into the ground.

Flying in that part of the Alaska Range was a challenge and rewarding, my passengers amiable, and the field camp one of the most luxurious I'd encountered. AGS put us up at a lodge on Farewell Lake. Most lakes in Alaska are shallow and dark, full of tannin from decaying vegetation. But Farewell was several shades of turquoise. From the air it looked like one of the hot springs in Yosemite. Unfortunately, the water wasn't even close to warm.

The lodge was owned by Stan Frost, the epitome of a big game hunter if I'd ever seen one, and his attractive wife and excellent cook, Marta. The Frosts catered primarily to hunters in the fall; however, because it was the only place to stay within 50 miles in any direction, they got a number of summer guests too. Hewn from logs, the buildings were rustic but comfortable. It didn't take long for the place to feel like home.

Good as life was, the closer it got to Alice's 1200-hour inspection and my trip to see Kathy, the less I cared about much of anything else. When the day finally came, I was standing in front of Craig's desk before Alice's rotor blades had come to a stop.

"Three-eight-seven's here," I said, nonchalantly. On the way through the hangar I was relieved to see there was still one helicopter sitting there and, from what I could see, it hadn't been cannibalized. Before Craig had a chance to respond, I added, "Any chance I can take her to Hinchinbrook for a few days? Maybe on a test flight or something."

"Aren't you gonna say hi first?" he asked. "Anyway, can't do it. Once Sparky's got that Wolfsburg radio in, that helicopter is going back to work. Could be as early as tomorrow." He grinned at me. "What's your hurry?"

"It's been over a month," I cautioned. "So don't mess with me."

Without a helicopter, getting to Kathy wasn't going to be easy, I thought. There weren't any roads anywhere near that part of the coast. The closest town was Cordova. I'd have to fly there, then charter a plane on floats, or a boat... which made me think of Vinny. He had a sailboat, the Toad, in Valdez. It wasn't as close to Hinchinbrook as Cordova, but we could drive there and it was still less than a day's sail away from the island.

"I can't, Tommy," Vinny said when I got him on the phone. "There's this big meeting with these really important guys. It could mean a lot of money."

"You're the only one who can help me out, Vinny," I told him. "You and the Toad. And, oh, did I mention that Chris says she can't wait to see you again."

"Asshole," was all he said.

The next day we were on our way to Hinchinbrook Island aboard his boat, an ugly little thing about 18 feet long and 10 feet wide. "She's beamy," Vinny told me when I mentioned that his boat was fat.

That evening, on an ingoing tide, we made our way up

the shallow inlet to Shelter Bay on Hinchinbrook. The island was everything Kathy had described, bright green mountains cloaked in radiant white snowfields, waterfalls, and wildlife everywhere. Only the bears didn't fit the descriptions in her letters. They were a lot bigger.

On the last day the four of us were on our way back to the girls' camp from one of their survey areas. Kathy and I had stopped near the top of a grassy knoll that overlooked Shelter Bay to take in the view. I was already beginning to miss her. My life was nothing but better with her around.

"You know, Kat," I began. "If you ever wanted to get married." For a moment she just looked at me, obviously surprised, then made an odd little sound. "Jesus, Kathy. You're laughing."

"No, I'm not," she laughed. "But..." There was an uncomfortable pause while she regained her composure. "I love you. I really do. But you caught me by surprise. And... well, I don't want to get married." Then she added quickly, "But if I did, it would be to you, honest."

Completely embarrassed, I added lamely, "I was just trying to let you know how I feel."

Later that day, Vinny and I were sailing up Orca Bay in the Toad. We'd consumed most of a bottle of rum and were having a great time singing along with Jimmy Buffett until the cassette machine ate the tape.

"There's more of them in a box below," Vinny told me.

"No problem," I said, stumbling to the companionway.

On my way back up from the cabin with several cassettes in hand, I couldn't help but notice the large red buoy a hundred feet or less behind Vinny. I knew we'd passed one more than half an hour ago, and that it was supposed to be the only marker in the channel. Then I noticed that the large metal tower of the buoy was leaning backwards at a precarious angle.

"Vinny!" was all I got out.

He saw the fear in my eyes and looked over his shoulder. Instantly Vinny threw the tiller over, bringing the bow around while he reached for the pull cord of the outboard motor. It roared to life, digging into the water and pushing us away. We came so close to the buoy, the little boat's stern rose on the swell of water built up by the swift-moving tide.

For most of the day we'd been sailing along at four or five knots, hull speed for the Toad, and making good time running in with the tide. But when the tide turned we didn't notice. Before long the little boat was being carried backwards faster than it could sail forward.

"That would have been pretty funny if we'd hit that goddamned channel marker, wouldn't it?" Vinny said once we were safe.

"It's almost like we were set up, wasn't it?" I agreed.

Actually, it wouldn't have been funny at all. The Toad's fiberglass transom would have split in two, and we'd have sunk in a few minutes.

Right around then I noticed Vinny's inflatable rubber boat, our only means of avoiding death in the frigid waters of the bay if we'd sunk, was rolled up in front of the Toad's little cabin.

"Where's the pump for that?" I asked.

"No idea," Vinny said casually, and we both broke out laughing.

Two days later I was back at work, shutting Alice down on a ridge in the Alaska Range to wait for my passengers. One more time I went over the scene with Kathy on Hinchinbrook Island, the one where I'd done such a half-ass job of asking her to marry me. It had been embarrassing, but I didn't regret it. She's a great girl, I said to myself. Then to Alice, "And I love her." As the rotor blades slowly swung to a stop, perfectly centered, ready to be tied down, I added affectionately, "I love you too, Alice."

I got back to Fairbanks a few days before Kathy. When she called from Anchorage, on her way from Hinchinbrook Island, I told her I'd be at the airport to pick her up. Unfortunately, I had to take a last minute flight to Delta Junction and was running late. On my way back to Fairbanks I monitored Approach Control's frequency. When an Alaska

Airlines pilot got on the radio, saying he was inbound from Anchorage, I knew it had to be Kathy's flight. After he received his clearance, I asked the pilot, in as professional manner as possible, if he could tell Kathy I'd be a little late picking her up.

"Well," she told me later. "I did feel kinda special when the pilot came on the intercom and told me, and everyone else on the plane, that you were going to be late. And that you felt bad because you hadn't seen me for so long."

Not long after Kathy and I got back to Fairbanks, the summer season began to wind down. People were coming and leaving before we even had a chance to have a beer together. Part of the problem was mine. If they didn't need me to fly, I was usually at our little house on the other side of the runway. There were a number of things that needed attention before winter. Kathy was also busy getting ready for her second year of graduate school, trying to set up her courses so she could get her degree in two years instead of the usual three or four.

If I wasn't at home I was in the air. Everyone except Craig and Rusty had left town for the winter, and there was a fair amount of flying during a normally slow time of year. I didn't mind doing it all because the fall colors were exceptional, especially around Delta. Golden birches and aspens filled the valley. Even the fallow barley fields were full of color, crimson bearberry, multihued willows of all shapes and sizes. Earlier in the year the fields were solid fireweed. Dropping down low level, about five feet above the endless blanket of brilliant purple flowers, the cockpit was filled with a soft purple glow.

In the beginning of October, Fairbanks had its first really cold day. It never got above freezing. When I flew up to Bettles at the end of the week there was snow on the ground. Winter was coming, reaching over the Brooks Range on its way south, and I wasn't ready. The thought of dressing up in layers of wool, of looking out the window at almost any hour of the day and seeing nothing but pitch black, was depressing. I didn't want to live in a place you couldn't feel the sun on your skin.

At the same time the temperature was dropping below freezing in Fairbanks, the south coast of Alaska was experiencing a heat wave. Homer's Flight Service Station was reporting 65 degrees, winds light and variable. When I learned that Kathy had a break in her class schedule, I suggested we go to Homer for a week or more. Do the drive we'd put off for the trip to New Zealand.

Rusty said he'd handle any flights that came up, so Kathy and I climbed into Spot and headed south down the Parks Highway. An hour later we crossed the Tanana River and started up the long incline to the Alaska Range, one of the few unpopulated areas of Alaska I didn't like, especially on the ground. It's flat, and you can't see five feet off the road because the stunted black spruce trees are so dense. The place gave me a weird kind of claustrophobia. Fortunately, the road was straight and we could drive fast.

Halfway to the mountains we passed the White Alice site on the Nenana River. Like the Defense Early Warning station on the North Slope that helped me out when I was stuck in a whiteout, the White Alice Communication Site was part of our national defense system. The line-of-sight radio stations linked the radar stations to Washington.

"Stick out like a sore thumb, don't they?" Kathy said, looking at the 50-foot-tall receivers and transmitters on either side of the site.

At the foothills of the Alaska Range we went by Healy, one of the few places on Earth that begged to be mined. Veins of coal 30 to 40 feet thick stick out of nearly every cut bank along the river that flows through town. And mine it they did. From the air you can see several square miles of the open-pit mine. You can also see that they've done a very good job of reclamation. Beside the active mining operations is a large grass-covered plateau, complete with small lake that used to be a mountain sitting on top of a large coal deposit.

From Healy we followed the Nenana River into the narrow entrance of Windy Pass. The road wound back and forth with the river, over bridges and through rock-cuts in the steep mountainsides. Below us the rapids of the Nenana filled the gorge with white water. After the pass it was a straight shot down the Chulitna River to Vinny's place in Anchorage, our destination for the night.

Cruising along at 80, a speed Spot seemed to like, we were there in time for dinner. Unfortunately, Vinny wasn't. He'd left a note saying he'd be gone for a few weeks and that we should make ourselves at home. His refrigerator was full but suspect, vintage milk and lots of aging meat, so we decided to go out for dinner.

Anchorage was crowded and dirty compared to the rest of the state, but it came with amenities. After September we were lucky to find oranges or iceberg lettuce in Fairbanks, but Anchorage's markets still had delicacies like papayas and kiwi fruit for a price. And there was no comparison when it came to going out for dinner.

We chose Simon and Seaforts, one of the most popular restaurants in town, and had to wait half an hour to be seated. But it was worth it. Our window table overlooked the calm waters of Cook Inlet from Knik Arm to McKenzie Point. Farther to the west the tall white flanks of Mount Susitna glowed red in the evening sun. And the food was excellent.

After dinner, with chocolate mousse and cognac lingering on our taste buds, we walked downtown. My first summer in Alaska, seven years earlier, I spent a lot of time in the bars along Fifth Avenue. Back when I thought that I should stay up all night because the sun did. Also, I felt comfortable in the seedy bars. Everyone I talked to was like me, a transient. With Kathy along, the nightlife wasn't as interesting as it used to be.

Kathy and I managed to have a good time anyway and began our trip down the Kenai Peninsula with sizeable hangovers. Fortunately, it didn't take long to leave the city behind, and once again we were alone with the grandeur of Alaska. The road to Homer followed the coast, cut out of solid rock for a lot of the first 50 miles because the Chugach

Mountains rise, literally, right out of Turnagain Arm, a large bay off Cook Inlet.

"What the hell is that?" I asked, looking across the mouth of Turnagain Arm. There appeared to be a wall of water stretching across the bay. Beginning a hundred feet from shore, it grew slowly into a vertical wave at least five feet high.

"Looks like a bore tide," she said.

"Must be," I agreed, remembering that, when water running out of a long bay like Turnagain runs into a tide coming up a long inlet, a wall of standing water can form where they meet.

Then Kathy added excitedly, "Do you see what I see?"

About 300 yards away, near the middle of the wave, there were two or three small sails bobbing all around.

"Are those sailboats?" I asked incredulously, thinking they were doomed if they'd gotten that close to the turbulent water.

Kathy was squinting into the morning light. "No," she said slowly. "I think they're windsurfers."

We pulled over to take a look. There were four people out there on windsurfers. They were dressed in heavy wetsuits and seemed to know what they were doing, flashing up and down the face of the endless wave. A little later on, at Bird Creek, where the mountains drew back from the ocean, we stopped at the general store and bought bread, ham, and a bottle of wine.

Both of us were still a little hung-over and thought a picnic down the road was in order; however, when we looked up at the steep ridge on the west side of Bird Creek, we changed our mind. With our lunch in a backpack we began climbing. Every step up the grassy slope made us feel better. On top of the ridge we didn't have to go far before running into enough fresh snow to block the trail. Which was perfect timing, because we were starving. On a dry spot of ground, out of the wind with our backs to a large warm rock, we sat in the sun, ate our sandwiches and drank the wine. Below us, the silvered surface of Turnagain Arm stretched from Cook Inlet to Portage

Glacier. Everywhere else, rugged mountains rose around us.

There is no comparing the reward of climbing a mountain to that of landing on top of it in a helicopter. When you land on a mountain ridge and get out, that's it, you're there, nice view, let's go. But climbing to the same spot, you get to know that mountain from bottom to top. There are hundreds of views instead of one, and an equal amount of interesting experiences. It seemed that my appreciation of a view varied directly to the effort put into getting there.

A blast of cold air woke me from my nap. A moment later Kathy stretched, sat up and smiled. "Gettin' chilly," she commented. The sun was only halfway to the horizon, but the temperature had dropped 10 or 15 degrees while we'd dozed. It was near freezing.

We scrambled down the mountain, as much to stay warm as to get back on the road, then drove around the head of Turnagain Arm and followed the road south into the Kenai Mountains. We had to slow down at the first pass we came to. Along the sides, snowmobilers were unloading their machines, nearly plugging the road for a mile. The sound of revving engines bounced off the mountain walls around us, while oily smoke hung thick in the air. Dressed in their insulated suits, the riders had come all the way from Anchorage to try out the first snow of the season, even though there wasn't very much of it.

After the pass, the road opened up again until Sunrise and Hope, two old gold-rush towns. Sunrise had disappeared along with the mining in the area. The old moss-covered log cabins had lost their roofs and were rotting into the wild rose bushes that surrounded them. But Hope had fared better by taking advantage of its picturesque location on the south side of Turnagain Arm and keeping the spirit of its gold-mining past alive for tourists.

At the turnoff to Hope we had to slow down for a couple cars and a Winnebago slowly winding their way up Summit Pass. People came to the Kenai Peninsula from all over the state, and the world, to fish for salmon in its rivers or halibut in the sea, hunt bear and sheep in the mountains, or moose out on the flats, dig clams at the beaches, float the rivers and hike, or just admire the scenery. So there was almost always traffic to contend with.

A hundred miles later we were out of the mountains and slowing down for the first real town on our way to Homer. Soldotna, a roadside sprawl in the middle of an endless expanse of scrub forests, lakes and bogs had grown a lot in the last few years. Something that was hard to understand until you found out that the river running through town had some of the best salmon fishing in Alaska.

The line of strip malls, bars and restaurants was mercifully short, and then it was an easy drive down the sparsely populated coastline.

"I could never get tired of this," I said as we rounded the final bend in the long road to Homer.

Below us Kachemak Bay opened to the sea. A long skinny gravel bar formed by the ocean's currents jutted three miles into the mouth of the bay. Tucked in the lee of the tip of the spit, the town's fishing fleet rested safely in the harbor. Across the bay the Kenai Mountains rose 5,000 feet from the ocean to their granite peaks. Four glaciers flowed down the valleys between them.

The town of several thousand people was on the close side of the bay, built on a bluff above the spit. The population was an odd assortment. Hard-working fishermen, affluent retirees, Russian "Old Believers" and hippies all shared a common desire to live in one of the more picturesque places in Alaska.

The room we got in a bed-and-breakfast had a view of the bay, but it was small, expensive, and didn't even have a bathroom.

"Seventy-five bucks and we don't get a toilet," I complained.

"It's down the hall on the left," Kathy told me.

I couldn't remember anyone telling us where the bathroom was, or seeing it on our way to our room. "How do you know that?"

Kathy looked at me for a second. "Shit. I'm sorry, Tom. Jamie and I stayed here when…"

"In this room?" I asked, surprised at the coincidence more than upset. I knew they'd been to Homer.

She laughed, "No. Not in this room."

"That would be weird," I commented.

Homer was a pleasant change from Fairbanks. It was a lot warmer, in the high 50s, but a strong onshore breeze kept us in jackets. Almost two weeks later, after seeing as much of the Kenai Peninsula as we could, we were on our way back to Fairbanks. Kathy was driving as we crossed the Tanana Flats. It was five o'clock in the afternoon and already dark. The day had ended an hour earlier as we drove through the Alaska Range. No sunset, just a gradual loss of light. Other than a berm of dirty snow along the side of the road and a few stars in the sky, there wasn't much to see, or feel.

"We're going the wrong way," I told Kathy.

"What?"

I pointed to the downy line of ice crystals along the bottom of my side window. The heater was having a hard time keeping up with the cold. The temperature had to be well below zero. It was barely October.

"It's getting colder by the mile, and darker. We should be heading the other way," I told her.

Not far from Fairbanks we noticed a glow in the night sky above us. The aurora borealis was emerging. By the time we got to the edge of town it covered most of the upper atmosphere in an enormous, yellow-green cloud.

"Let's head to Musher's Field," she suggested.

Musher's Field is where the dogsled races are held in Fairbanks. It's wide open and beyond the glare of city lights. When we got there the aurora was the only thing we could see. All that remained of the night sky was a dark ring along the horizon. As we pulled into the middle of the field and turned off the headlights, the unearthly glow began to descend. Shards of light appeared below it. Slowly the radiant shafts joined into luminous veils, gently twisting in a celestial breeze, morphing continuously from blues to yellows, purples to green, with every gentle shade in between.

"Amazing," I said. Everywhere the strange and beautiful colors shimmered and pulsed, slowly descending, surrounding us as they came right down to the ground.

It was incredible. I'd never seen, or even heard of, anything like it. The luminous veils of living color were all we could see.

"Do you hear that?" Kathy asked, rolling down her window. Along with the frigid air a strange sound flowed through the opening. A light sizzling noise, like ice crystals blowing across hard-packed snow.

Too see and hear something like that in the middle of an artic night, where nothing moves, there is no sound, and the only color is black, was remarkable. But when I opened my eyes the next morning sometime around noon, the magic was gone. The sky outside was one color, gray. Winter already, I thought, as Kathy stirred.

"Don't wake up," I told her. "Wherever you are has got to be better than this." But she sat up and looked out the window anyway.

"Hey! It snowed," she exclaimed. "Let's go skiing."

When we left for Homer there was no snow. Now there was over a foot of it on the ground. Everything was soft and white. With only two or three hours of daylight left, we got our cross-country skis out of storage and took off around the airport.

"What a difference a little snow makes," Kathy said, our skis gliding effortlessly along an unplowed road near the end of the runway.

She was right. The world around us was bright and cheery. We left the road and skied into the woods, following the most open path. In a thick stand of spruce a gust of wind set off a cascade of snow from the top of a tree. For a moment we were alone in a sea of shimmering ice crystals.

Winter for me was about the same as it had been the year before, a lot of sleeping and hanging out with Craig, who had recently found out he was going to be a father. But things weren't going that well for Kathy. They'd given her an office at the university to work on her thesis, but it was in the basement. There were no windows. When she left for school and came back it was dark. In between she was underground. Sometimes the better part of a week went by for Kathy without anything but artificial light.

Life got even better for me in January when the Army Corps of Engineers asked Craig for a helicopter to support their snow pillow project. Snow pillows are six-by-six-foot stainless steel envelopes placed around the watershed west of Fairbanks. By measuring the change in pressure when they were covered with snow, the scientists were trying to predict how much runoff there would be in the spring.

It was a treat to be flying so early in the year, but cold. The heaters weren't great in Alice. With the wind-chill factor, it was often 30 or 40 degrees below zero in the chin bubble. At that temperature the tail rotor pedals under my feet, metal bars one inch wide, felt like branding irons. They drew off that much heat, even through heavy winter boots with three-quarter-inch wool liners and two layers of thick wool socks.

Oddly enough, it was difficult to navigate around the small mountains west of Fairbanks. They were round and relatively featureless, with no rhyme or reason to their drainages. Valleys and ridges twisted and turned among each other in extremely deceptive ways. Neither logic nor intuition worked all the time. Even my dependable map was fallible with everything covered in snow.

Landings weren't easy either. The engineers liked to check the pillows after a heavy snowfall. Usually it was soft powder that billowed up while we were still 20 or 30 feet from our intended landing spot. At that point I just held the power setting and flew the helicopter into the snow. Hoping we weren't on a slope steep enough to roll us over.

- 14 -

DEATH IN THE FAMILY

The first sign of spring came in April, in the form of "breakup fever." Breakup is the time of the year ice leaves the rivers of Alaska. It is dramatic. For six months the rivers are as still as the frozen world around them; then the snow begins to melt, trickling in channels underneath the snow, feeding small streams and rivers until the pressure builds and the ice begins to break.

Reports as sharp as a rifle shot, low rumbles and deep booms accompany the ice as it splits and moves. Sometimes the rivers come to life slowly, grinding, pushing, mounding up in dams that flood the riverbanks. The blockages move, break and form new dams until the flow of ice and water becomes unstoppable. Other times it lets go in a matter of minutes. But it's always an impressive sight.

Breakup is an undeniable sign of change. It's also a momentous social occasion. Everyone knows that spring, summer and the multitude of outdoor activities are never far behind. People change, become more social and do things other than eat and sleep.

In varying degrees it is a psychological awakening. For most it is a celebration of survival, some see it simply as the changing of seasons and adjust, but for a few it is a breaking point. Like removing the lid from a pressure cooker, they explode. People around Fairbanks call it breakup fever.

The case of it that made the front page of the Fairbanks News Miner in early April involved a woman and a man who lived about 15 miles out on the Chena Hot Springs Road. The state troopers got a call about the man dragging himself down the road, bleeding profusely. It turned out he'd been shot three times. The rounds that hit him were slugs from a large-bore shotgun, at close range, that had left gigantic holes in the guy's

246

torso and thigh. He told the troopers that his girlfriend had shot him.

According to the paper, when the troopers arrived at the couple's home the woman admitted she had shot the man, and accused him of infidelity. She said she had planned to leave him that summer. But one nice warm day, when everyone else was feeling great, she shot him. "I wasn't going to kill him," she was reported to have said. "I was just trying to shoot his balls off."

Actual evidence that breakup was beginning came on an afternoon flight to a gold claim northeast of Fairbanks. While my passengers checked the thick overburden of ice covering the stream they mined, trying to figure out when they'd be able to come back and get to work, I took my shotgun and went looking for a cabin I'd seen as we were landing.

I found it easily, not far down the stream in a small thicket of black spruce trees. The cabin was smaller than it looked from the air, about the size of a bedroom. The log walls were less than five feet tall, the door even lower, and there was only one small window on the south side. Underneath it, a wild rose grew in a decaying flower box. The scene was cute, in a romantic and nostalgic way, but I'd just finished a winter in a good-sized city and found that too confining. I couldn't imagine what would happen to me during five or six months alone in the claustrophobic cabin with nothing but my mind for company.

It was obvious no one had been around for a long, long time. Rust had eaten holes in the solitary enameled plate left on the roughhewn table. The cast-iron stove against the wall was mostly a pile of rust and pieces on the plank floor. Back outside, I looked around and saw what appeared to be a clearing a little farther from the stream. Another cabin or outbuilding, I thought, and decided to take a look.

As I pushed through the prickly little spruce trees separating me from the clearing, something stopped me. A sound, or smell, it didn't matter. I chambered a round in my shotgun and moved the safety to fire. Ten feet later I was in the clearing staring at the mangled carcass of a moose.

The full-grown animal had been ripped apart by a bear. There was blood everywhere, bright red, freshly torn meat. My grip on the gun tightened. The bear might not be far away. If he was close, he probably wasn't happy about being driven off his meal.

I looked behind me quickly, then around the small clearing. There weren't any buildings, only spruce trees as thick as dog fur and awfully close. I tried to listen, but there was only a rushing sound in my ears. Breathe, I told myself, feeling light-headed as I began backing into the woods the way I'd come, looking around constantly, hoping my luck would hold until I got away from the bear's food.

At the stream I began loping through the rotten snow, held close to the bank by the dense spruce. Twice I slipped into the stream and both times my foot went through the ice. In a minute my toes ached, but stopping wouldn't do any good. By the time I got to the helicopter the whole foot was numb, and I was dragging it as much as walking. But I felt good. Running into that bear kill had been exciting. And falling through the ice on the stream meant that we were well into the thaw cycle. Breakup had already begun.

Within a week there was a reddish hue in the deciduous trees on the south facing ridges. Sap was beginning to flow. Then the fluffy white buds began to show on the willows around town. Finally I heard the welcome honking of geese as they came down the Tanana River on their way to the breeding grounds on Minto Flats.

Like the migrant waterfowl, Tundra's seasonal pilots and mechanics began to return. Johnny Burns and Baldini were first. Burns had spent the winter in Florida, Baldini on the west coast of Africa. A few days later John Russell arrived. He'd been in Africa too, but on the other side of the continent from Baldini. Rusty was back from a good showing in the Iditarod and working full time again. Almost overnight the hangar came back to life with marathon parties and endless foosball tournaments.

Not everything was the same. Ray was no longer our director of maintenance, and I was going to miss him. He epitomized what a head of maintenance should be, experienced and resourceful. Ray knew his helicopters and, unlike a lot of maintenance personnel, could communicate with pilots. He understood that mechanics see problems and pilots feel them.

Ray moved on to another job and Chuck, who had worked for Tundra for a few years, became our new head of maintenance. No one else really wanted the job, but Chuck seemed like a good choice because he was organized, had even managed to update the microfiche files and parts inventory. Regrettably, it turned out that was all he wanted to do, have an organized office.

With no one in charge, Mike Parker took over the maintenance responsibilities in the hangar and developed what became known as roll-around supervising. He had an office chair, a big gray one with armrests and solid wheels that turned in any direction, and he seldom got out of it. Instead, Mike rolled from helicopter to work bench to the next helicopter, discussing what each mechanic was doing and offering advice.

Mike's system worked well. From the reassuring hum of the wheels on his chair as he glided effortlessly around the hangar, to his uncharacteristically considerate demeanor while dealing with his subordinates, the other mechanics grew so fond of him they became known as "The Parkerettes."

During a lull in activities around Tundra I took Kathy to the Pump House, a relatively new and upscale restaurant outside of town on the Chena River. They'd taken an old gold-rush era building that housed water pumps, gutted the interior and rebuilt it, then furnished it with antiques from that time period. The place was a bit touristy, but comfortable.

The night was warm and the ice was gone, so we took our drinks and sat outside for a while to watch the river flow.

"Oh, I forgot to tell you," Kathy said. "Mom called. She's going to Hawaii for a week and wants me to come along. Dad can't go, last minute kind of thing. Anyway, I don't think she'd mind if you came along. What do you think? Lie in the sun on a nice hot beach, drink Mai Tai's."

"For a week?" I asked.

Hawaii always sounded good to me, and I got along well enough with her mom. But it was spring in Fairbanks, what I'd been waiting for all winter, and it was happening fast. If you have the patience, you can literally watch the buds unfold in late April, early May. I didn't want to miss that.

"Why not?" she smiled.

There were a few flights scheduled in the next week or two, and the phone was ringing a lot, but there were plenty of pilots around with nothing to do. I was thinking seriously about joining her until I remembered that we also had recurrent training and FAA check rides coming up.

"Sounds good," I told her. "But I'll have to see what Craig's got going on."

It wasn't good. Recurrent training was going to begin before Kathy even left for Hawaii. The check rides with the Federal Aviation Administration were scheduled right after that. The summer season was beginning early this year, Craig told me, and we weren't ready.

Recurrent training, the review of flight procedures and Federal Aviation Regulations, was always difficult. Whether through macabre design or the nature of inept bureaucratic legalese, the language of the FARs was basically indecipherable. Understanding them was difficult, but figuring out their intent wasn't. It appeared to me that all the rules and regulations were not much more than an elaborate framework designed to assign blame, almost always to the pilot.

The FAA check ride we took after recurrent training wasn't something I looked forward to either. But this year was different. Craig had applied for, and received, his check airman designation from the Federal Aviation Administration. He was going to be giving the check rides this year.

I always looked forward to flying with Craig. We both prided ourselves on being smooth, being as gentle on the controls as we could. A lot of pilots move the cyclic around all over the cockpit just to stay in one place. That worked, but they didn't have what we called good pilot technique.

The day Craig and I went out together was perfect for flying, sunny, cool and calm.

"Where to?" I asked once we were in the air.

"Head on out to the butte," he told me.

The butte was one of several small hills in the middle of the Tanana flats, a place we both used to train new pilots. When we got there Craig told me to make an approach to the small clearing on top of the butte. The landing went well and he took the controls.

"I'm gonna do the nose around," he said. "And I'm using that rock over there." One of the first things the FAA check pilot did in a typical check ride was have us pick the helicopter up and hover back and forth, then side to side, to show we could control it. "Check it for me, will ya."

I opened my door and leaned out. "Back a bit. Okay, to the left a foot. Okay, you're right over it."

Once the tail rotor was directly over the rock he'd indicated, Craig hovered the helicopter's nose 360 degrees, trying to keep the tail rotor in its position over the rock. He couldn't see behind the cockpit, so he had to do it by ground reference.

"How'd I do?" he asked when he had completed the circle.

"A nine," I told him. The tail rotor strayed from the rock once, but less than six or eight inches.

"You got an eight," he told me when I'd finished the same maneuver.

"What do you mean an eight?" I protested. "How far was I from the rock?"

"A mile," he said. But when I continued to glare at him, he conceded, "Not that much. But it happened a couple times."

Before long, we were down to one of the last things the FAA examiners checked us for, the ability to control the aircraft to a successful landing in the event of an engine failure. Usually the check pilot picked a landing spot, an area without trees at least 100 feet across. Then he'd have us fly by it 1,000 feet in the air. As we went by the spot the check airman rolled the throttle off. Because the forced landing area was well behind us by that time, we had to enter a 180-degree turn that was timed to end right over the chosen spot. Around 50 feet above the ground the examiner would instruct us to roll the power back on.

Craig and I made it more of a challenge. After I picked the place I wanted him to land, Craig flew towards it at treetop level. As he passed the spot he rolled the throttle off and lowered the collective. At that point, all he had was airspeed to get back to the forced landing area. Immediately he did a steep climb. Near the top, with our airspeed at zero, he twisted the aircraft around and leveled it. Then he nosed it over into a steep dive. When we were less than a hundred feet above the ground he pulled the nose up and flared the aircraft, bleeding off the airspeed just in time to land in the middle of the clearing I had picked.

It was a fast maneuver and he'd done it perfectly, rolling out at the peak on a good approach angle with enough time to get his airspeed back and make a smooth deceleration to a hover. I ended up a little slow at the top and almost fell through, losing another point to Craig.

The final thing we did had nothing to do with the FAA check ride, but it was my favorite, a true test of how smooth a guy's flying could be, and it was my turn to go first. At 500 feet, about a quarter of a mile away from my chosen landing spot, I pulled back on the cyclic, slowed down to 60 mph and took some of the power out. That was the last move of the collective I was allowed to make until the flare for landing. The rest of the approach, downwind, crosswind and final legs, had to be completed without any additional power adjustments. The one who ended up closest to his landing spot won. When I was done Craig grudgingly gave me a 10, but I still lost overall by two points.

After all the pilots had finished recurrent training and passed their check rides, we had a party. It was the beginning of another summer, new jobs with different people in unusual places, and some fat paychecks. It was also the last time we'd all be together until the end of the summer. Russell was taking some guys out to the Ray Mountains the next day, the beginning of his contract with Anaconda Copper, and Rusty was going out a few days later.

The next night none of us felt like doing much of anything. I didn't even want to cook. Kathy and her mother were still in Hawaii, so I went out for a quiet dinner at the Fox Roadhouse with Craig and Sheryl. Near the end of the meal Craig got a phone call from Tundra. The FAA had called the hangar to say that Russell was overdue on his flight plan.

Pilots go past the time they say they'll be back on a regular basis. Usually they are home and simply forget to close their flight plans. Or they are on the ground where they were working, unable to take off for one reason or another and out of radio contact. But if an aircraft is overdue because it has crashed, survivors need help immediately.

After paying for the meal we drove to the hanger. John was working in Bandana Creek on the south side of the Ray Mountains. I'd been there a few times and knew that if he'd had a problem on the ground, a dead battery or something like that, they wouldn't be able to establish radio contact. There were mountains between Bandana and the nearest Flight Service Station. It was also remote, not on any of the regular flight paths. So John wouldn't be able to relay a message through another aircraft. That's what I thought. They were stuck at Bandana Creek with no radio contact.

Craig didn't want to speculate.

As soon as we got to the hangar he called the Flight Service Station in Tanana, the one closest to Bandana Creek. They had gotten a call from John around four-thirty. He'd radioed a request to extend his flight plan. They also said that a few hours later, just before dark, they heard a helicopter pass to the north of them, the route Russell would have flown to get back to Fairbanks.

It was good news he'd extended his flight plan. We

knew they were okay less than four hours ago. But neither Craig nor I liked the fact flight service had heard a helicopter go by around dark. We agreed it could just as easily have been another helicopter, and that John most likely would have contacted flight service on his way to Fairbanks; however, it was a critical unknown.

I still thought Russell and his passengers were at Bandana Creek. Regardless, no matter what we thought, there wasn't anything we could do before sunrise. If they were at Bandana Creek they were safe. Looking for them anywhere else at night, especially in the dark mountains, would be too risky.

Craig took off with the first sign of light on the horizon. He went by himself. There were only two passengers with Russell. If his helicopter was having problems, Craig could bring them back in one aircraft.

I got to the hangar not too long after Craig left. The secretary had arrived a few minutes earlier.

"The FAA called," she said, obviously concerned. "Someone picked up an ELT north of Tanana."

All commercial aircraft are equipped with an ELT, Emergency Locator Transmitter. It sends a signal that sounds like a car alarm on other aircrafts' VHF radios. The closer you get to an activated ELT the louder it gets. They can be turned on manually or by sudden impact.

Early in the afternoon the Federal Aviation Administration called again. Craig had relayed a message through flight service that he'd found John and his passengers. They had hit the side of a mountain on their way back to Fairbanks. All of them were dead.

An hour later Craig landed and I went to meet him. Neither of us could maintain eye contact. We knew each other too well to conceal what we felt, and it hurt.

I thought I'd gotten used to sudden death in Vietnam. Final and unfair as it seemed to be, I always understood it. But this wasn't combat where death was random and everywhere. We had control of our environment. The odds were in our favor. All we had to do to survive was be good pilots, and John was one of the best.

"We're going to need two aircraft," Craig told me as a state trooper and a guy in a black suit, obviously FAA, walked up to us. There had to be an inspection of the crash site before the bodies could be removed from the aircraft.

Craig took off with his two passengers while I followed alone in Alice. For brief moments I'd forget Russell was dead. Then I'd remember and my stomach would tighten in a knot. How could this have happened to him, I kept asking myself. John always knew what was going on. It was inconceivable that something catastrophic could have caught him by surprise. I could see him grinning, so damned confident.

From the air, what little I could see on the side of the mountain didn't look like one of our aircraft. It didn't look like anything, I thought. It certainly wasn't the helicopter that was in the hangar yesterday morning, the red, white and blue Hughes 500 we called Elizabeth. It looked more like... I couldn't believe what was happening. I was making an argument that it wasn't John's helicopter. That this was some kind of mistake.

I landed and let my helicopter cool for an extra minute or two before shutting it down, and didn't get out until the blades had been stopped for a while. The smell of jet fuel was everywhere and grew stronger as I approached the site. The fuel cell must have ruptured. They had hit hard. I didn't want to keep walking but knew that if I stopped I would not be able to get going again.

Even up close the helicopter looked more like something crumpled and dropped than an aircraft. It was on its left side, half buried in the snow. All I could see was part of the belly, the engine compartment and the passengers' door. Almost nothing remained of the cockpit. No doors or windshield, just the instrument panel sticking up from the floor in front of Gary, the guy in the copilot's seat. He and Russell were good friends. They'd worked together last summer. Gary's girlfriend was back at the hangar waiting for him. He was frozen solid, his arms crossed at chest level, like he was pushing something away. My heart sank. Gary had seen it coming.

Because the helicopter was on its left side, the side John was sitting on, I didn't see him until I got to the front of the wreckage. His head and left shoulder were in the snow. What I saw were his hands. John was still flying the helicopter, right hand griping the cyclic, left hand where the collective would have been. From the positions they were in, it looked to me as if he was pulling up on the collective to climb, and rolling the cyclic hard to the left. John had also seen it coming.

I couldn't stay there. Overwhelmed, I kept moving around the front of the helicopter and up the slope they'd run into. To my left was the open door of the passenger compartment. From above the wreckage, I could see inside. Tangled in a cargo net was the other guy. I didn't know him, didn't want to see any more, but before I could look away I saw large purple and blue welts where his jacket and shirt had ridden halfway up his back. Shit, I said under my breath. I knew John and Gary had died instantly, but he might have lived long enough to know what was happening.

The helicopter's tail boom was sticking out of the snow uphill and to the left of the wreckage. Needing a distraction, I walked over to look. Surprisingly, the tail rotor blades were undamaged, meaning they weren't turning very fast when the tail boom hit the ground. Maybe the tail boom came off in flight, I thought. My spirits actually rose, thinking that it might have been a mechanical failure that killed them instead of pilot error. Then I realized that, if the tail rotor came off in flight, it wouldn't be in front of the helicopter. They must have hit so hard it tore off and kept going.

A little farther up the mountain I turned and sat, overlooking the crash site. The slope we were on was rounded and gentle. It stretched away in a long, uninterrupted white ridge towards Bandana Creek. The way they'd come. There weren't any trees, even bushes, only a few alders sticking a foot or two above the snow in the drainage off to my left.

Whiteout conditions. But Russell wouldn't have fallen for that. He worked out of Bandana Creek the previous summer. This was the way he'd gone back and forth to Fairbanks all the time. He knew the area well and would have had a route to follow when the weather was bad.

I turned around and looked up the mountain in the direction they were heading. His helicopter was on the cusp of a gentle ridge that got steeper as it went up the mountain. The valley to my right led to the pass that John would have been heading for. They'd hit around 2,600 feet, high enough to clear the pass if they'd just been off to the right several hundred feet.

It had to have been a whiteout, I thought dejectedly. I'd heard the FAA guy tell Craig that the clock in the helicopter had stopped right around seven, well past sunset. And the Flight Service Station in Tanana had said there were snow showers in the area around then. The light would have been low, no terrain features, only snow.

It still didn't make sense. John had been going too fast. If he'd been in a whiteout he would have slowed down. Then it dawned on me. Maybe it was something similar to what happened to me about the same time a year ago in the White Mountains, where the valley became a ridge right before my eyes.

Either way, I decided, from what I'd seen the only explanation for their deaths was inadvertent flight into the ground. Feeling a little less overwhelmed, I walked back down the mountain to the crash site.

"Come on, big fella," I heard the state trooper say as I got closer. He and Craig were having a hard time getting the guy out of the passenger compartment.

"Need any help?" I asked.

"Got it," the trooper said.

By that time I was standing beside the wreckage. John was out of the helicopter, lying on his side in the snow a few feet away and facing me. There wasn't much blood, or damage of any kind, but none of the features of his face looked familiar. His skin was pale, hair dark and thinner. And his eyes were one color, a mottled gray, void of everything my friend had been.

Because the dead men were frozen in such awkward positions we couldn't fit all of them inside the helicopters. Craig got John in the back of his Hughes, but Gary and the other guy had to ride on my cargo racks. The FAA inspector rode back to Fairbanks with me too. It was the most uncomfortable flight of my life.

That night I called John's parents and told them what had happened. They were missionaries working in Africa. Nice people who had helped others all their lives and loved their son very much. Then I called Kathy and got on the next flight to Hawaii.

In a Japanese restaurant just off Waikiki Beach, I drank a bit more sake than Kathy or her mother and fell behind them on the walk along the beach to our hotel. A path of silver moonlight stretched across the ocean, following me as I walked barefoot in the sand. With a final glance at Kathy and Helen, I stopped, slipped out of my clothes and into the sea. When it was deep enough I dove, felt the cool water wash over my face and swam towards the light.

When my arms grew tired I rolled on my back and, rocking gently in the ocean swells, whispered to the moon, "It's good to be alive.

END OF AN ERA

It was summer in Fairbanks when Kathy and I got back from Hawaii. The days were warm and evenings long. I was flying almost every day, and when I wasn't up in the air, Kathy and I were outside, running, riding our bikes, or taking care of things around the house. When I had a day off we often floated the Chena from Fort Wainwright through Fairbanks to within a couple hundred yards of our house.

There were fewer parties at the hangar after John died. It seemed that Kathy and I went out less too. But that probably had more to do with our relationship than anything. We enjoyed each other's company and found that most of the things we liked to do didn't need other people.

We still liked to sit in the sun behind the hangar with the Tundroids and a cold beer or two. And seldom turned down an invitation to play pool at Pikes Landing, or volleyball at the Howling Dog for shots of whisky. But we didn't go out of our way to find new friends or look for parties, at least not the type that lasted all night.

Seemingly little had changed at Tundra, but now and then I would see a sadness creep into someone's eyes and know they were thinking about John. I missed him too, thought about him a lot, but I didn't seem to be taking it as hard as some people. For a while I thought it was because they were closer to him, or that maybe there was resentment because of his affair with Darcie. But it didn't take long to realize it was about acceptance.

If I hadn't been there, reached conclusions about what happened on the side of that mountain, seen the body that wasn't John anymore, it might have been different. However, as improbable as his death might have been, it wasn't the mystery to me it appeared to be for some.

Another thing making it easier for me was that I knew exactly how he died. There was no doubt in my mind that it had been painless. John had been extremely busy right up to the split second he died.

Craig seemed to be in a similar state of mind. During a lull in a conversation, he asked, "Have you been talkin' to Russell?"

"Almost every day," I told him. "You too, huh?"

"Uh-huh," he smiled. "It's like he's right there in front of me."

"Yeah," I agreed. "It's pretty natural. In a weird kind of way."

"Must be we don't want to let him go," Craig sighed.

We sat in silence for a moment, feeling the void he'd left. "Speaking of not letting go," he added, picking up a "Chinaman's cap" that had been sitting on his desk by the phone. It was the control switch for the cyclic trim motors of a Hughes 500, a little conical piece of metal on top of the cyclic that looks exactly like a miniature straw hat. "FAA guy walked in here last week," Craig continued. "Put this down on my desk and asked what it was. Like he'd found some evidence. 'Where'd you get this?' I asked him. He told me they'd pried it outta Russell's fingers."

"Must have been pretty intense," I said. "I mean, dying like that. I've sure been close, but..."

"Yeah," Craig agreed. "I think I might've actually died in my near-death experience."

"What?" I asked, thinking Craig was going on some fanciful journey.

"Wasn't even supposed to be there," he said.

"Where?" I asked, beginning to lose my patience.

"With Tinker. Near the Hobo Woods in the Mushroom," Craig told me, like I was supposed to have known all along.

The Mushroom was an umbrella-shaped bend in the Saigon River northwest of Cu Chi. Hobo Woods was a name adapted from a similar sounding Vietnamese word that designated a forest in the Mushroom. And Tinker was a pilot Craig flew with. So Craig was talking about a mission he and Tinker were on in Vietnam.

"Tinker was flying?" I asked. The Charlie Model gunship Craig and Tinker were in had two pilots, along with two door gunners and lots of rockets in pods attached to both sides of the helicopter.

"Yeah," Craig said. "Next thing I know, there's this guy right in front of us with an RPG. We're only a hundred feet off the ground, but Tinker noses it over. Put us in a dive straight at him."

"That's when you died?" I asked, trying to keep the story moving.

"No, damn it," he replied. "The guy swung 'round and shot at us. Looked like it was gonna hit right on the nose."

"Well?"

I actually felt more sympathetic than my curt request implied. A rocket-propelled grenade almost got me once. Missed by two or three feet. It was definitely scary, but I certainly didn't feel like I'd died.

"Must have gone between the skids," Craig said. "But that's when I died. When I thought the RPG hit us."

"What do you mean, you died?" I asked, choosing to be curious.

"It was like I drifted off to sleep or somethin'. I just sorta left my body and was someplace else. It was real comfortable. Warm."

"That's what being dead was to you?" I was beginning to lose interest again.

"Not there. But ahead of me was this… it wasn't really a tunnel, more of a lighter place. But I wanted to go there. I had this feelin' that everything I knew, every thought I'd had, everyone I've ever known, was just ahead of me there." Craig paused. "Then I was back in the helicopter and we were pulling out of the dive."

"What happened to the guy with the rocket?"

"Don't know."

"Your near-death experience was a lot more interesting than mine," I conceded.

That was the first time we had really sat down and talked about John, or life and death, since he died. Things were returning to normal, but always changing. By the end of the summer Craig and Sheryl had a baby girl, Cammie, and they all but disappeared, completely wrapped up in their daughter. That winter Kathy graduated with her master's degree in wildlife biology and range management, and her parents decided to sell their house on Lake Michigan. Along with the announcement, there was a color brochure from the real-estate company that had the listing.

I picked the pamphlet up, admiring the spacious mansion, tennis court and swimming pool. "Sure is a nice place," I said.

"Yeah," Kathy agreed as I handed it to her.

For a long time she stared at the picture of her parents' home, deep in thought.

"You okay?" I asked.

She looked at me, then back at the picture, and said, "You know. It would be a great spot for a wedding." I laughed, not really sure what she was talking about. "What's it been?" she continued evenly. "Two years, a little more?" She looked at me again and smiled. "You're not perfect, but we seem to get along okay. And you said you wanted to get married if I did. Right?"

The ceremony took place at her parents' home in front of the tall living room windows. It had been overcast all day and even rained earlier, but as Kathy said, "I do," the room lit up in bright sunlight. I shit you not.

Two days later we were back in Alaska. Two years later Kathy still worked for the Forest Service while I continued to fly for them. But it was a different job. The original field crews, Rocky, Tim, Linda, even Chris, had moved on. Fred and Ken spent most of the summer in Anchorage and had left Kathy in charge. With new, and much younger, people making up the FSL crews, we began to feel more like parents than anything else. Tundra had changed too. Johnny Burns married his longtime girlfriend from Kansas and settled down, a little. Ken moved back to the Gulf of Mexico, then Ernie. Everyone had gone their own way except Craig and Sheryl, who were full-time parents.

Five years after we met, Kathy and I left Alaska with no regrets, knowing well that the good times we shared with our friends were as unique as the characters that came together to do what they did best. Enjoy life. However long it lasts.

THE END

CPSIA information can be obtained at www.ICGtesting.com
Printed in the USA
LVOW06s1557090913

351652LV00002B/394/P